Grandville

by Bryan Talbot

DARK HORSE BOOKS®

Dedicated to the memory of
Ian McKie (1951–2009)

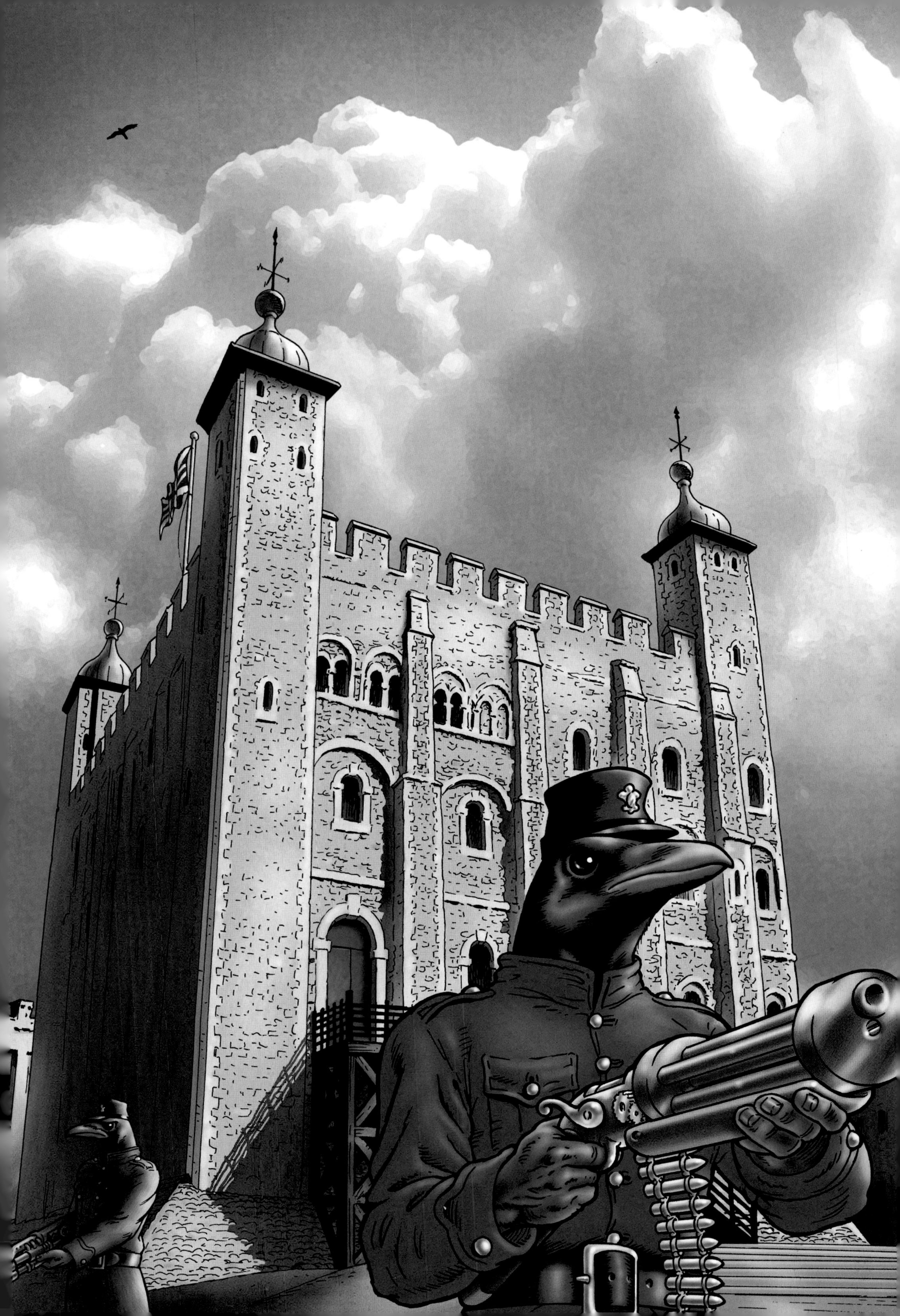

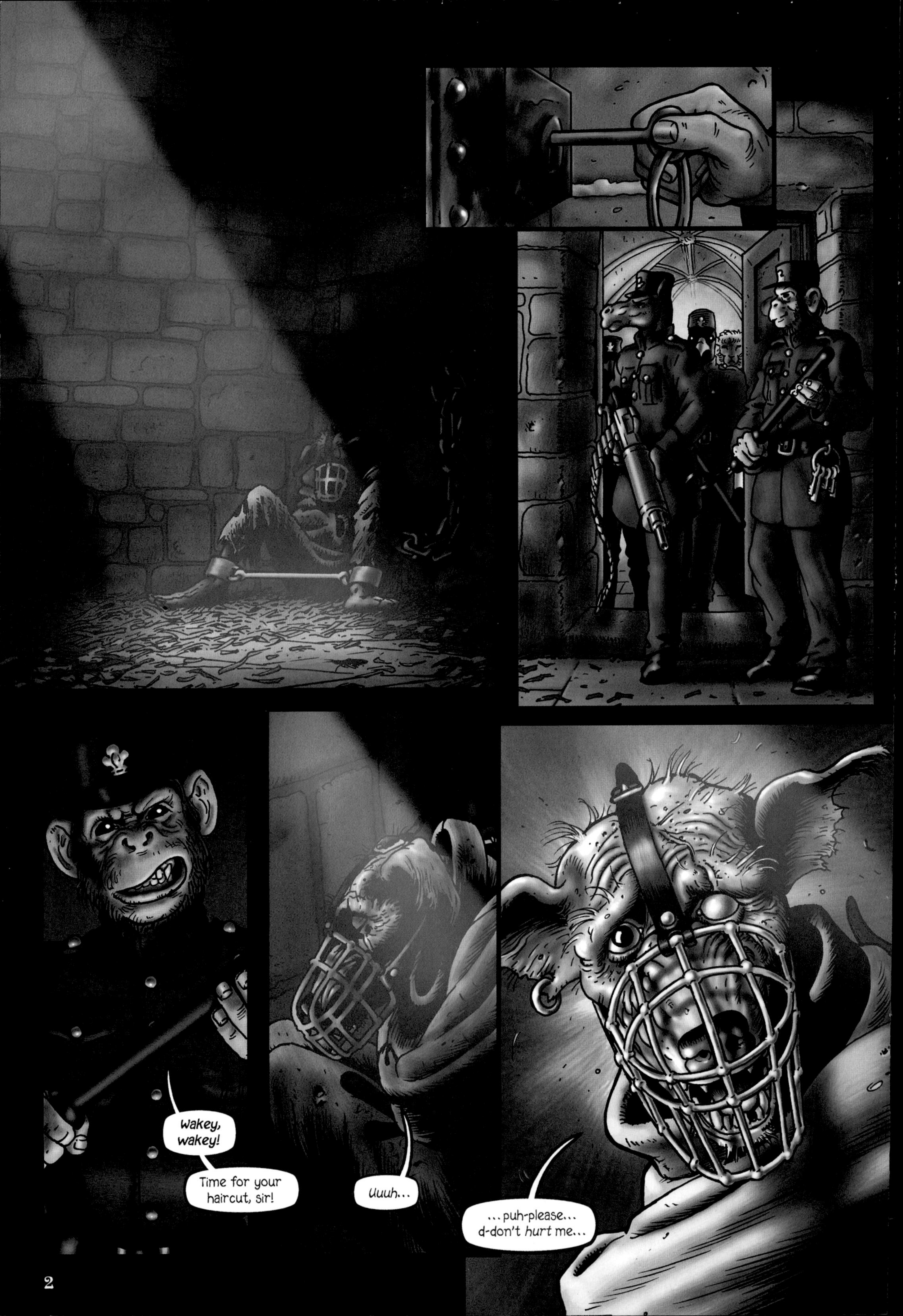
Wakey, wakey!
Time for your haircut, sir!
Uuuh...
...puh-please... d-don't *hurt* me...

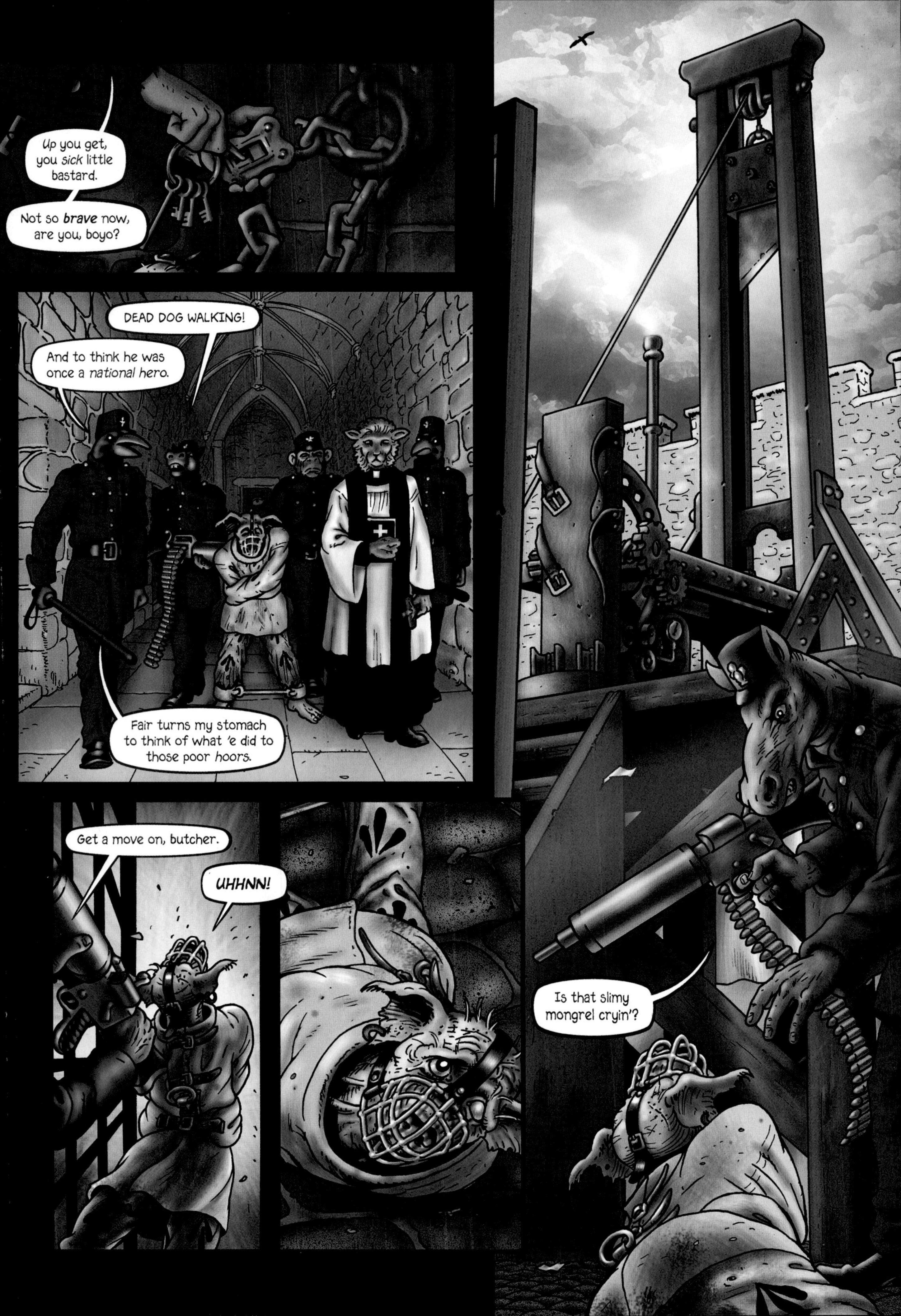
Up you get, you sick little bastard.
Not so brave now, are you, boyo?
DEAD DOG WALKING!
And to think he was once a national hero.
Fair turns my stomach to think of what 'e did to those poor hoors.
Get a move on, butcher.
UHHNN!
Is that slimy mongrel cryin'?

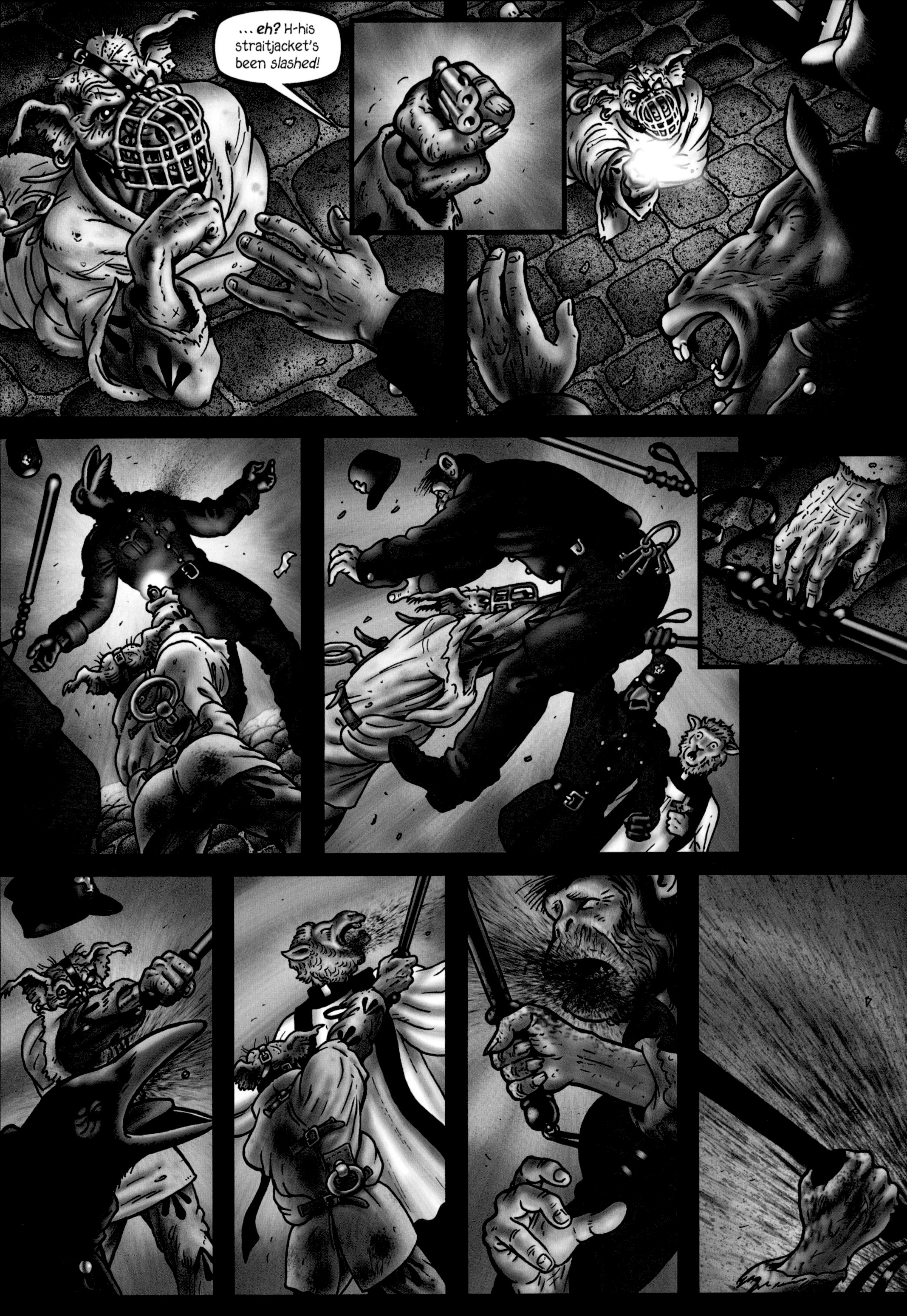
... eh? H-his straitjacket's been slashed!

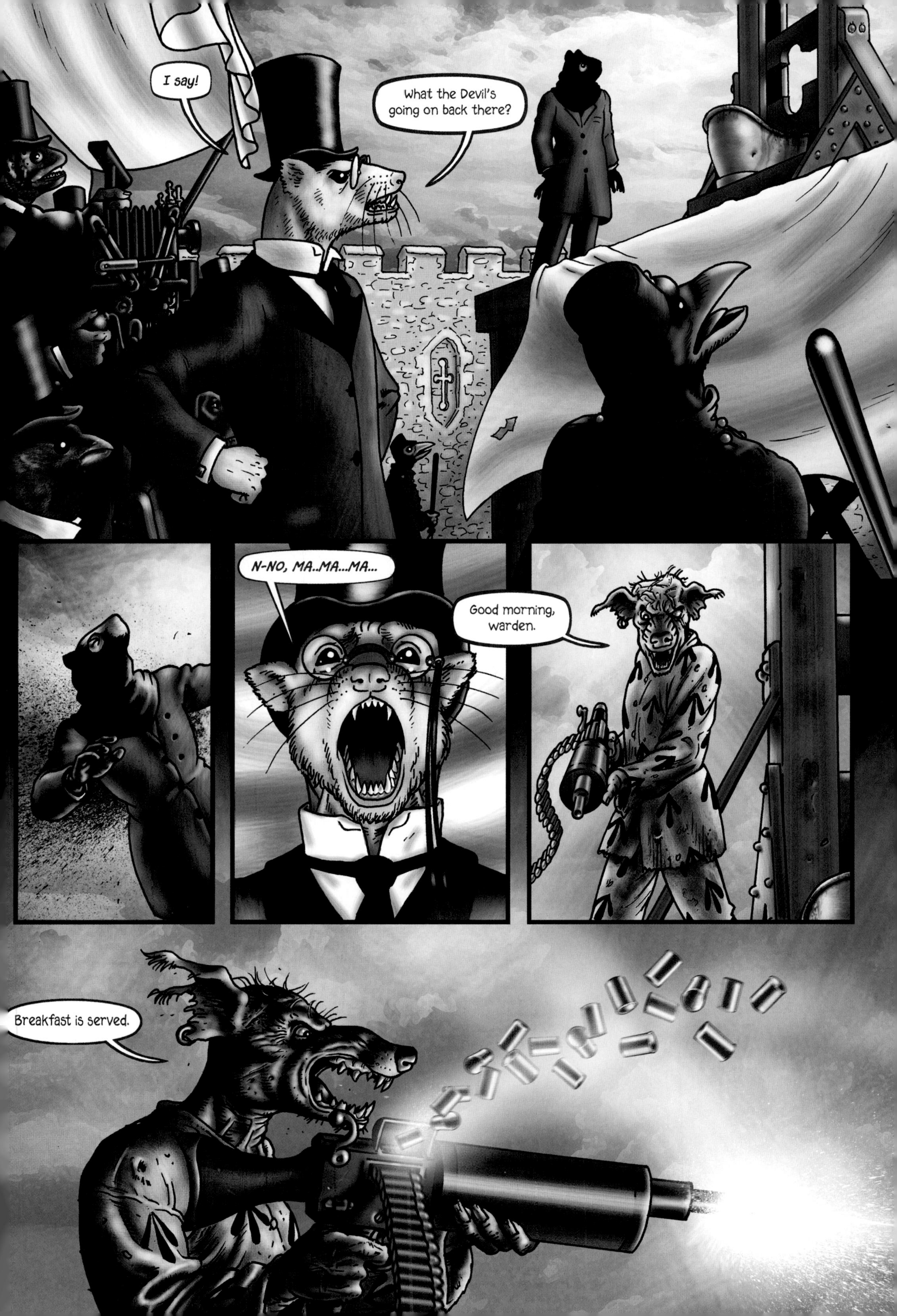
I say!
What the Devil's going on back there?
N-NO, MA..MA...MA...
Good morning, warden.
Breakfast is served.

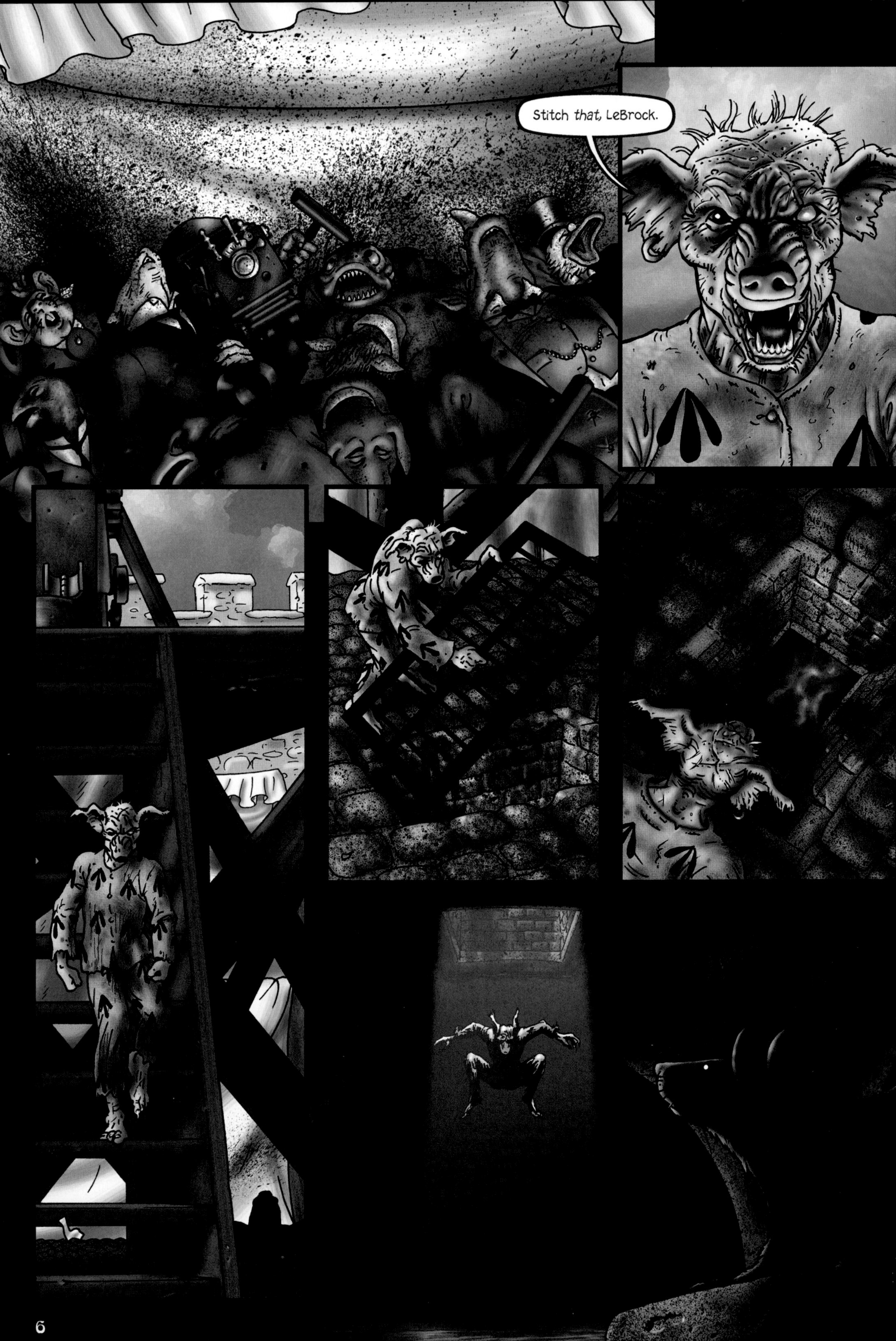
Stitch *that,* LeBrock.

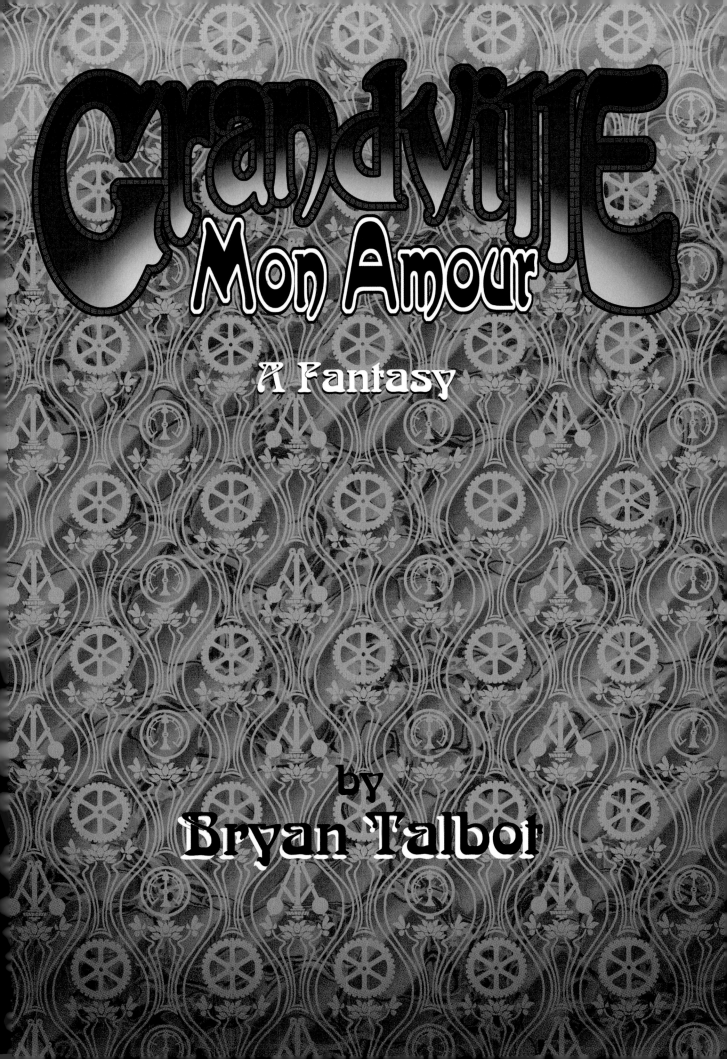

Grandville
Mon Amour

A Fantasy

by
Bryan Talbot

Script, art & book design: Bryan Talbot

Colouring on pages 94 to 96: Alwyn Talbot
Bryan Talbot lettering font produced by Comicraft
Colour flats: Jesse Kindzierski & Jordan Smith
French Advisors: Marie-Paul Brown & Eric Bufkens

Art Nouveau steampunk pattern by Bryan Talbot,
based on the endpapers of "Dampf und Elektricität:
die Technik im Anfange des XX Jahrhunderts."
Berlin: W. Herlet. [c. #1900]

Sincere acknowledgements for proof-reading,
comments on the work-in-progress, and other important input to
William Atherton, Chaz Brenchley, Alison Brown,
Dan Franklin, Stephen Holland, Dr. Mel Gibson,
Dr. Mary Talbot, and Chris Warner

No doughfaces were harmed in the making of this book

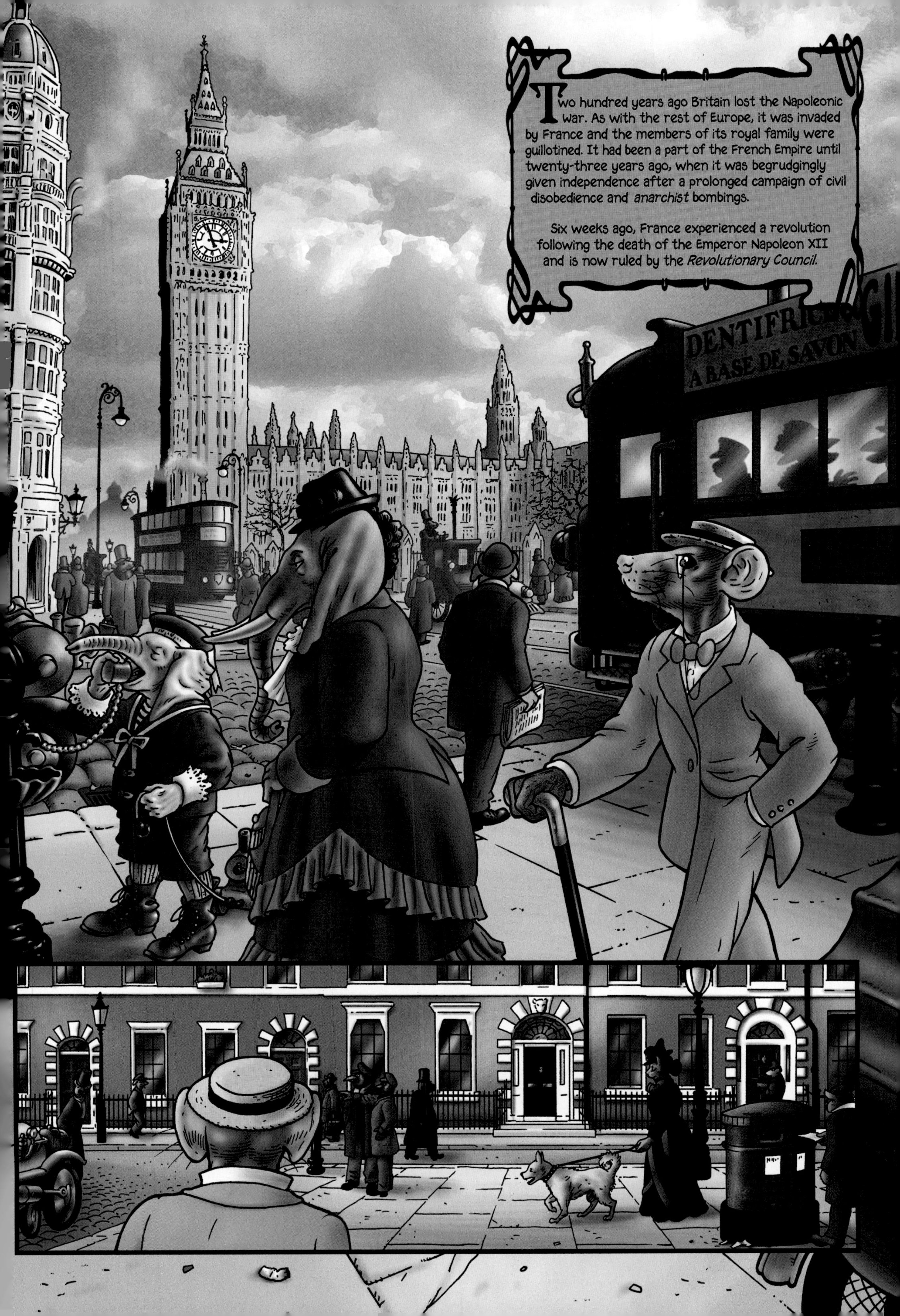
Two hundred years ago Britain lost the Napoleonic war. As with the rest of Europe, it was invaded by France and the members of its royal family were guillotined. It had been a part of the French Empire until twenty-three years ago, when it was begrudgingly given independence after a prolonged campaign of civil disobedience and *anarchist* bombings.
Six weeks ago, France experienced a revolution following the death of the Emperor Napoleon XII and is now ruled by the *Revolutionary Council*.
DENTIFRIC
A BASE DE SAVON

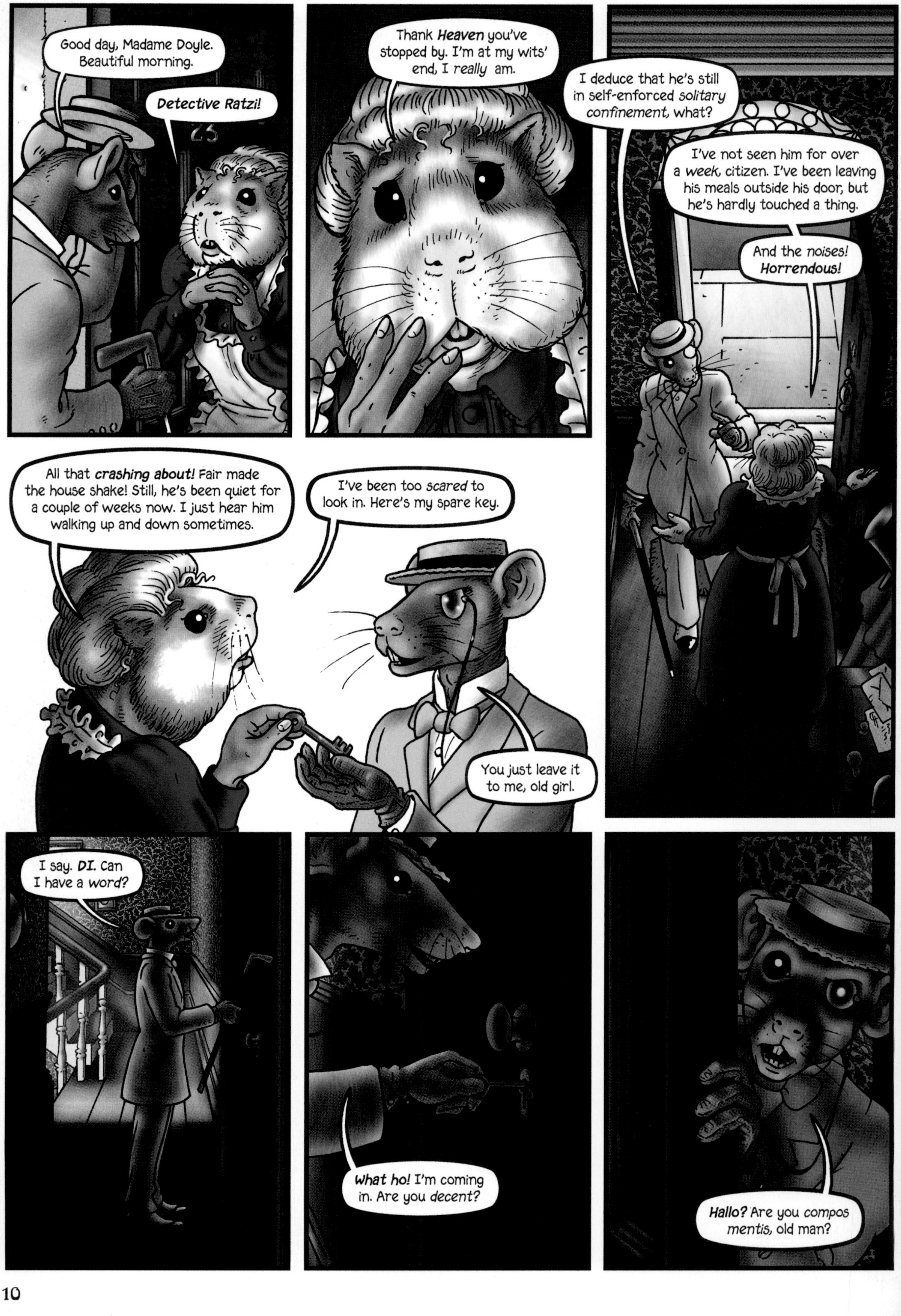

Good day, Madame Doyle. Beautiful morning.
Detective Ratzi!
Thank **Heaven** you've stopped by. I'm at my wits' end, I *really* am.
I deduce that he's still in self-enforced *solitary confinement*, what?
I've not seen him for over a *week*, citizen. I've been leaving his meals outside his door, but he's hardly touched a thing.
And the *noises!* **Horrendous!**
All that ***crashing about!*** Fair made the house shake! Still, he's been *quiet* for a couple of weeks now. I just hear him walking up and down sometimes.
I've been too *scared* to look in. Here's my spare key.
You just leave it to me, old girl.
I say. ***DI.*** Can I have a *word?*
What ho! I'm coming in. Are you *decent?*
Hallo? Are you *compos mentis*, old man?

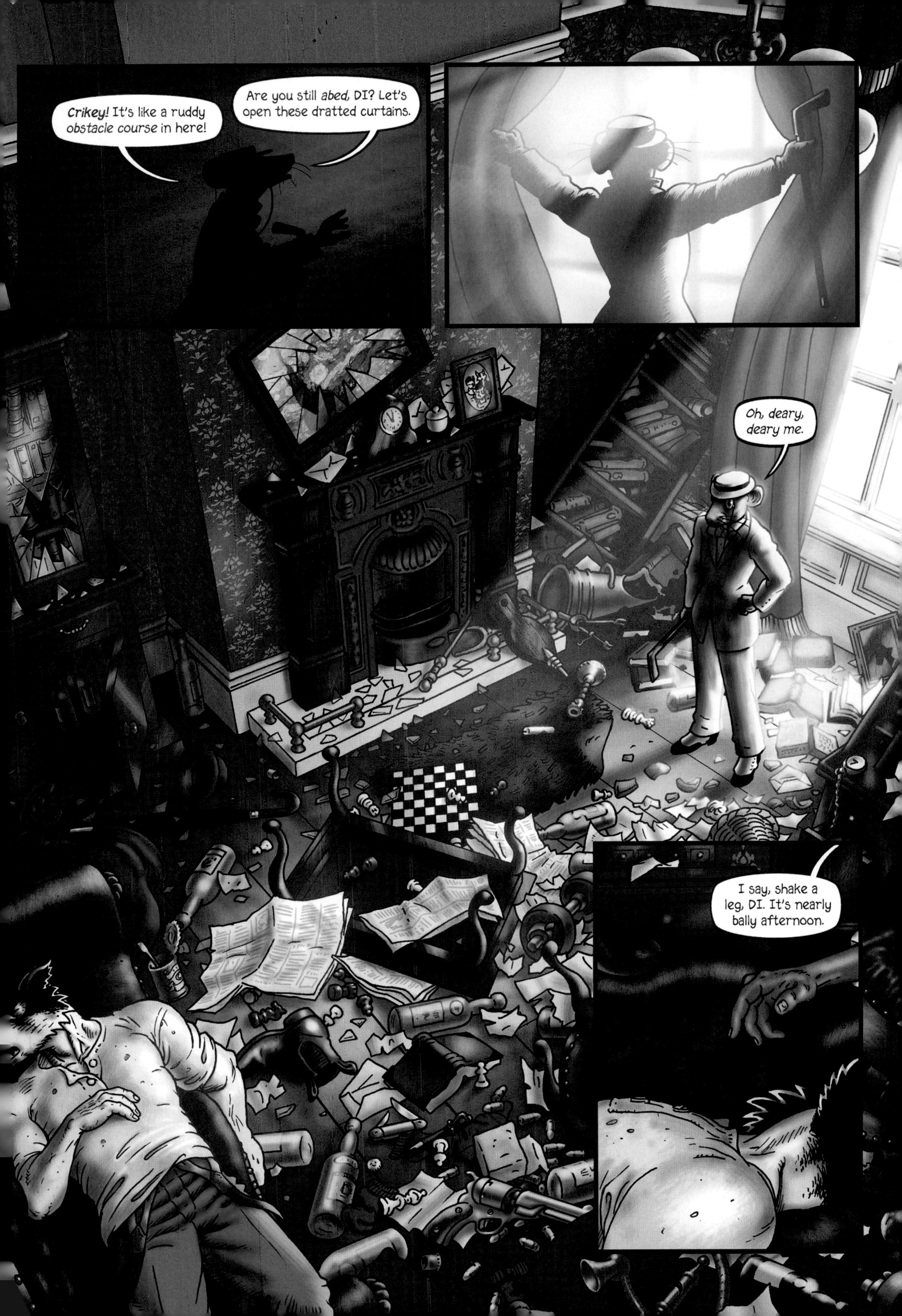

Crikey! It's like a ruddy obstacle course in here!
Are you still abed, DI? Let's open these dratted curtains.
Oh, deary, deary me.
I say, shake a leg, DI. It's nearly bally afternoon.

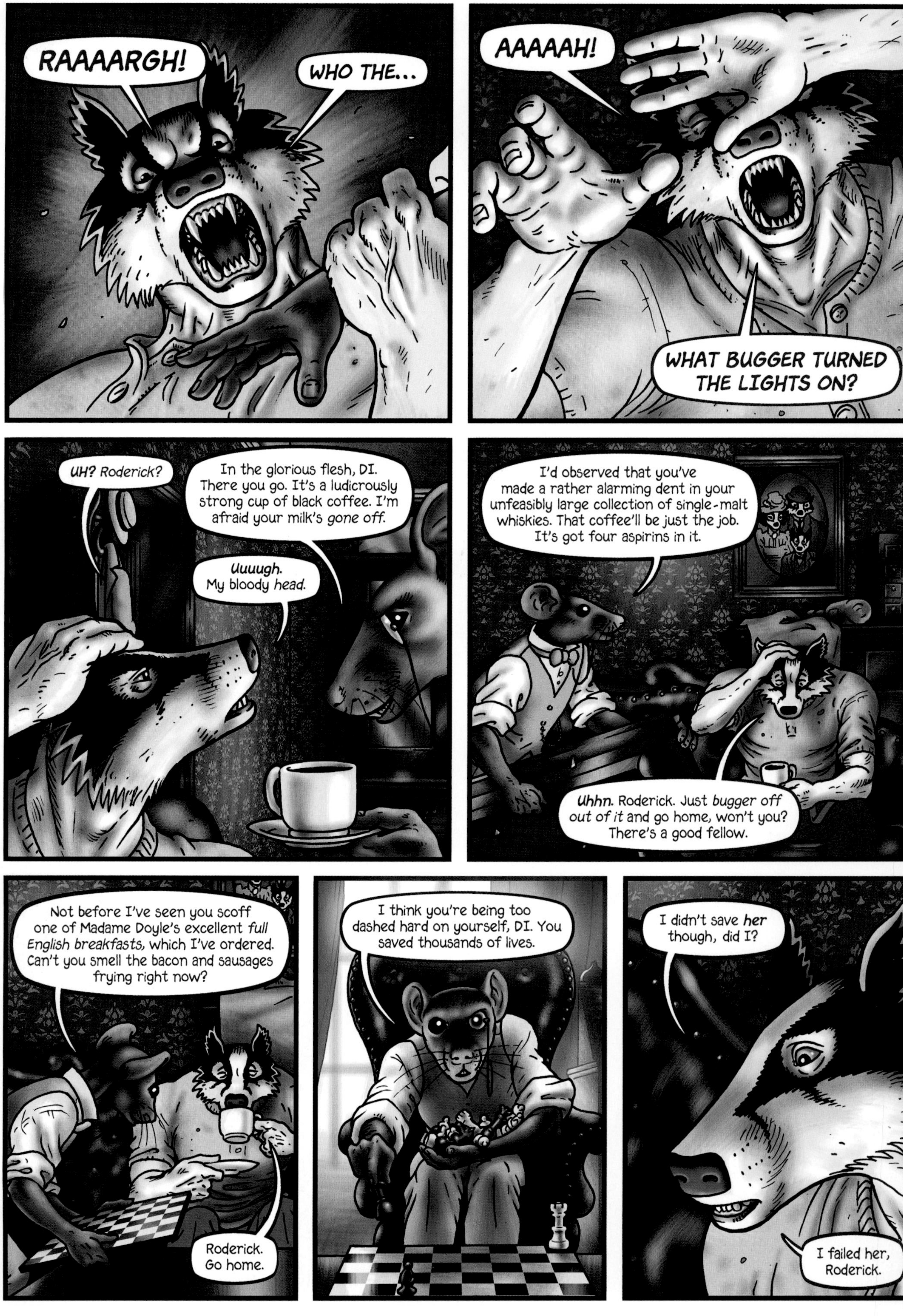
RAAAARGH!
WHO THE...
AAAAAH!
WHAT BUGGER TURNED THE LIGHTS ON?
UH? Roderick?
In the glorious flesh, DI. There you go. It's a ludicrously strong cup of black coffee. I'm afraid your milk's gone off.
Uuuugh. My bloody head.
I'd observed that you've made a rather alarming dent in your unfeasibly large collection of single-malt whiskies. That coffee'll be just the job. It's got four aspirins in it.
Uhhn. Roderick. Just bugger off out of it and go home, won't you? There's a good fellow.
Not before I've seen you scoff one of Madame Doyle's excellent full English breakfasts, which I've ordered. Can't you smell the bacon and sausages frying right now?
Roderick. Go home.
I think you're being too dashed hard on yourself, DI. You saved thousands of lives.
I didn't save her though, did I?
I failed her, Roderick.

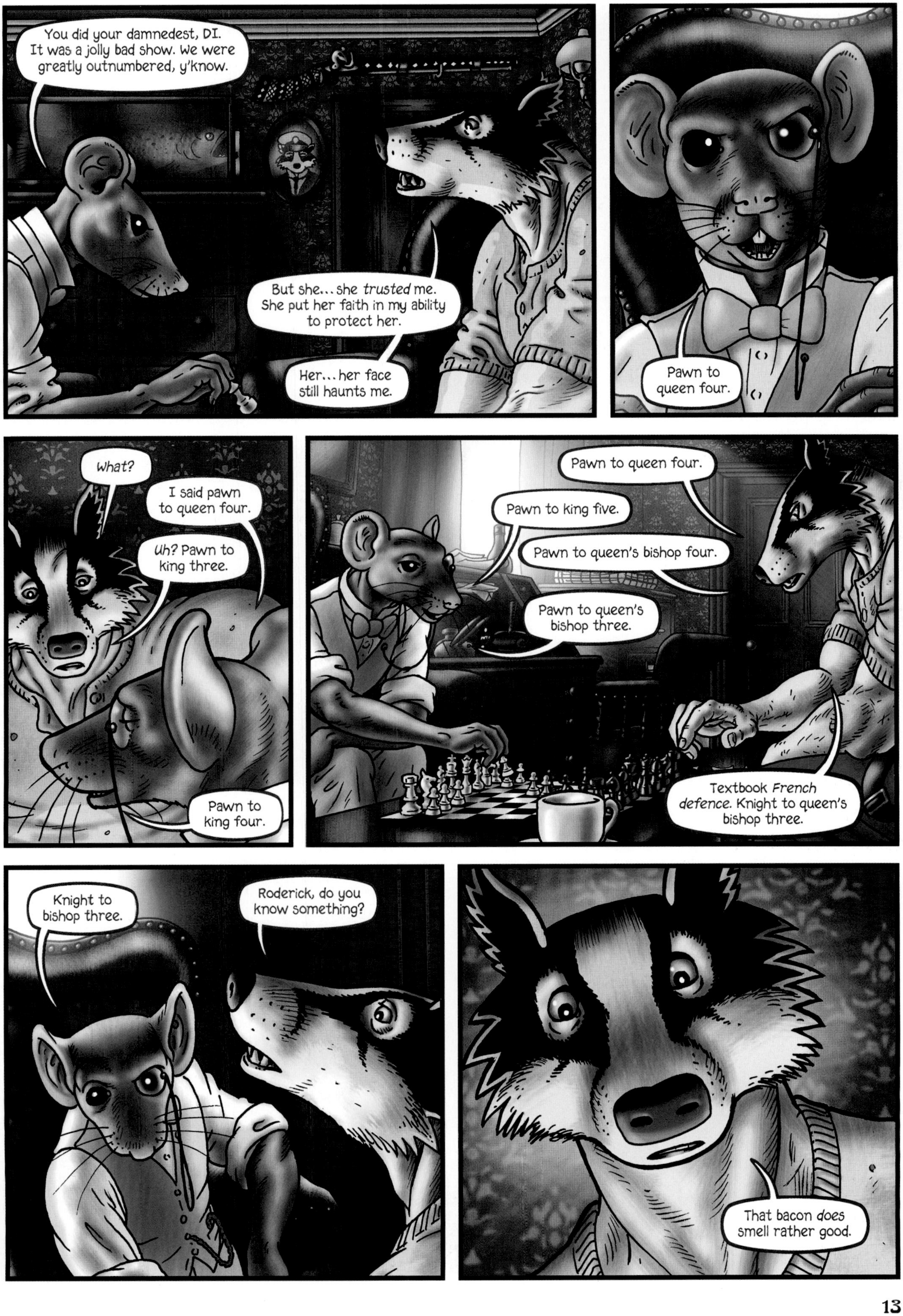

You did your damnedest, DI. It was a jolly bad show. We were greatly outnumbered, y'know.
But she... she *trusted* me. She put her faith in my ability to protect her.
Her... her face still haunts me.
Pawn to queen four.
What?
I said pawn to queen four.
Uh? Pawn to king three.
Pawn to king four.
Pawn to queen four.
Pawn to king five.
Pawn to queen's bishop four.
Pawn to queen's bishop three.
Textbook *French defence*. Knight to queen's bishop three.
Knight to bishop three.
Roderick, do you know something?
That bacon *does* smell rather good.

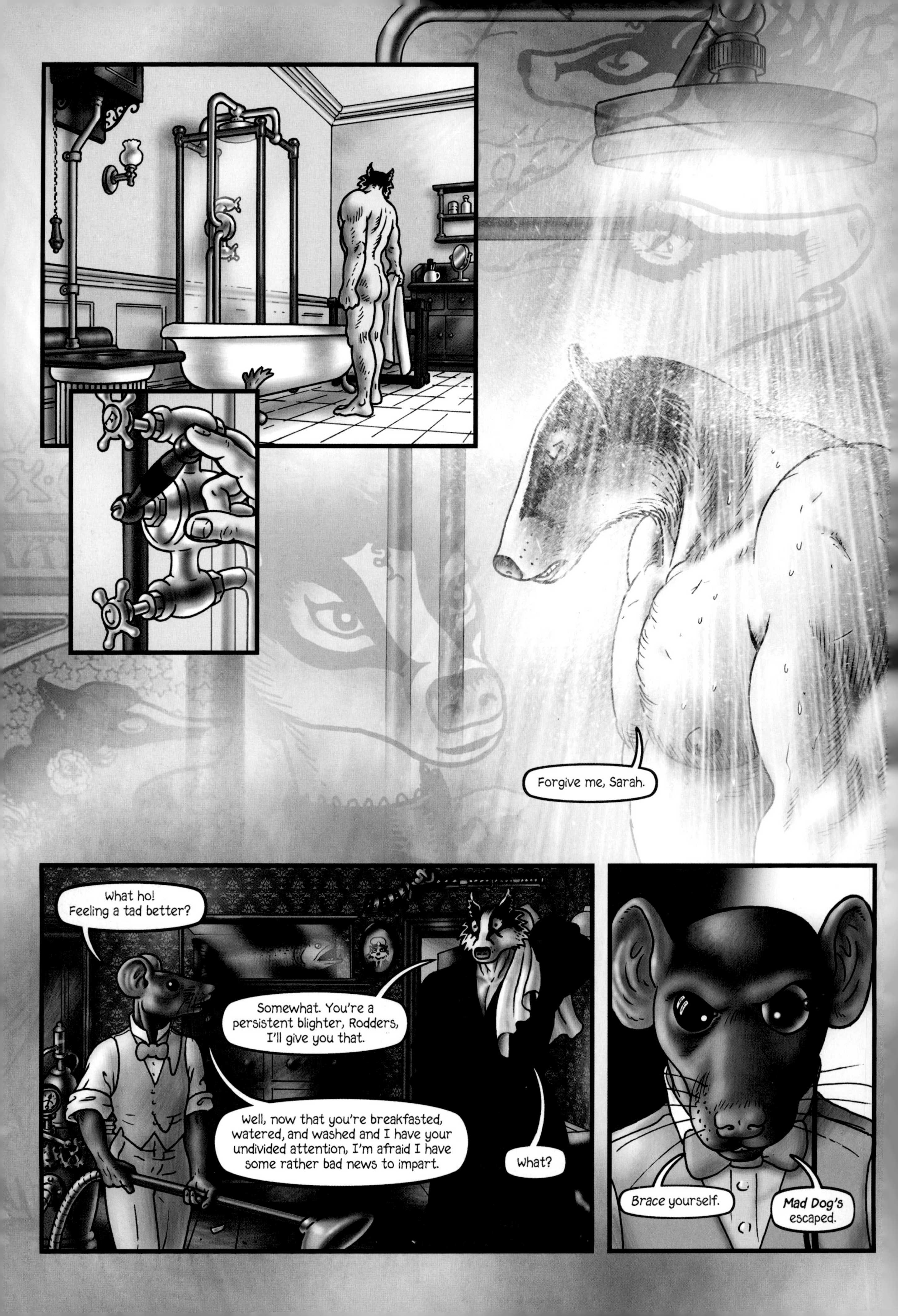
Forgive me, Sarah.
What ho!
Feeling a tad better?
Somewhat. You're a persistent blighter, Rodders, I'll give you that.
Well, now that you're breakfasted, watered, and washed and I have your undivided attention, I'm afraid I have some rather bad news to impart.
What?
Brace yourself.
Mad Dog's escaped.

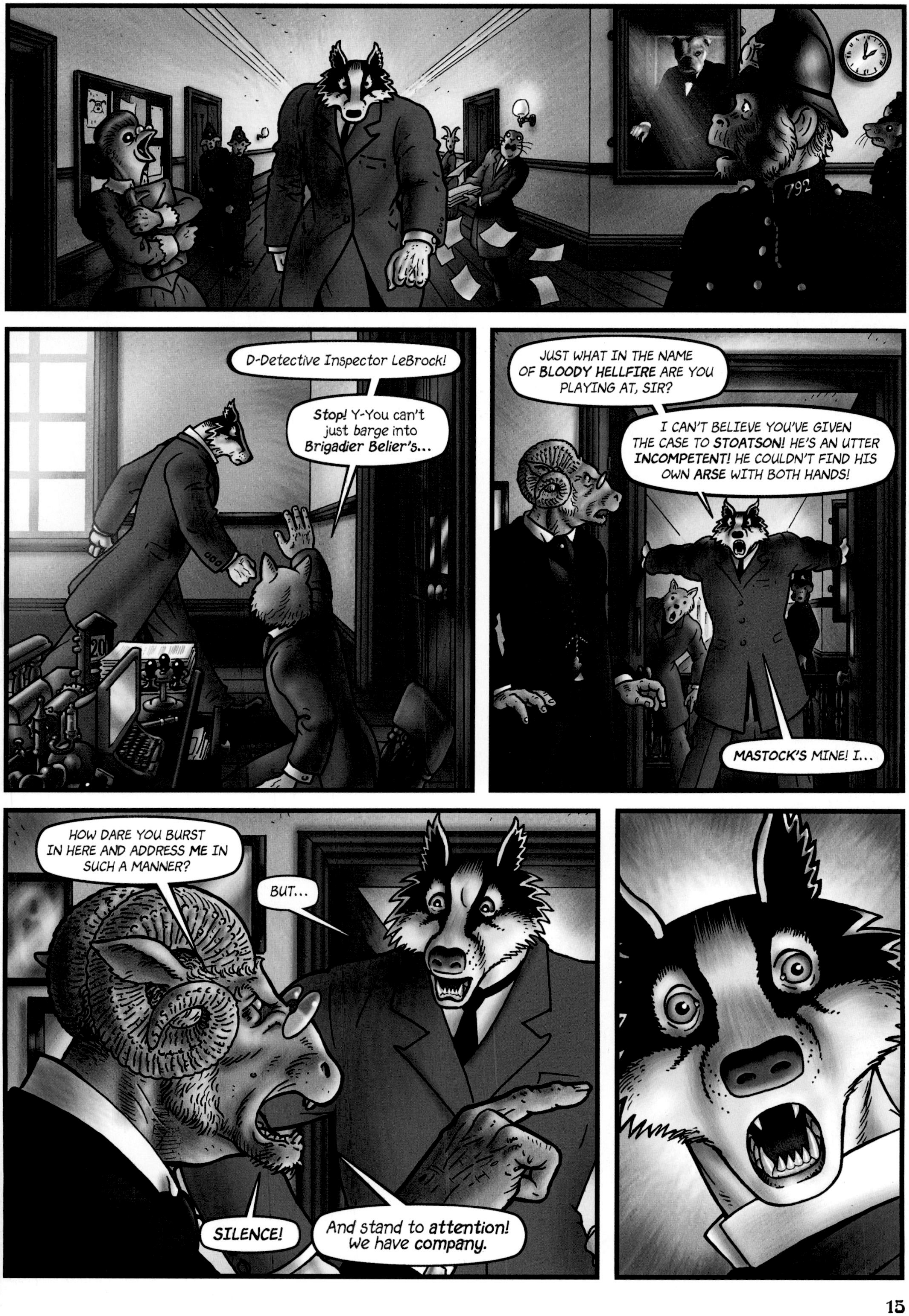

D-Detective Inspector LeBrock!
Stop! Y-You can't just barge into Brigadier Belier's...
JUST WHAT IN THE NAME OF BLOODY HELLFIRE ARE YOU PLAYING AT, SIR?
I CAN'T BELIEVE YOU'VE GIVEN THE CASE TO STOATSON! HE'S AN UTTER INCOMPETENT! HE COULDN'T FIND HIS OWN ARSE WITH BOTH HANDS!
MASTOCK'S MINE! I...
HOW DARE YOU BURST IN HERE AND ADDRESS ME IN SUCH A MANNER?
BUT...
SILENCE!
And stand to attention! We have company.

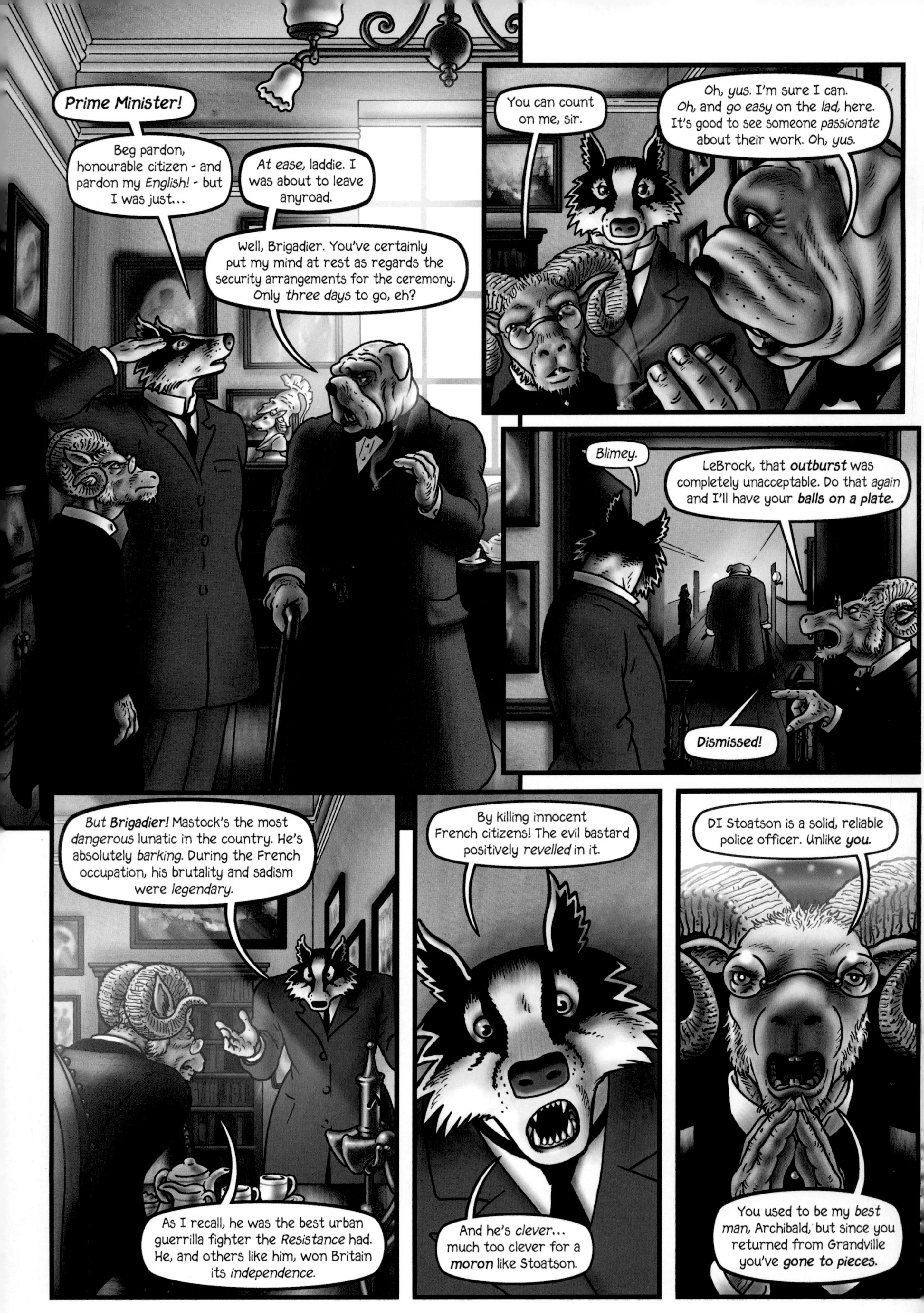
Prime Minister!
Beg pardon, honourable citizen - and pardon my *English!* - but I was just...
At ease, laddie. I was about to leave anyroad.
Well, Brigadier. You've certainly put my mind at rest as regards the security arrangements for the ceremony. Only *three days* to go, eh?
You can count on me, sir.
Oh, *yus*. I'm sure I can. *Oh,* and *go easy* on the *lad,* here. It's good to see someone *passionate* about their work. Oh, *yus.*
Blimey.
LeBrock, that **outburst** was completely unacceptable. Do that *again* and I'll have your **balls on a plate.**
Dismissed!
But **Brigadier!** Mastock's the most *dangerous* lunatic in the country. He's absolutely *barking.* During the French occupation, his brutality and sadism were *legendary.*
As I recall, he was the best urban guerrilla fighter the *Resistance* had. He, and others like him, won Britain its *independence.*
By killing innocent French citizens! The evil bastard positively *revelled* in it.
And he's *clever...* much too clever for a **moron** like Stoatson.
DI Stoatson is a solid, reliable police officer. Unlike ***you.***
You used to be my *best man,* Archibald, but since you returned from Grandville you've ***gone to pieces.***

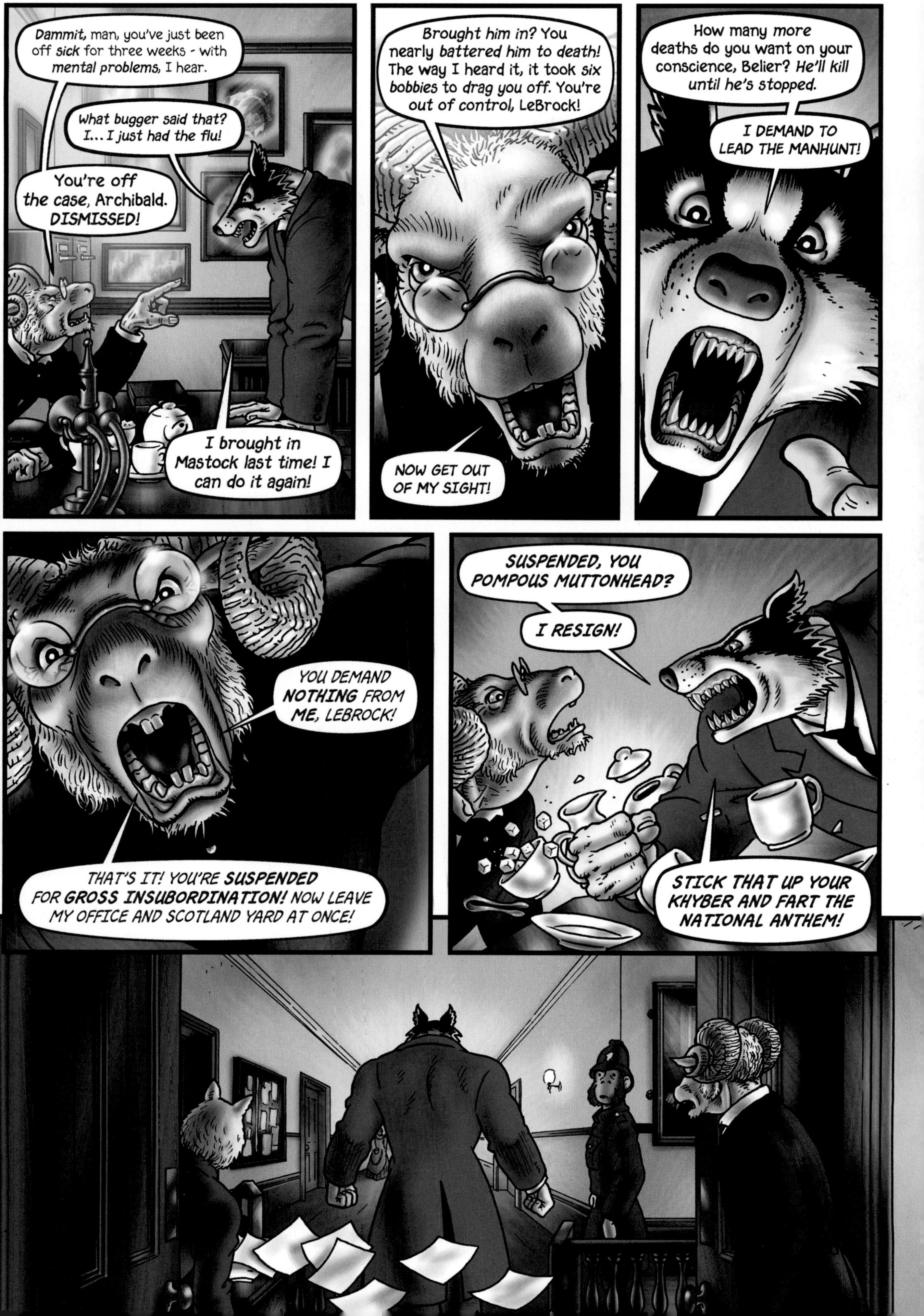
Dammit, man, you've just been off sick for three weeks - with mental problems, I hear.
What bugger said that? I... I just had the flu!
You're off the case, Archibald. DISMISSED!
I brought in Mastock last time! I can do it again!
Brought him in? You nearly battered him to death! The way I heard it, it took six bobbies to drag you off. You're out of control, LeBrock!
NOW GET OUT OF MY SIGHT!
How many more deaths do you want on your conscience, Belier? He'll kill until he's stopped.
I DEMAND TO LEAD THE MANHUNT!
YOU DEMAND NOTHING FROM ME, LEBROCK!
THAT'S IT! YOU'RE SUSPENDED FOR GROSS INSUBORDINATION! NOW LEAVE MY OFFICE AND SCOTLAND YARD AT ONCE!
SUSPENDED, YOU POMPOUS MUTTONHEAD?
I RESIGN!
STICK THAT UP YOUR KHYBER AND FART THE NATIONAL ANTHEM!

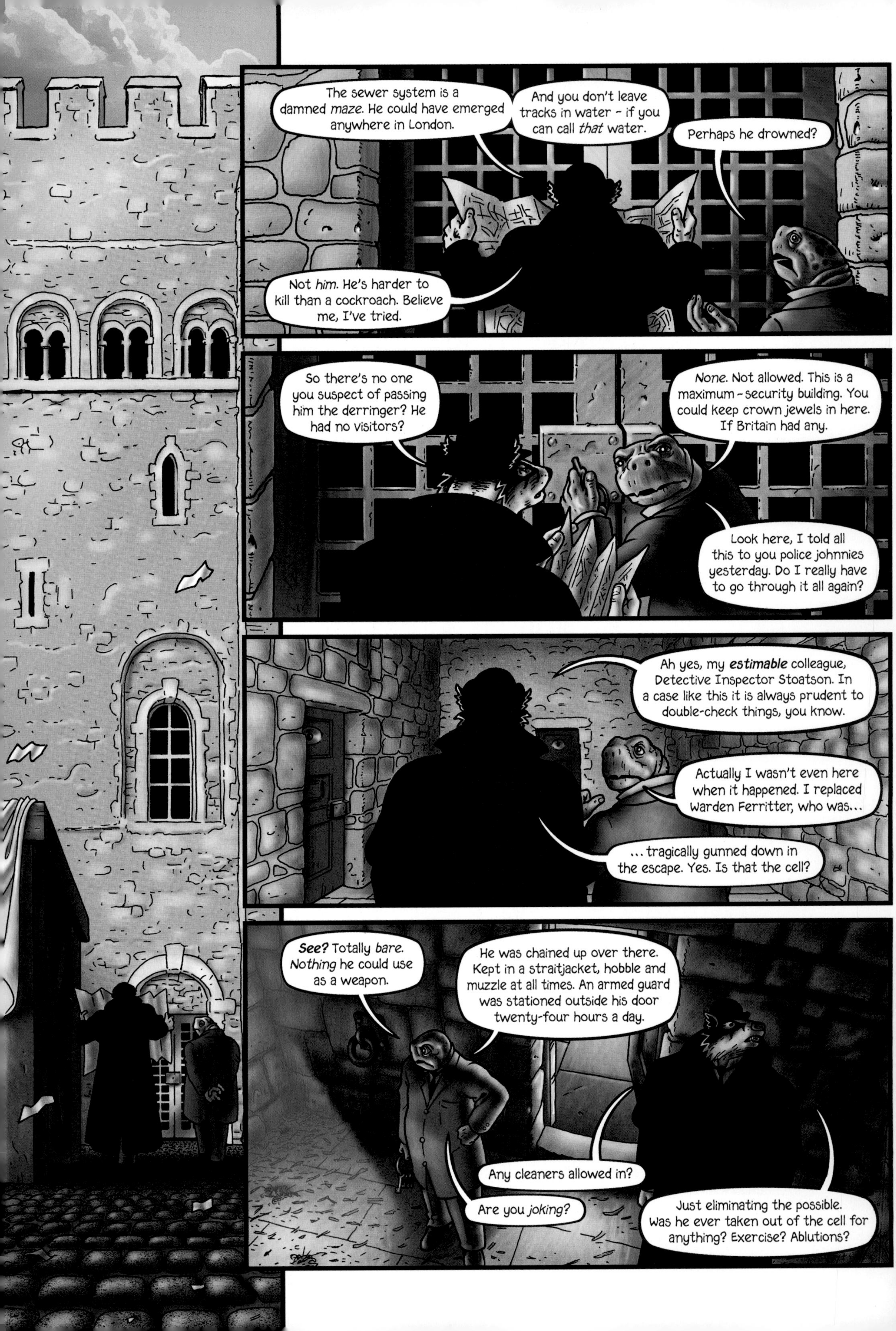
The sewer system is a damned *maze*. He could have emerged anywhere in London.
And you don't leave tracks in water - if you can call *that* water.
Perhaps he drowned?
Not *him*. He's harder to kill than a cockroach. Believe me, I've tried.
So there's no one you suspect of passing him the derringer? He had no visitors?
None. Not allowed. This is a maximum-security building. You could keep crown jewels in here. If Britain had any.
Look here, I told all this to you police johnnies yesterday. Do I really have to go through it all again?
Ah yes, my ***estimable*** colleague, Detective Inspector Stoatson. In a case like this it is always prudent to double-check things, you know.
Actually I wasn't even here when it happened. I replaced Warden Ferritter, who was...
...tragically gunned down in the escape. Yes. Is that the cell?
See? Totally *bare*. *Nothing* he could use as a weapon.
He was chained up over there. Kept in a straitjacket, hobble and muzzle at all times. An armed guard was stationed outside his door twenty-four hours a day.
Any cleaners allowed in?
Are you *joking*?
Just eliminating the possible. Was he ever taken out of the cell for anything? Exercise? Ablutions?

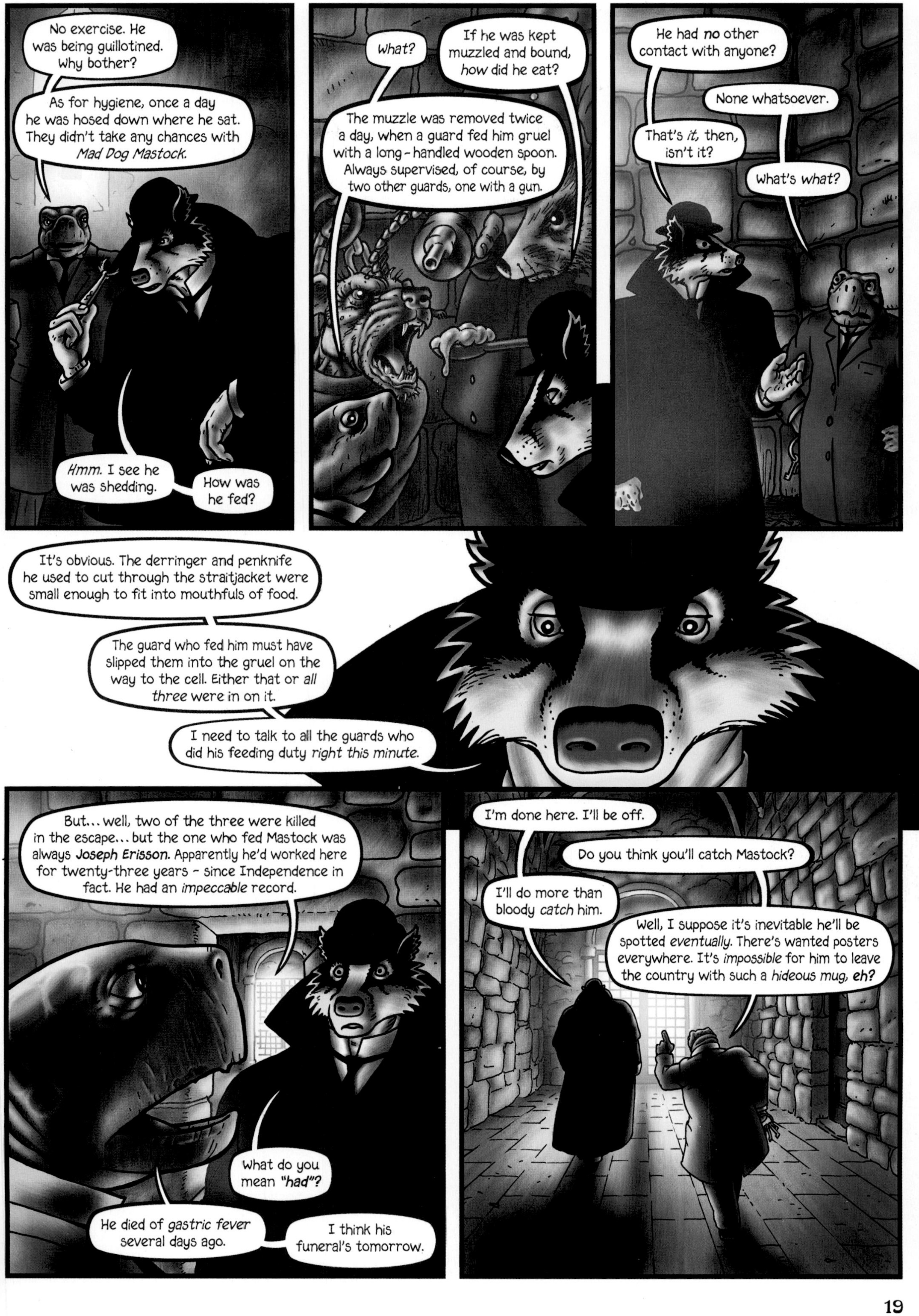

No exercise. He was being guillotined. Why bother?
As for hygiene, once a day he was hosed down where he sat. They didn't take any chances with *Mad Dog Mastock.*
Hmm. I see he was shedding.
How was he fed?
What?
If he was kept muzzled and bound, *how* did he eat?
The muzzle was removed twice a day, when a guard fed him gruel with a long-handled wooden spoon. Always supervised, of course, by two other guards, one with a gun.
He had **no** other contact with anyone?
None whatsoever.
That's *it*, then, isn't it?
What's *what?*
It's obvious. The derringer and penknife he used to cut through the straitjacket were small enough to fit into mouthfuls of food.
The guard who fed him must have slipped them into the gruel on the way to the cell. Either that or *all three* were in on it.
I need to talk to all the guards who did his feeding duty *right this minute.*
But... well, two of the three were killed in the escape... but the one who fed Mastock was always **Joseph Erisson.** Apparently he'd worked here for twenty-three years - since Independence in fact. He had an *impeccable* record.
What do you mean **"had"?**
He died of *gastric fever* several days ago.
I think his funeral's tomorrow.
I'm done here. I'll be off.
Do you think you'll catch Mastock?
I'll do more than bloody *catch* him.
Well, I suppose it's inevitable he'll be spotted *eventually.* There's wanted posters everywhere. It's *impossible* for him to leave the country with such a *hideous mug,* **eh?**

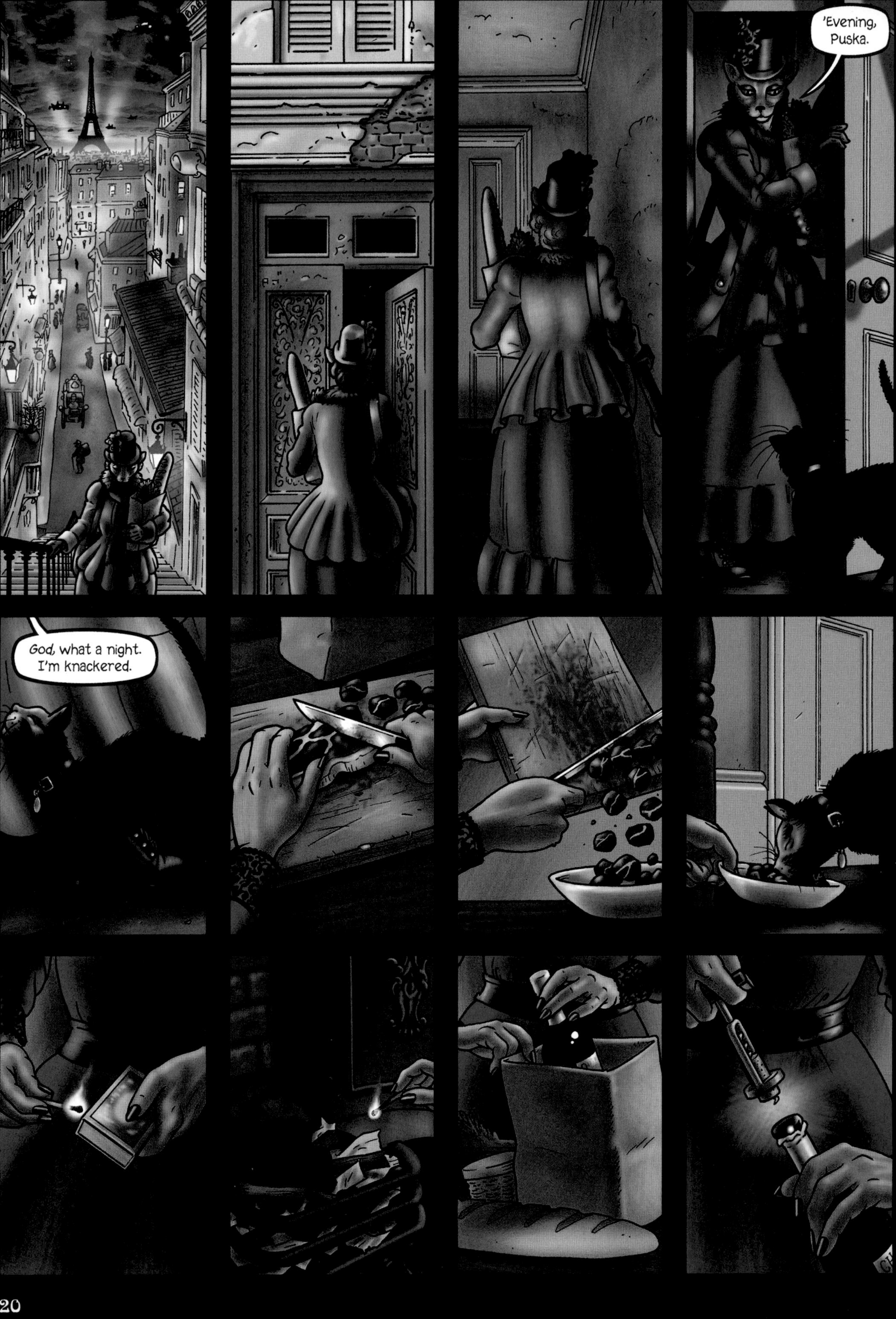
'Evening, Puska.
God, what a night. I'm knackered.

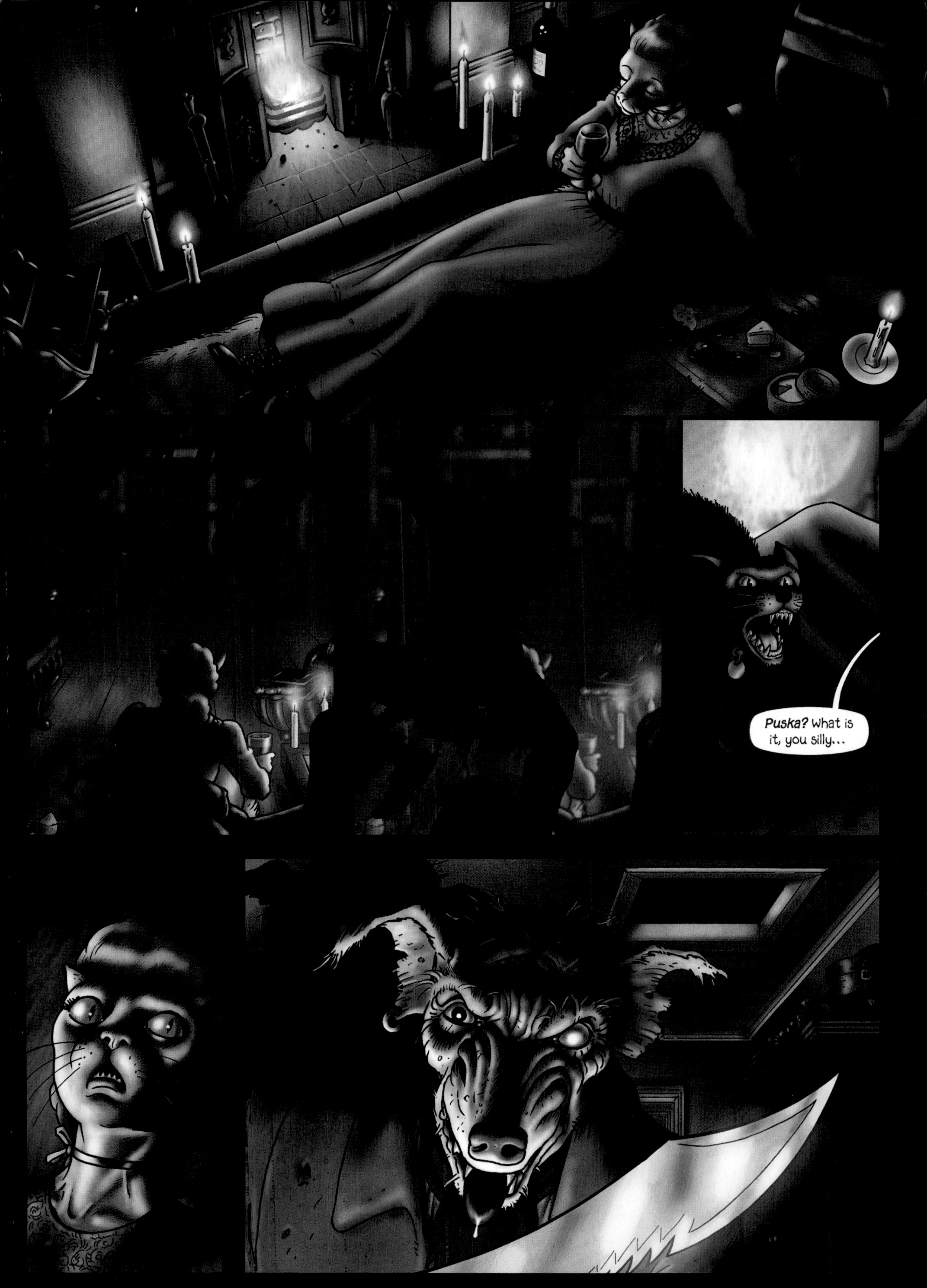
Puska? What is it, you silly...

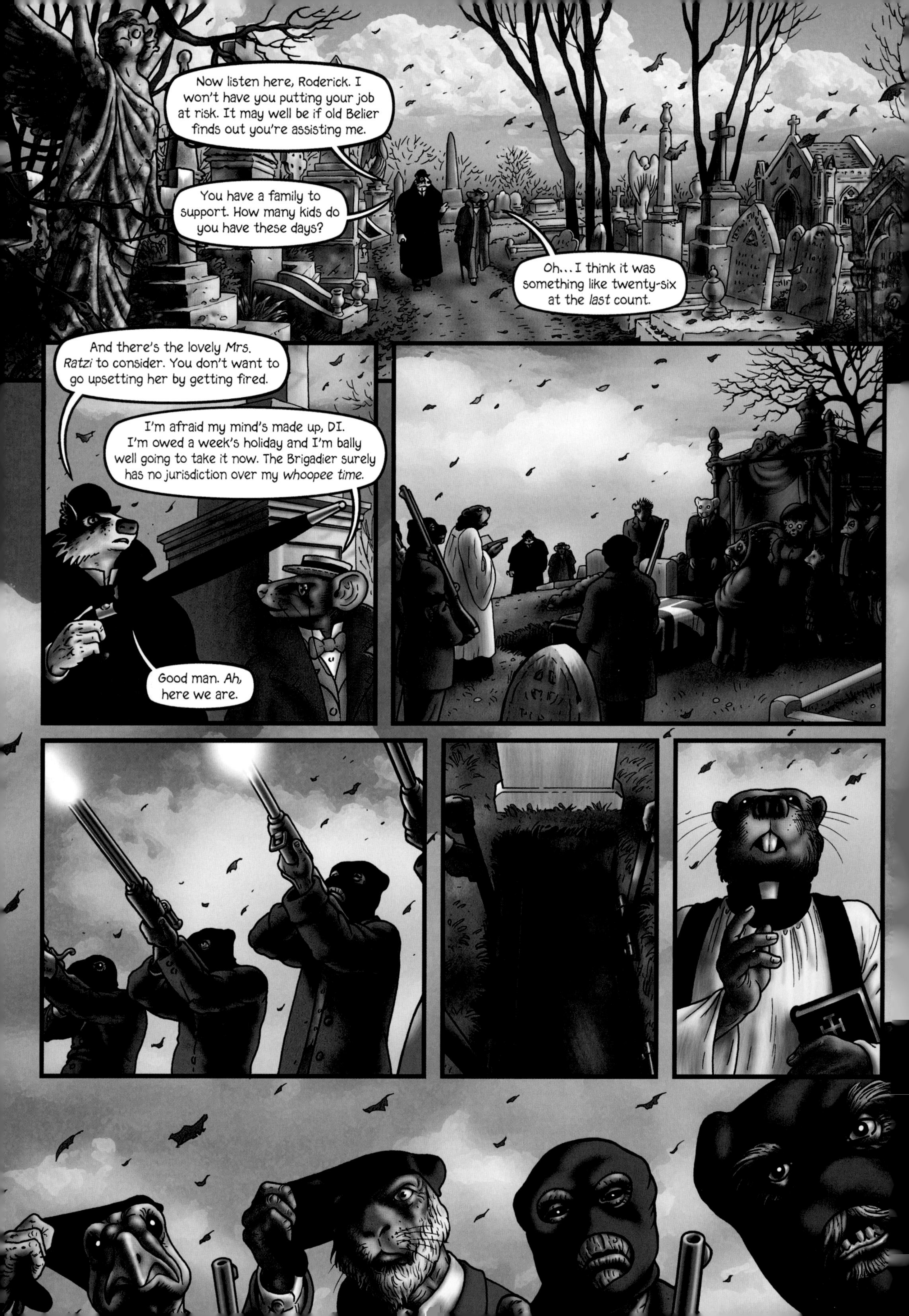

Now listen here, Roderick. I won't have you putting your job at risk. It may well be if old Belier finds out you're assisting me.
You have a family to support. How many kids do you have these days?
Oh... I think it was something like twenty-six at the *last* count.
And there's the lovely Mrs. *Ratzi* to consider. You don't want to go upsetting her by getting fired.
I'm afraid my mind's made up, DI. I'm owed a week's holiday and I'm bally well going to take it now. The Brigadier surely has no jurisdiction over my *whoopee time.*
Good man. *Ah,* here we are.

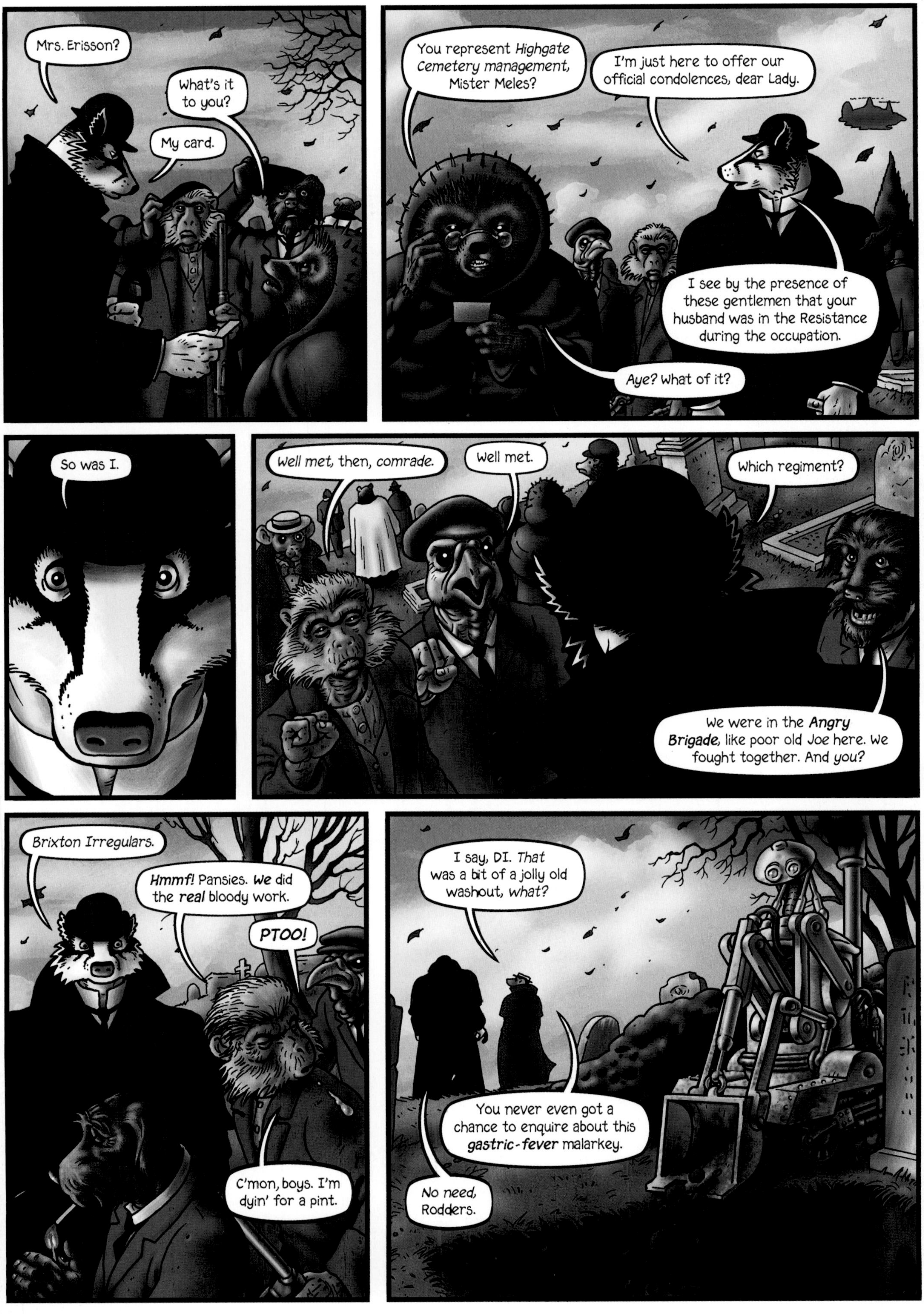
Mrs. Erisson?
What's it to you?
My card.
You represent *Highgate Cemetery management*, Mister Meles?
I'm just here to offer our official condolences, dear Lady.
I see by the presence of these gentlemen that your husband was in the Resistance during the occupation.
Aye? What of it?
So was I.
Well met, then, comrade.
Well met.
Which regiment?
We were in the **Angry Brigade**, like poor old Joe here. We fought together. And *you?*
Brixton Irregulars.
Hmmf! Pansies. **We** did the ***real*** bloody work.
PTOO!
C'mon, boys. I'm dyin' for a pint.
I say, DI. *That* was a bit of a jolly old washout, *what?*
You never even got a chance to enquire about this ***gastric-fever*** malarkey.
No need, Rodders.

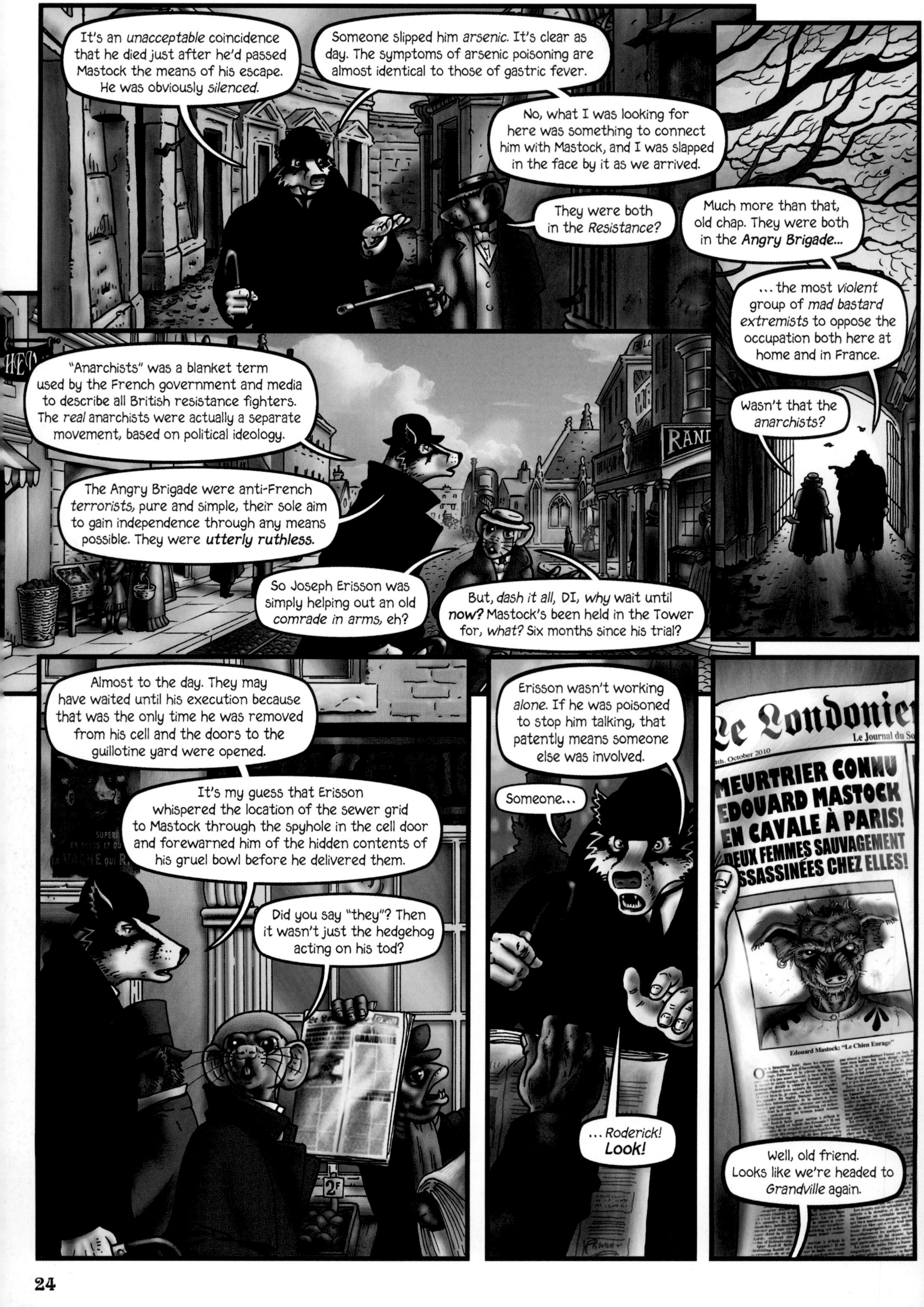

It's an *unacceptable* coincidence that he died just after he'd passed Mastock the means of his escape. He was obviously *silenced.*
Someone slipped him *arsenic.* It's clear as day. The symptoms of arsenic poisoning are almost identical to those of gastric fever.
No, what I was looking for here was something to connect him with Mastock, and I was slapped in the face by it as we arrived.
They were both in the *Resistance?*
Much more than that, old chap. They were both in the ***Angry Brigade...***
...the most *violent* group of *mad bastard extremists* to oppose the occupation both here at home and in France.
Wasn't that the *anarchists?*
"Anarchists" was a blanket term used by the French government and media to describe all British resistance fighters. The *real* anarchists were actually a separate movement, based on political ideology.
The Angry Brigade were anti-French *terrorists,* pure and simple, their sole aim to gain independence through any means possible. They were ***utterly ruthless.***
So Joseph Erisson was simply helping out an old *comrade in arms,* eh?
But, *dash it all,* DI, *why* wait until **now?** Mastock's been held in the Tower for, *what?* Six months since his trial?
Almost to the day. They may have waited until his execution because that was the only time he was removed from his cell and the doors to the guillotine yard were opened.
It's my guess that Erisson whispered the location of the sewer grid to Mastock through the spyhole in the cell door and forewarned him of the hidden contents of his gruel bowl before he delivered them.
Did you say "they"? Then it wasn't just the hedgehog acting on his tod?
GRANDVILLE
2F
Erisson wasn't working *alone.* If he was poisoned to stop him talking, that patently means someone else was involved.
Someone...
...Roderick! ***Look!***
Le Londonier
Le Journal du So
October 2010
MEURTRIER CONNU EDOUARD MASTOCK EN CAVALE À PARIS!
DEUX FEMMES SAUVAGEMENT ASSASSINÉES CHEZ ELLES!
Edouard Mastock: "Le Chien Enragé"
Well, old friend. Looks like we're headed to *Grandville* again.

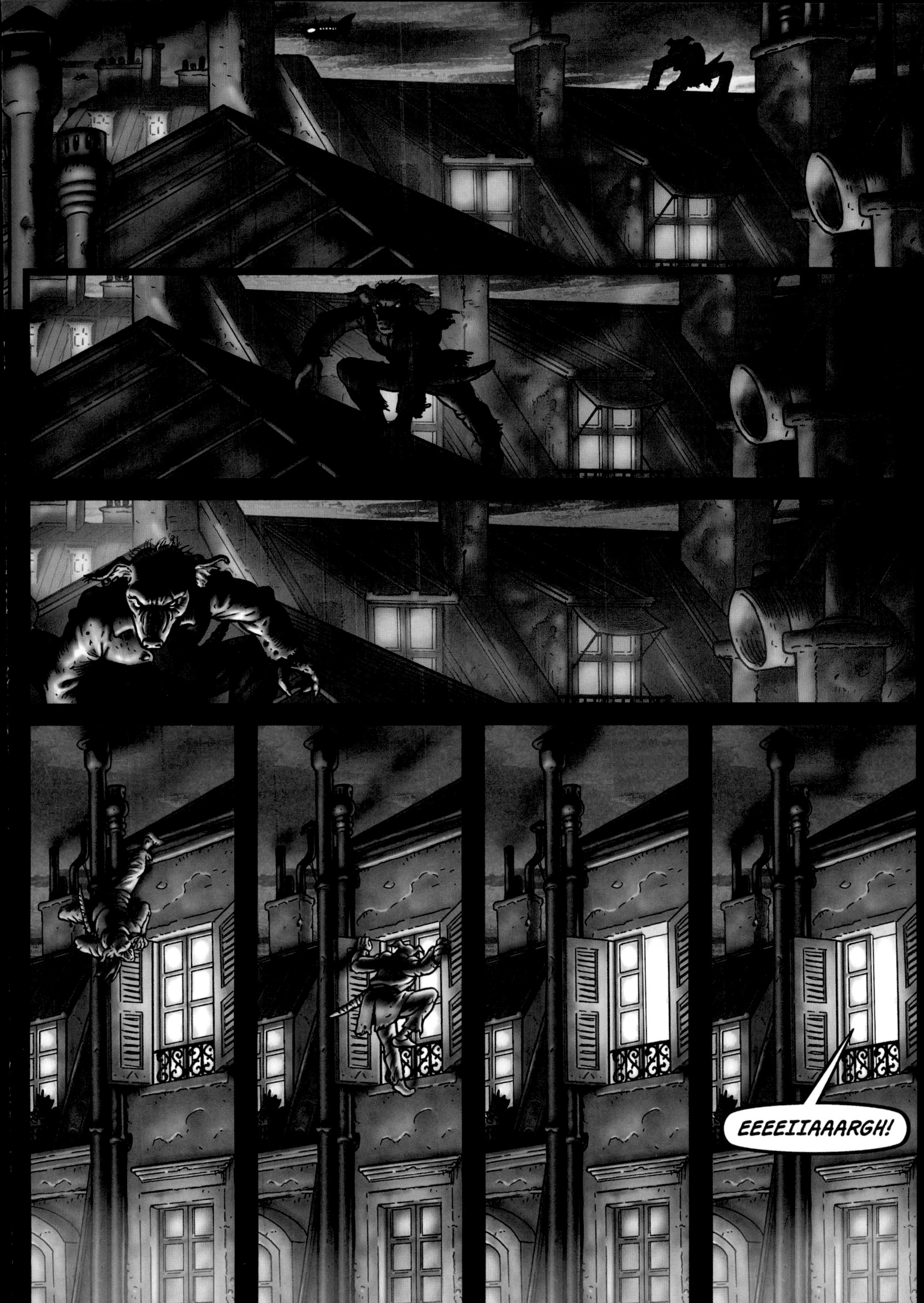
EEEEIIAAARGH!

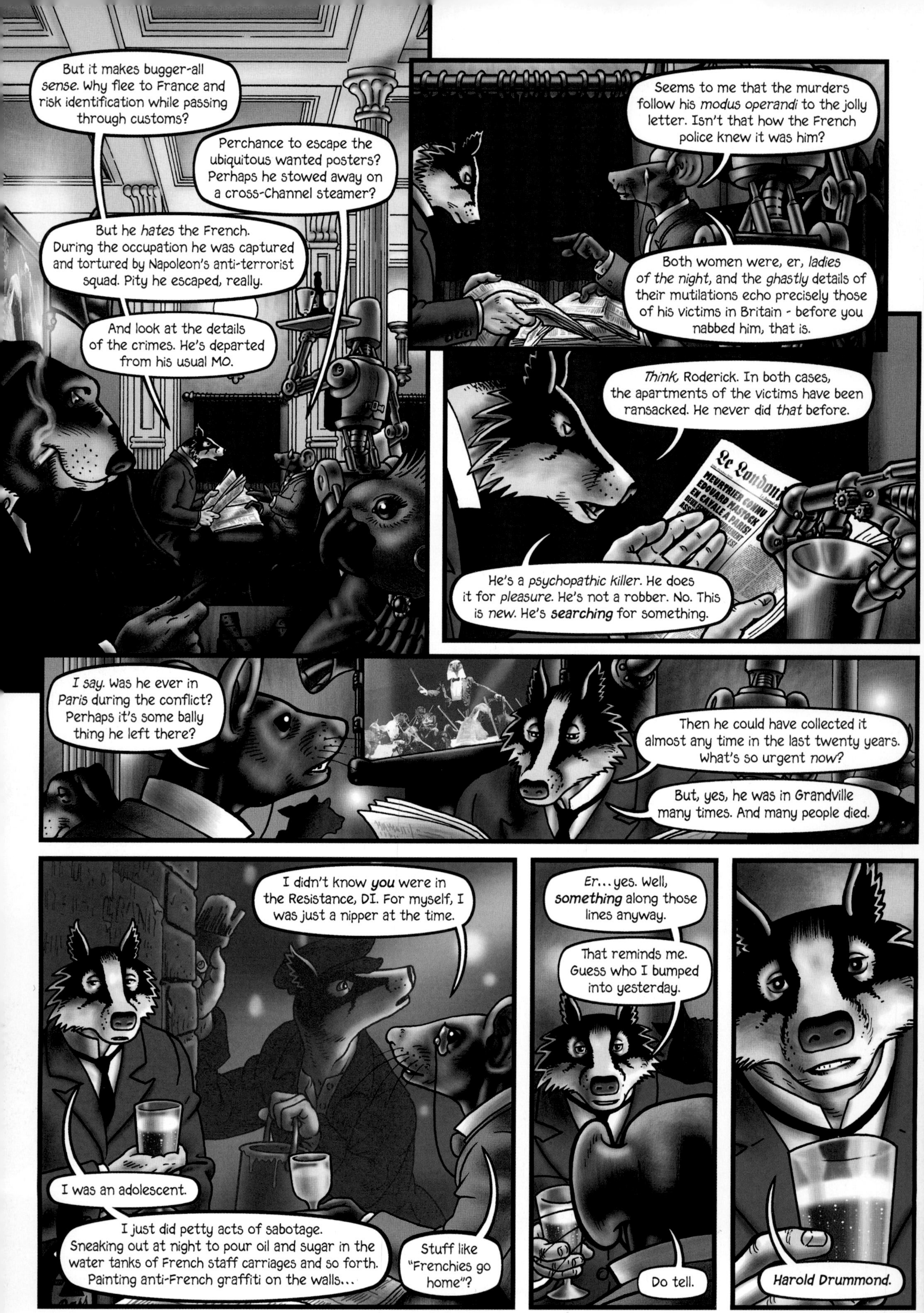

But it makes bugger-all *sense*. Why flee to France and risk identification while passing through customs?
Perchance to escape the ubiquitous wanted posters? Perhaps he stowed away on a cross-Channel steamer?
But he *hates* the French. During the occupation he was captured and tortured by Napoleon's anti-terrorist squad. Pity he escaped, really.
And look at the details of the crimes. He's departed from his usual MO.
Seems to me that the murders follow his *modus operandi* to the jolly letter. Isn't that how the French police knew it was him?
Both women were, er, *ladies of the night*, and the *ghastly* details of their mutilations echo precisely those of his victims in Britain - before you nabbed him, that is.
Think, Roderick. In both cases, the apartments of the victims have been ransacked. He never did *that* before.
He's a *psychopathic killer*. He does it for *pleasure*. He's not a robber. No. This is *new*. He's **searching** for something.
I say. Was he ever in *Paris* during the conflict? Perhaps it's some bally thing he left there?
Then he could have collected it almost any time in the last twenty years. What's so urgent *now*?
But, yes, he was in Grandville many times. And many people died.
I didn't know **you** were in the Resistance, DI. For myself, I was just a nipper at the time.
I was an adolescent.
I just did petty acts of sabotage. Sneaking out at night to pour oil and sugar in the water tanks of French staff carriages and so forth. Painting anti-French graffiti on the walls...
Stuff like "Frenchies go home"?
Er... yes. Well, **something** along those lines anyway.
That reminds me. Guess who I bumped into yesterday.
Do tell.
Harold Drummond.

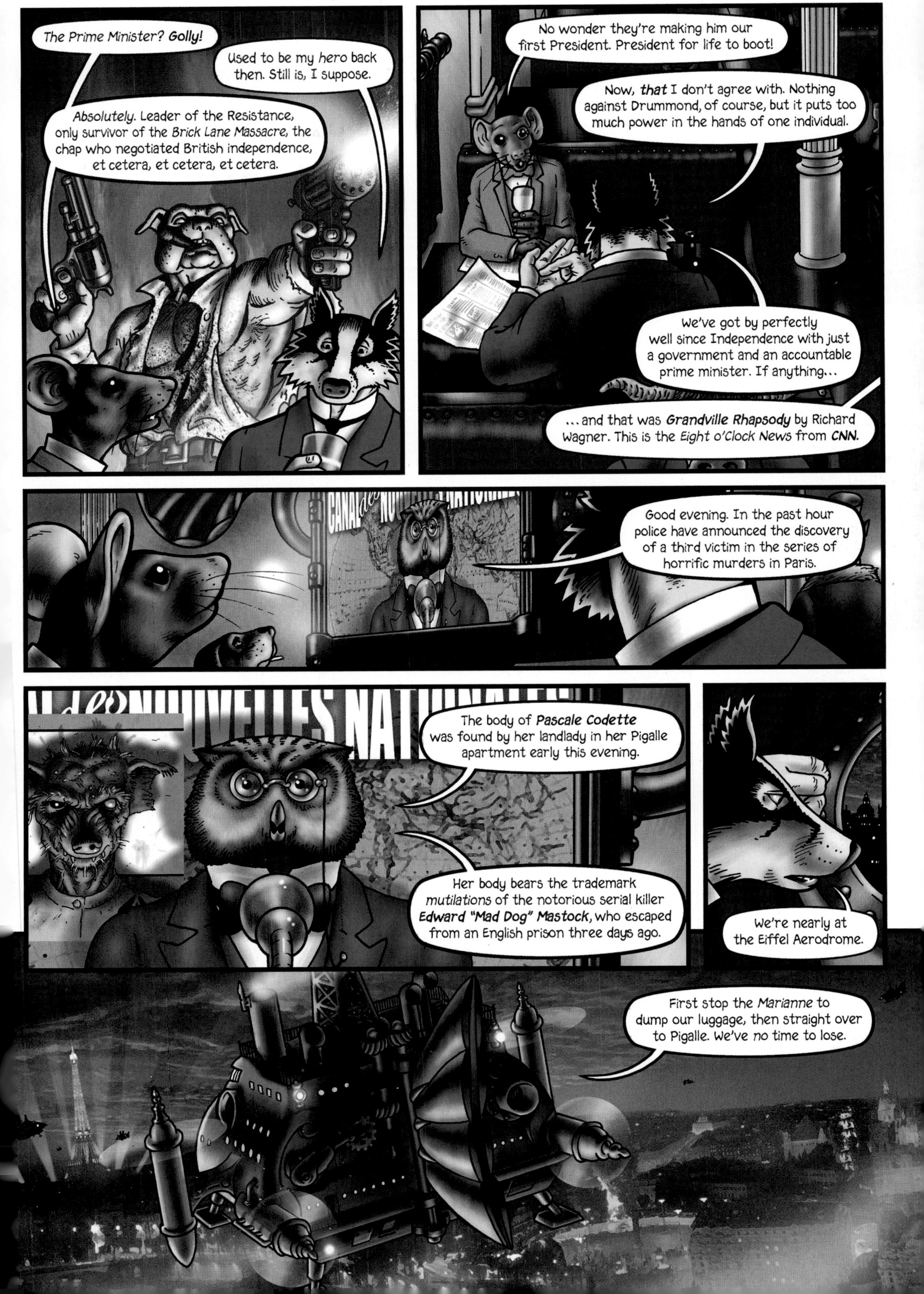
The Prime Minister? **Golly!**
Used to be my *hero* back then. Still is, I suppose.
Absolutely. Leader of the Resistance, only survivor of the *Brick Lane Massacre*, the chap who negotiated British independence, et cetera, et cetera, et cetera.
No wonder they're making him our first President. President for life to boot!
Now, ***that*** I don't agree with. Nothing against Drummond, of course, but it puts too much power in the hands of one individual.
We've got by perfectly well since Independence with just a government and an accountable prime minister. If anything...
...and that was ***Grandville Rhapsody*** by Richard Wagner. This is the *Eight o'Clock News* from ***CNN***.
Good evening. In the past hour police have announced the discovery of a third victim in the series of horrific murders in Paris.
The body of ***Pascale Codette*** was found by her landlady in her Pigalle apartment early this evening.
Her body bears the trademark *mutilations* of the notorious serial killer ***Edward "Mad Dog" Mastock***, who escaped from an English prison three days ago.
We're nearly at the Eiffel Aerodrome.
First stop the *Marianne* to dump our luggage, then straight over to Pigalle. We've *no* time to lose.

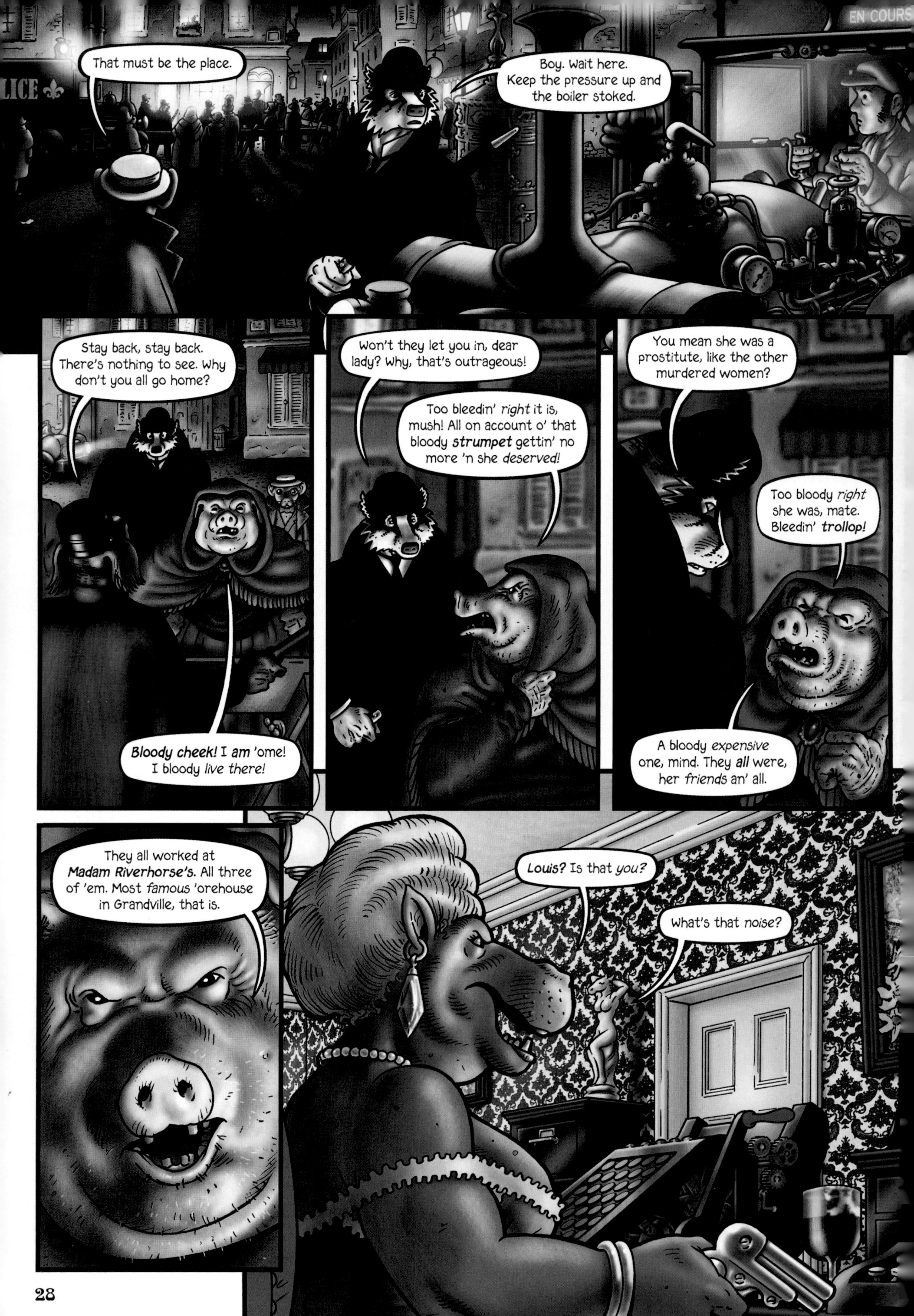

EN COURS
LICE
That must be the place.
Boy. Wait here.
Keep the pressure up and the boiler stoked.
Stay back, stay back. There's nothing to see. Why don't you all go home?
Bloody cheek! I **am** 'ome! I bloody *live there!*
Won't they let you in, dear lady? Why, that's outrageous!
Too bleedin' *right* it is, mush! All on account o' that bloody ***strumpet*** gettin' no more 'n she *deserved!*
You mean she was a prostitute, like the other murdered women?
Too bloody *right* she was, mate. Bleedin' ***trollop!***
A bloody *expensive* one, mind. They **all** were, her *friends* an' all.
They all worked at ***Madam Riverhorse's.*** All three of 'em. Most *famous* 'orehouse in Grandville, that is.
Louis? Is that *you?*
What's that *noise?*

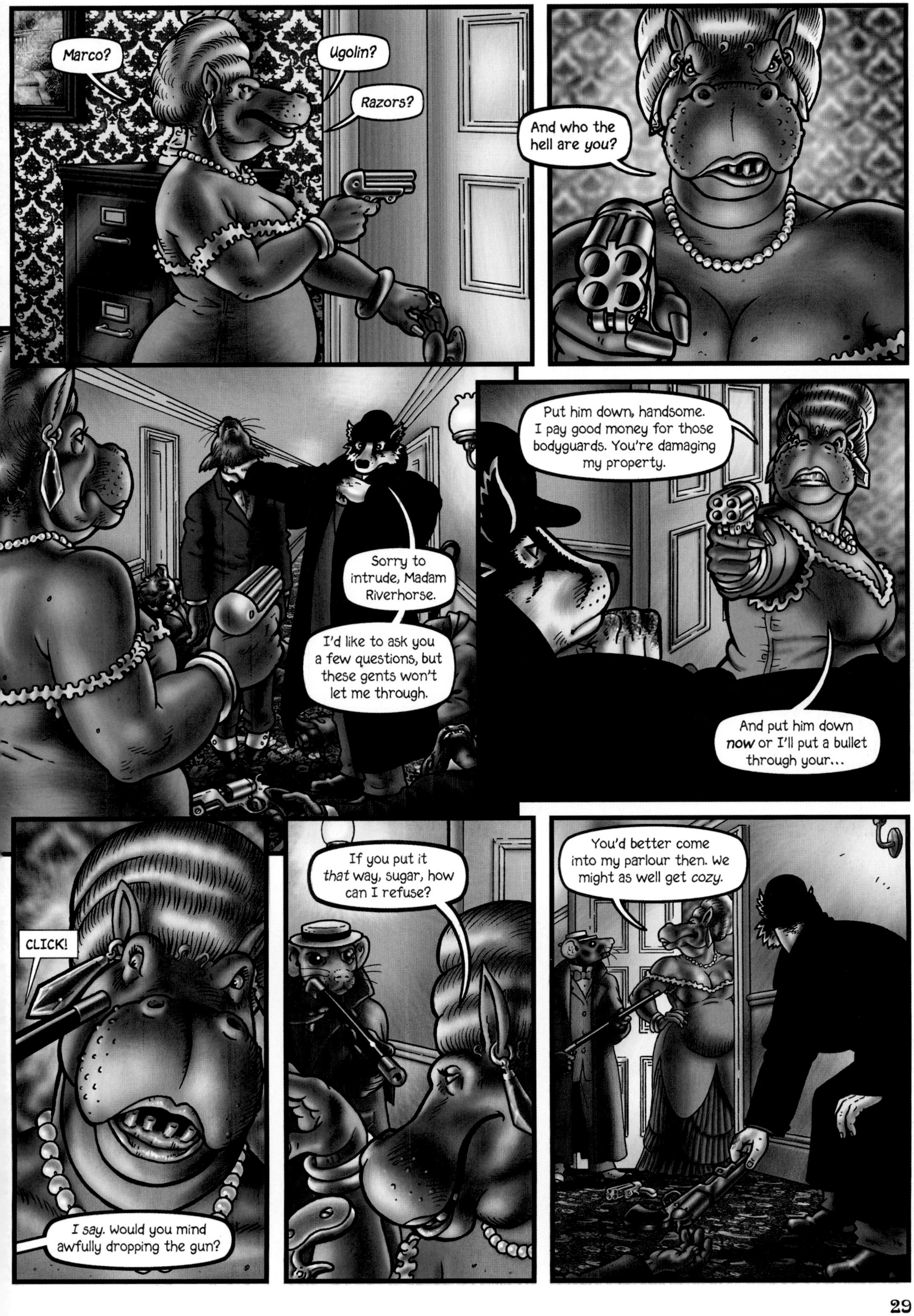
Marco?
Ugolin?
Razors?
And who the hell are you?
Sorry to intrude, Madam Riverhorse.
I'd like to ask you a few questions, but these gents won't let me through.
Put him down, handsome. I pay good money for those bodyguards. You're damaging my property.
And put him down *now* or I'll put a bullet through your...
CLICK!
I say. Would you mind awfully dropping the gun?
If you put it *that* way, sugar, how can I refuse?
You'd better come into my parlour then. We might as well get *cozy.*

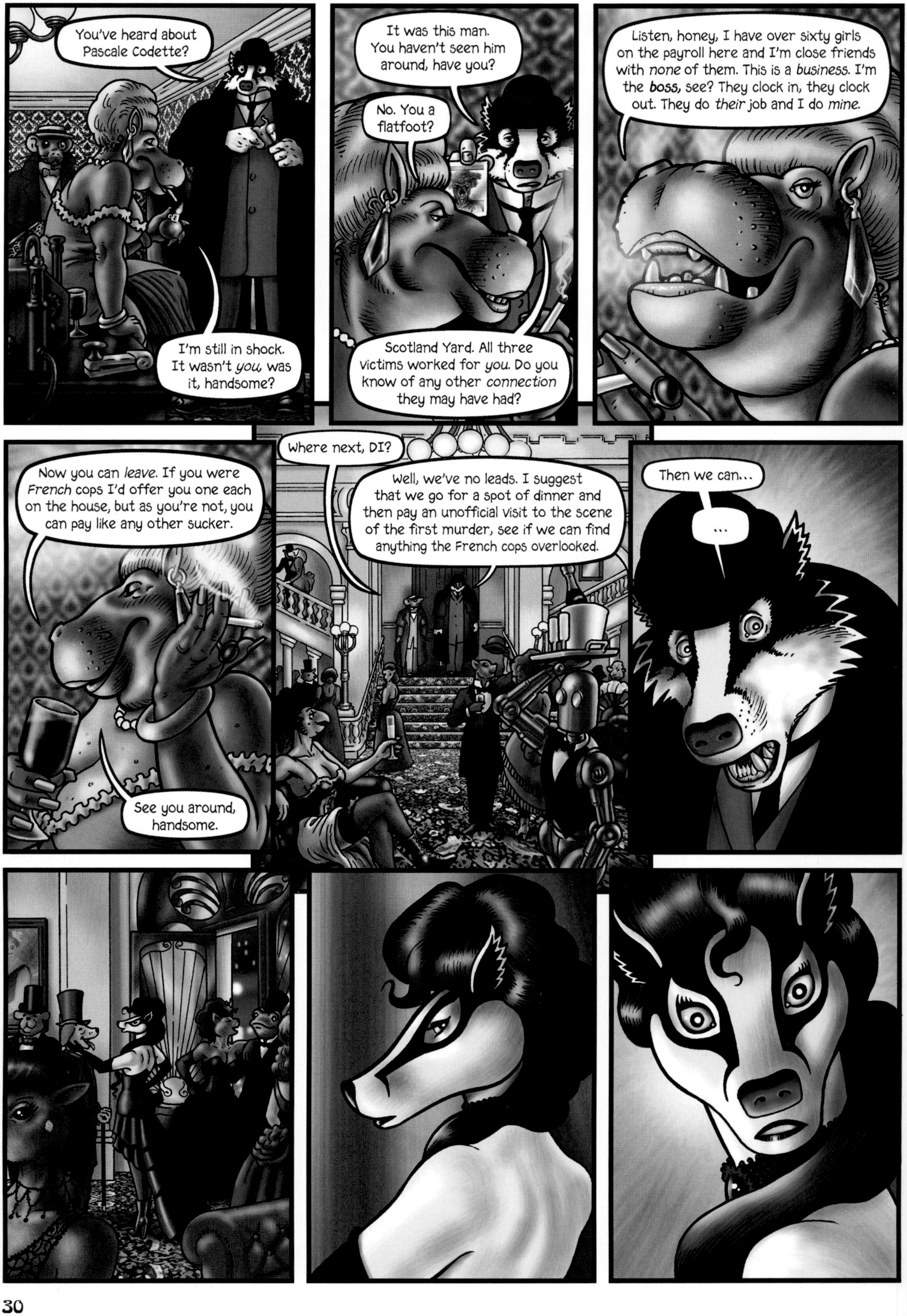
You've heard about Pascale Codette?
I'm still in shock. It wasn't *you*, was it, handsome?
It was this man. You haven't seen him around, have you?
No. You a flatfoot?
Scotland Yard. All three victims worked for *you*. Do you know of any other *connection* they may have had?
Listen, honey, I have over sixty girls on the payroll here and I'm close friends with *none* of them. This is a *business*. I'm the ***boss***, see? They clock in, they clock out. They do *their* job and I do *mine*.
Now you can *leave*. If you were *French* cops I'd offer you one each on the house, but as you're not, you can pay like any other sucker.
See you around, handsome.
Where next, DI?
Well, we've no leads. I suggest that we go for a spot of dinner and then pay an unofficial visit to the scene of the first murder, see if we can find anything the French cops overlooked.
Then we can...
...

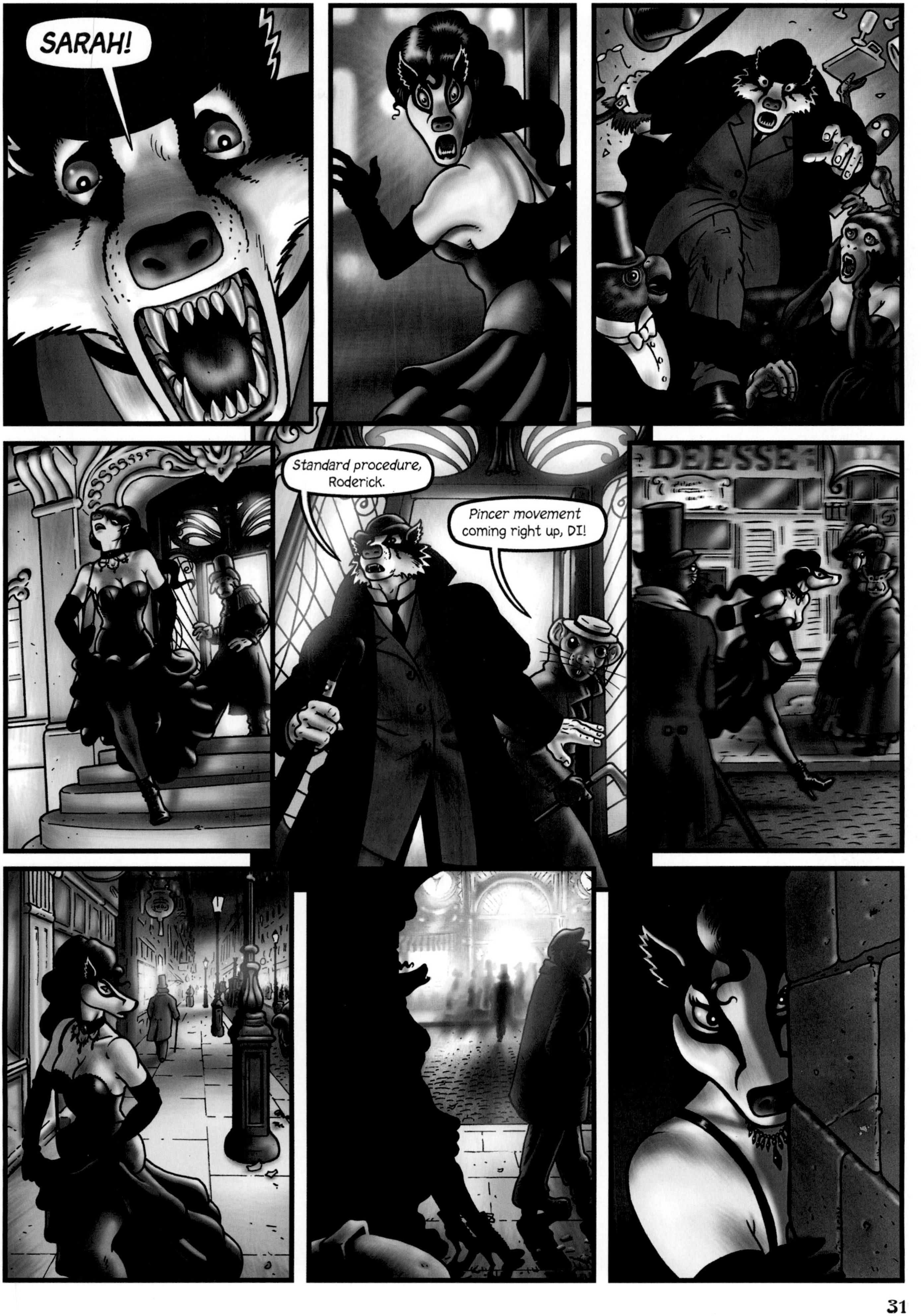
SARAH!
Standard procedure, Roderick.
Pincer movement coming right up, DI!
DEESSE

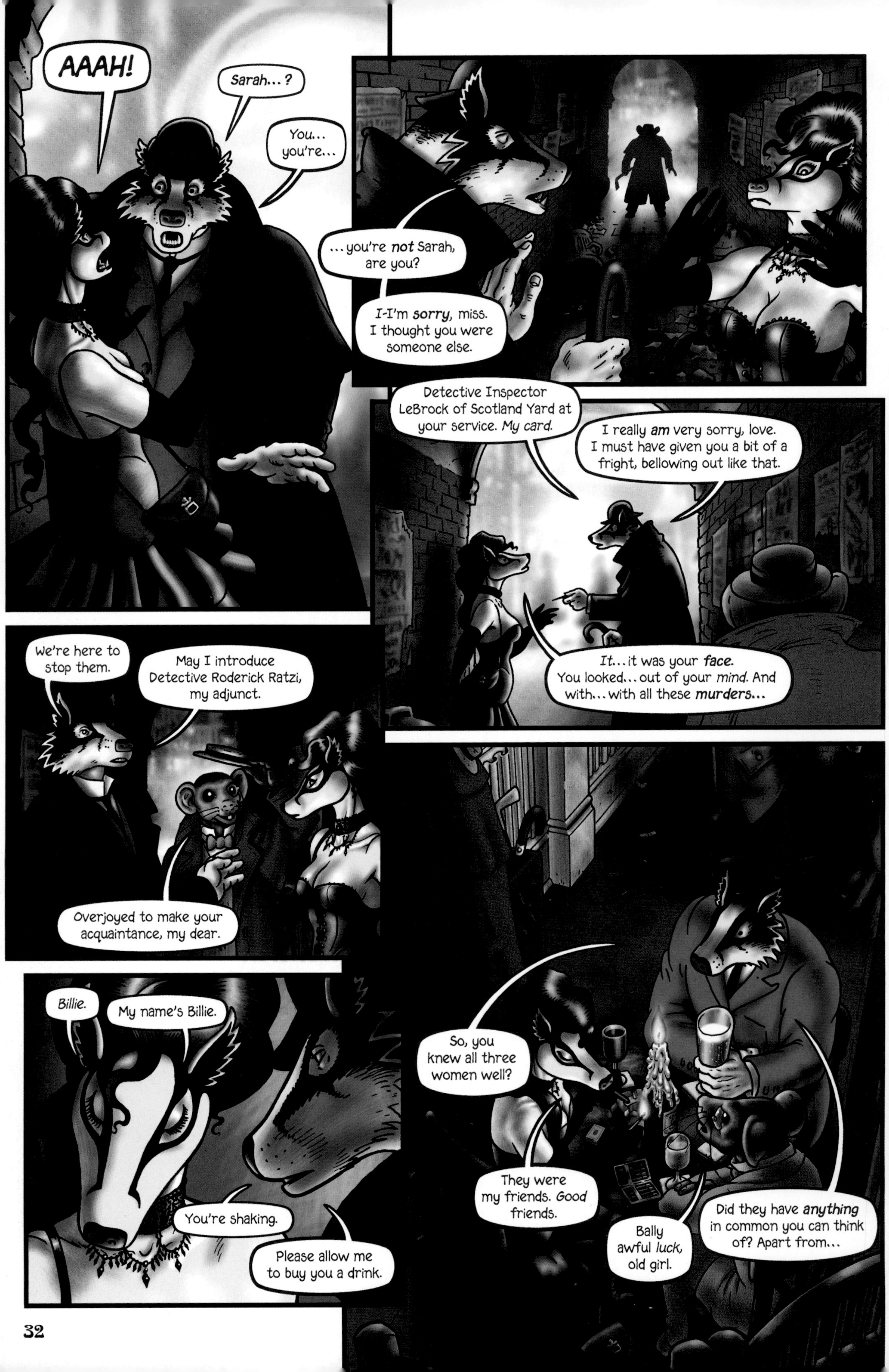
AAAH!
Sarah...?
You... you're...
...you're **not** Sarah, are you?
I-I'm **sorry**, miss. I thought you were someone else.
Detective Inspector LeBrock of Scotland Yard at your service. *My card.*
I really **am** very sorry, love. I must have given you a bit of a fright, bellowing out like that.
It... it was your **face**. You looked... out of your *mind*. And with... with all these **murders**...
We're here to stop them.
May I introduce Detective Roderick Ratzi, my adjunct.
Overjoyed to make your acquaintance, my dear.
Billie.
My name's Billie.
You're shaking.
Please allow me to buy you a drink.
So, you knew all three women well?
They were my friends. *Good* friends.
Bally awful *luck*, old girl.
Did they have **anything** in common you can think of? Apart from...

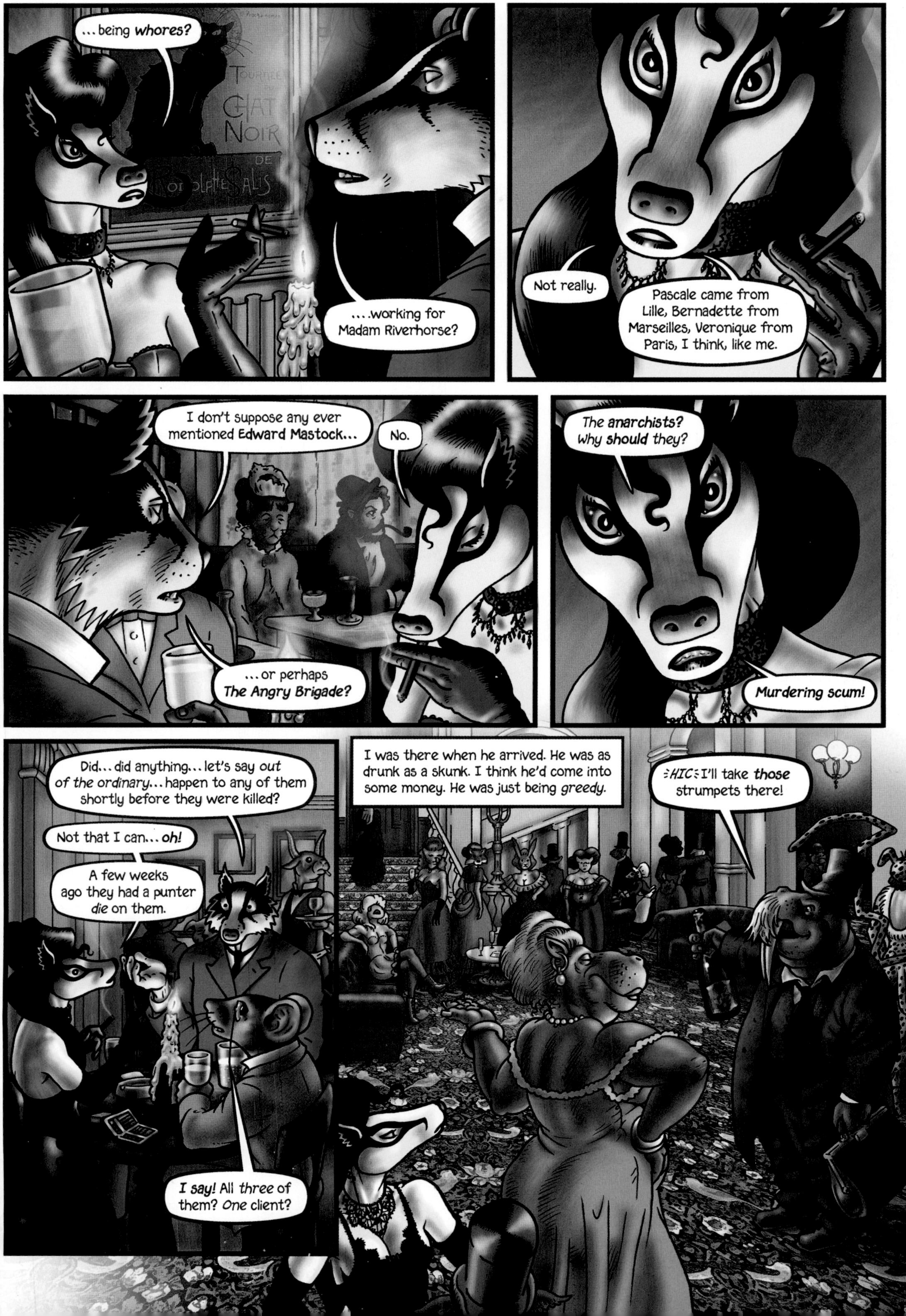

...being *whores?*
TOURNÉE DU CHAT NOIR DE RODOLPHE SALIS
....working for Madam Riverhorse?
Not really.
Pascale came from Lille, Bernadette from Marseilles, Veronique from Paris, I think, like me.
I don't suppose any ever mentioned **Edward Mastock**...
No.
...or perhaps *The Angry Brigade?*
The **anarchists?** *Why* **should** *they?*
Murdering scum!
Did... did anything... let's say *out of the ordinary*... happen to any of them shortly before they were killed?
Not that I can... ***oh!***
A few weeks ago they had a punter *die* on them.
I say! All *three* of them? *One* client?
I was there when he arrived. He was as drunk as a skunk. I think he'd come into some money. He was just being *greedy.*
HIC I'll take ***those*** strumpets there!

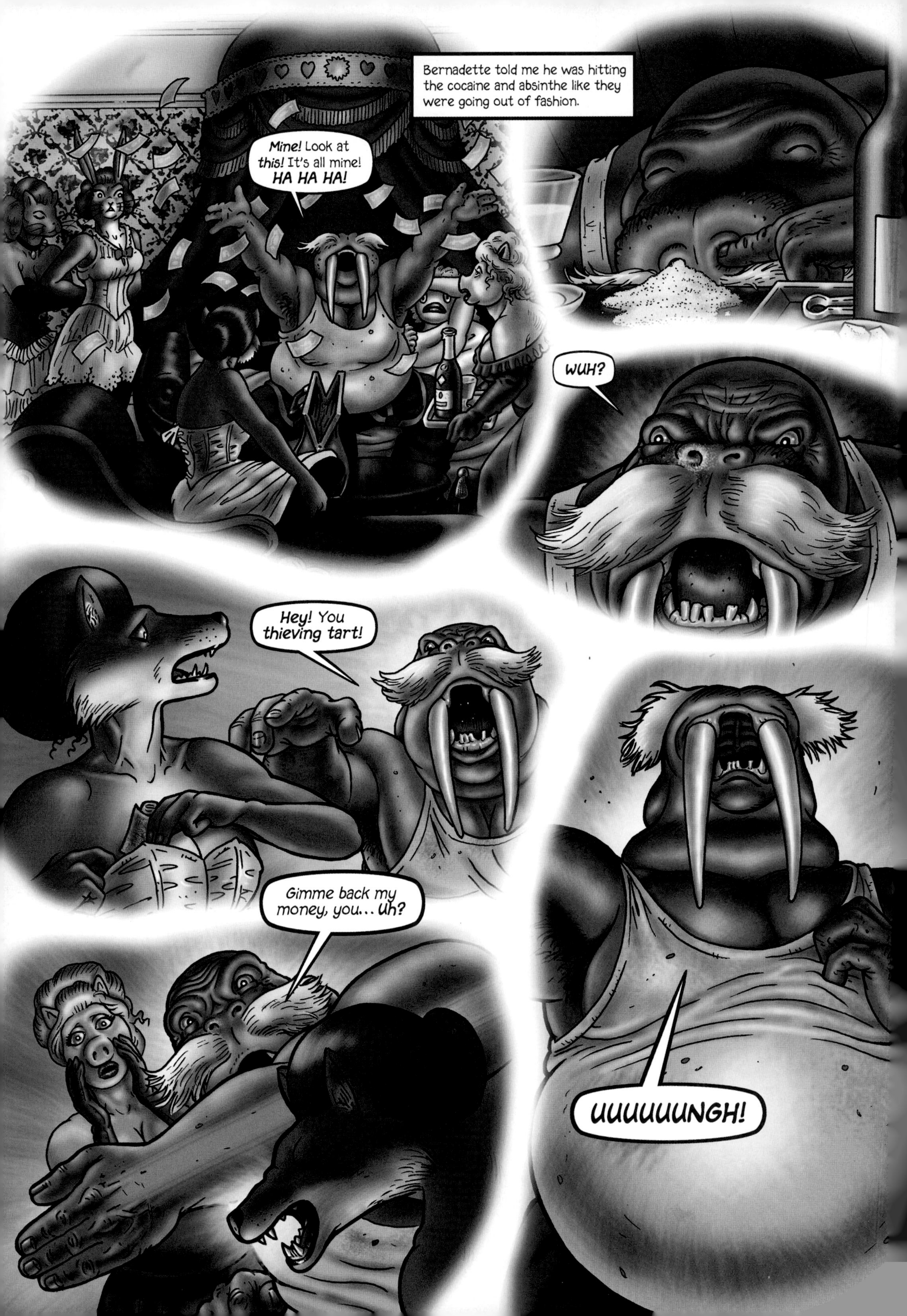
Bernadette told me he was hitting the cocaine and absinthe like they were going out of fashion.
Mine! Look at this! It's all mine! HA HA HA!
WUH?
Hey! You thieving tart!
Gimme back my money, you... uh?
UUUUUUNGH!

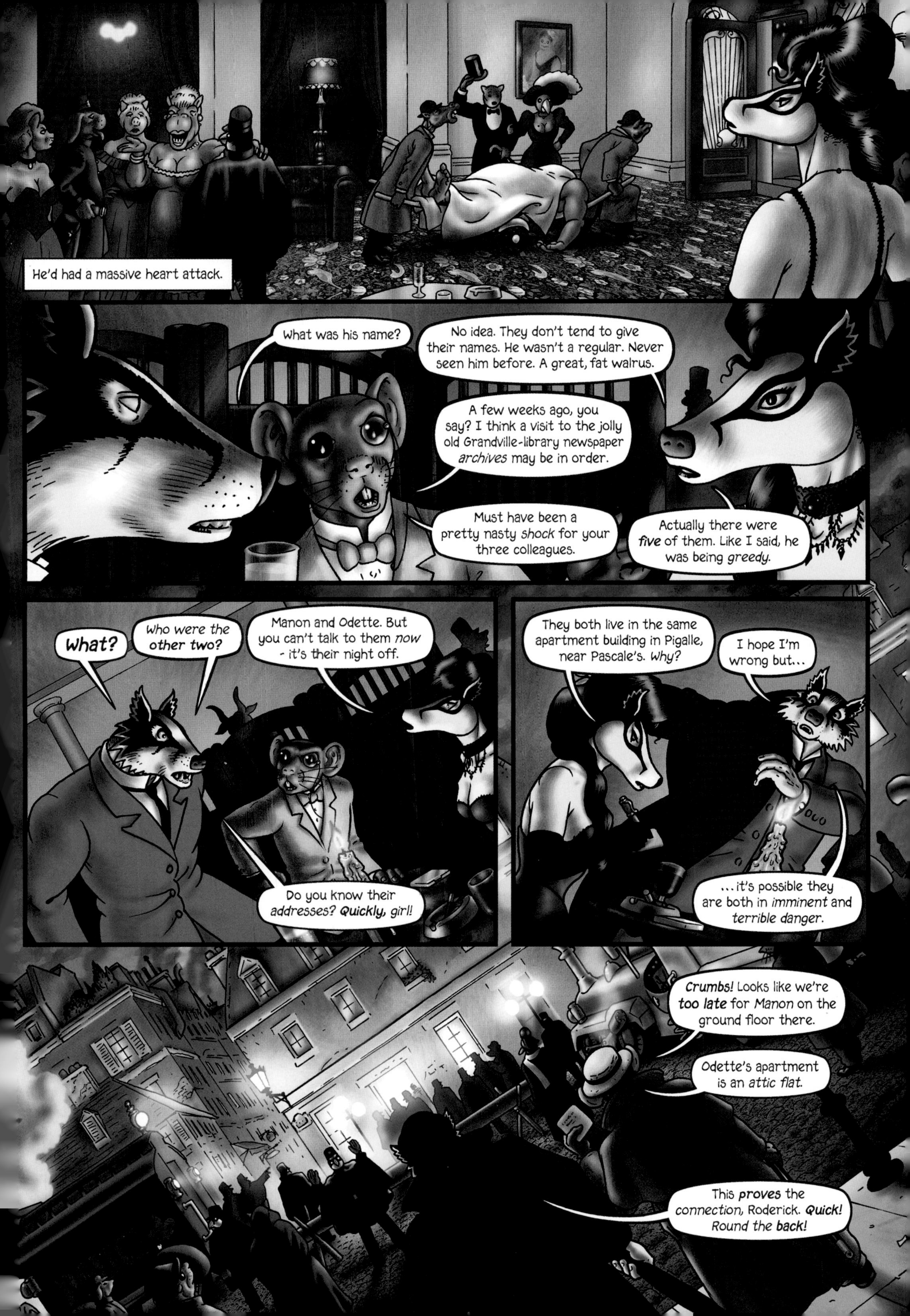

He'd had a massive heart attack.
What was his name?
No idea. They don't tend to give their names. He wasn't a regular. Never seen him before. A great, fat walrus.
A few weeks ago, you say? I think a visit to the jolly old Grandville-library newspaper *archives* may be in order.
Must have been a pretty nasty *shock* for your three colleagues.
Actually there were ***five*** of them. Like I said, he was being *greedy*.
What?
*Who were the **other two**?*
Manon and Odette. But you can't talk to them *now* - it's their night off.
Do you know their *addresses? **Quickly**, girl!*
They both live in the same apartment building in Pigalle, near Pascale's. *Why?*
I hope I'm wrong but...
...it's possible they are both in *imminent* and *terrible danger*.
Crumbs! Looks like we're ***too late*** for Manon on the ground floor there.
Odette's apartment is an *attic flat*.
This ***proves*** the *connection*, Roderick. ***Quick!*** *Round the **back!***

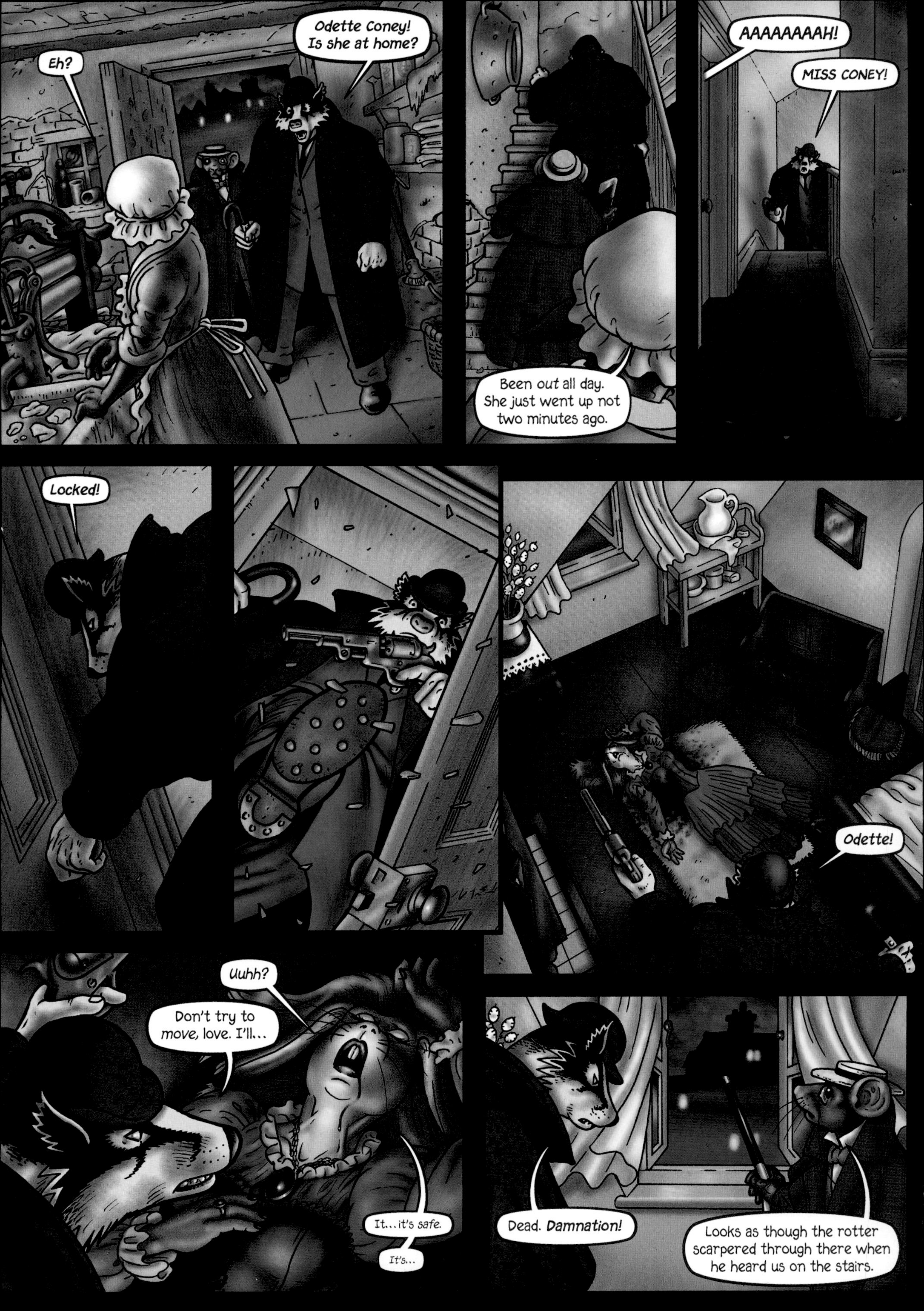
Eh?
Odette Coney! Is she at home?
Been out all day. She just went up not two minutes ago.
AAAAAAAAAH!
MISS CONEY!
Locked!
Odette!
Uuhh?
Don't try to move, love. I'll...
It...it's safe.
It's...
Dead. Damnation!
Looks as though the rotter scarpered through there when he heard us on the stairs.

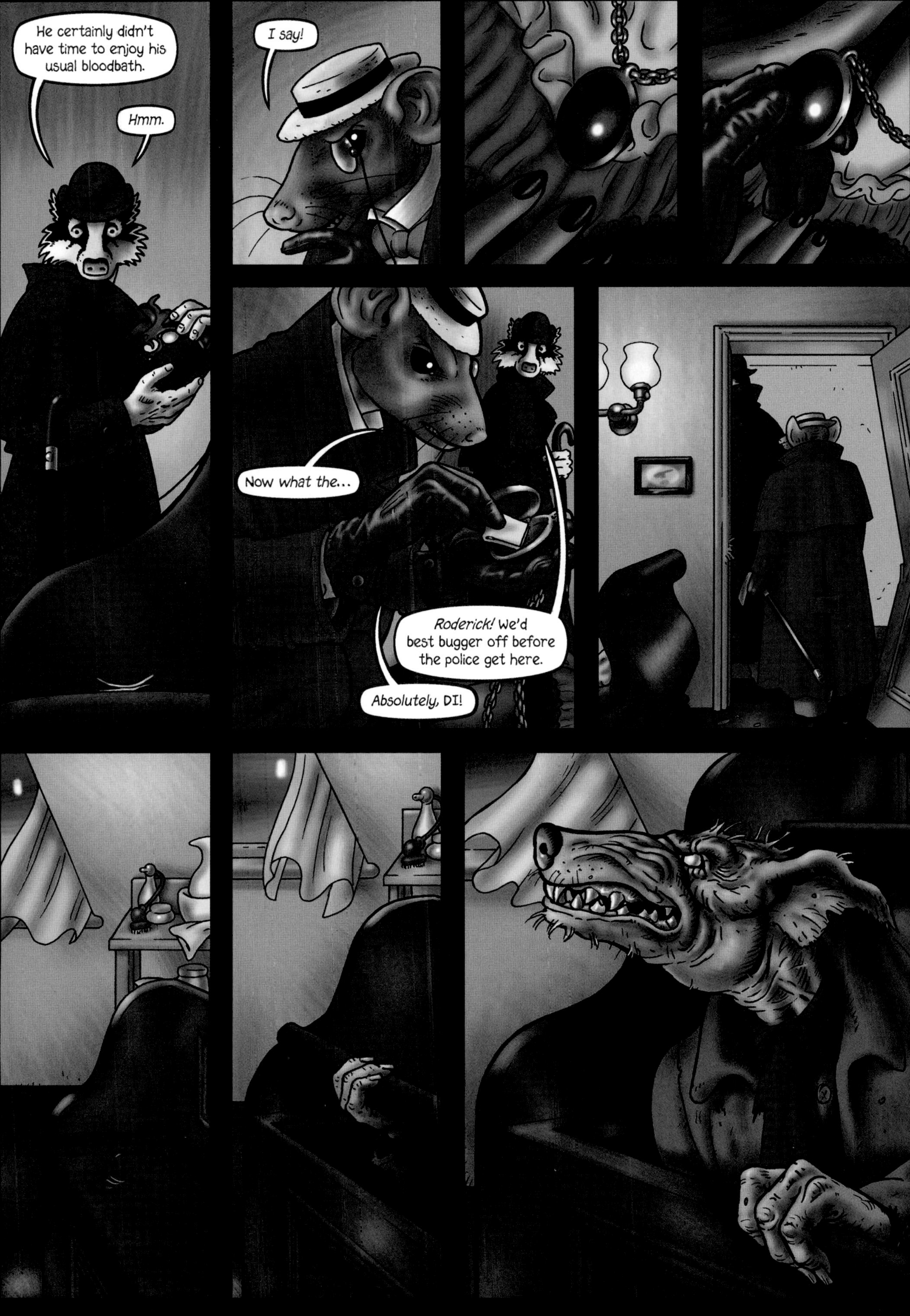
He certainly didn't have time to enjoy his usual bloodbath.
Hmm.
I say!
Now what the...
Roderick! We'd best bugger off before the police get here.
Absolutely, DI!

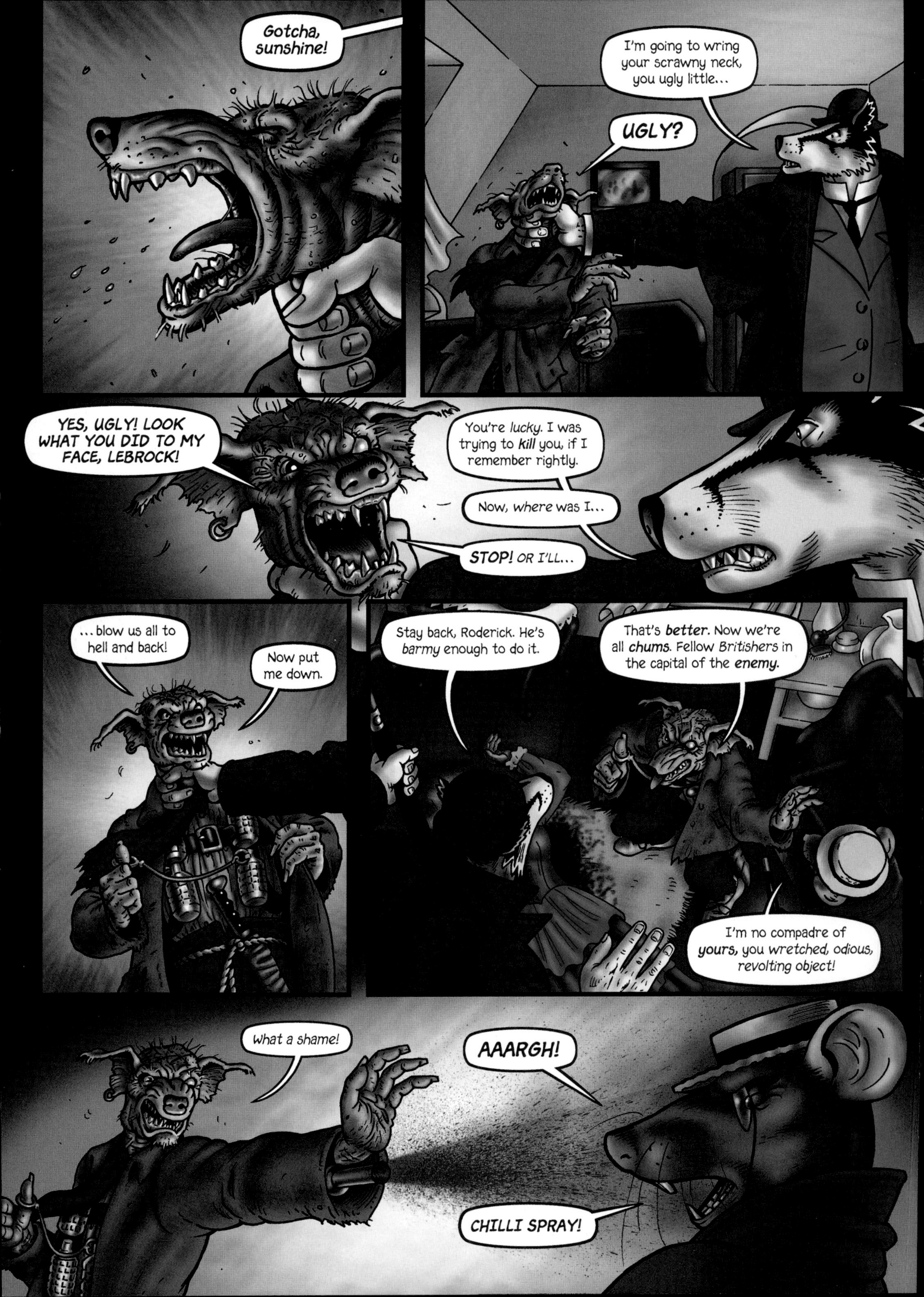
Gotcha, sunshine!
I'm going to wring your scrawny neck, you ugly little...
UGLY?
YES, UGLY! LOOK WHAT YOU DID TO MY FACE, LEBROCK!
You're *lucky*. I was trying to ***kill*** you, if I remember rightly.
Now, *where* was I...
STOP! OR I'LL...
...blow us all to hell and back!
Now put me down.
Stay back, Roderick. He's *barmy* enough to do it.
That's ***better***. Now we're all ***chums***. Fellow *Britishers* in the capital of the ***enemy***.
I'm no compadre of ***yours***, you wretched, odious, revolting object!
What a shame!
AAARGH!
CHILLI SPRAY!

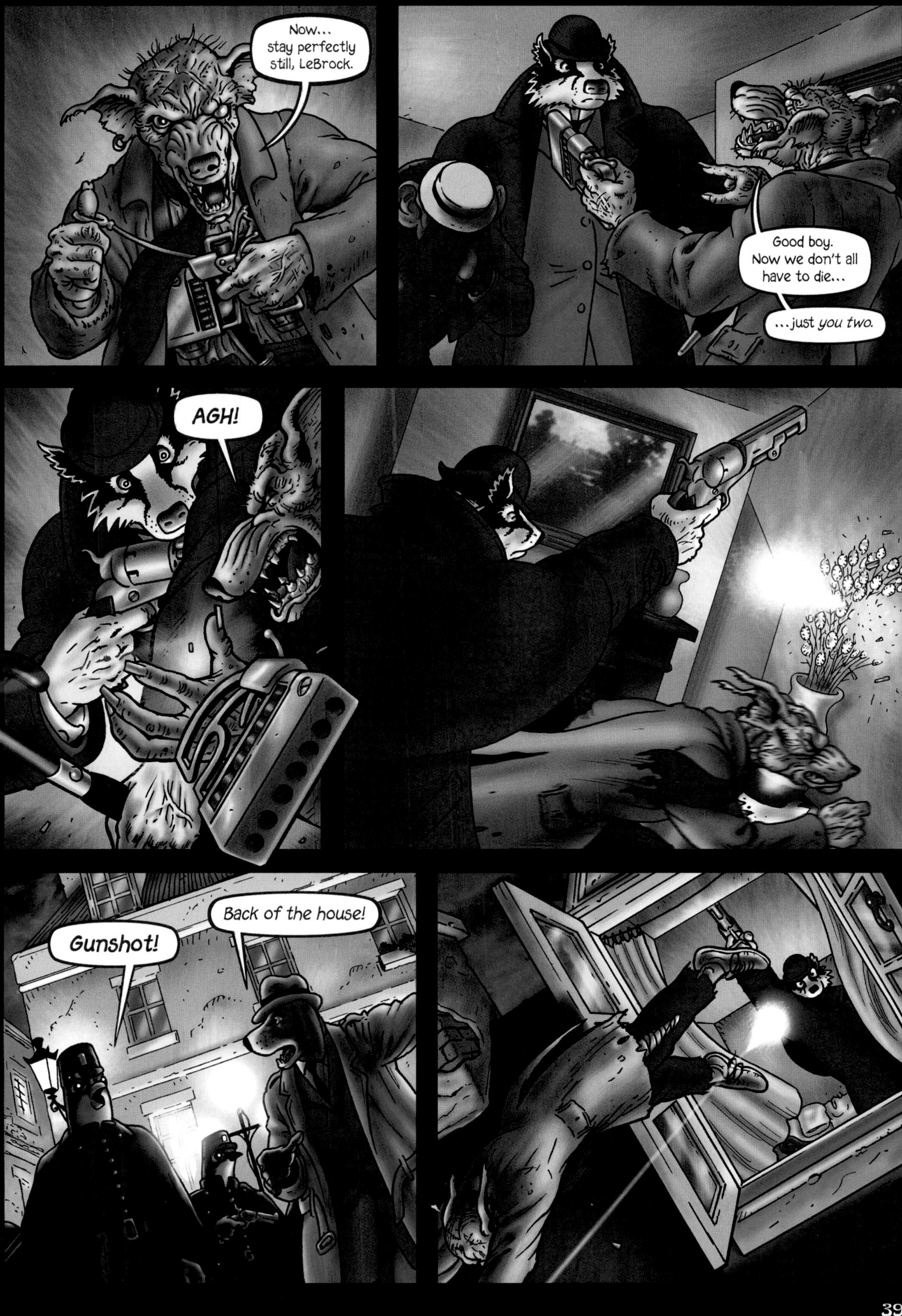
Now... stay perfectly still, LeBrock.
Good boy. Now we don't all have to die...
...just *you two.*
AGH!
Gunshot!
Back of the house!

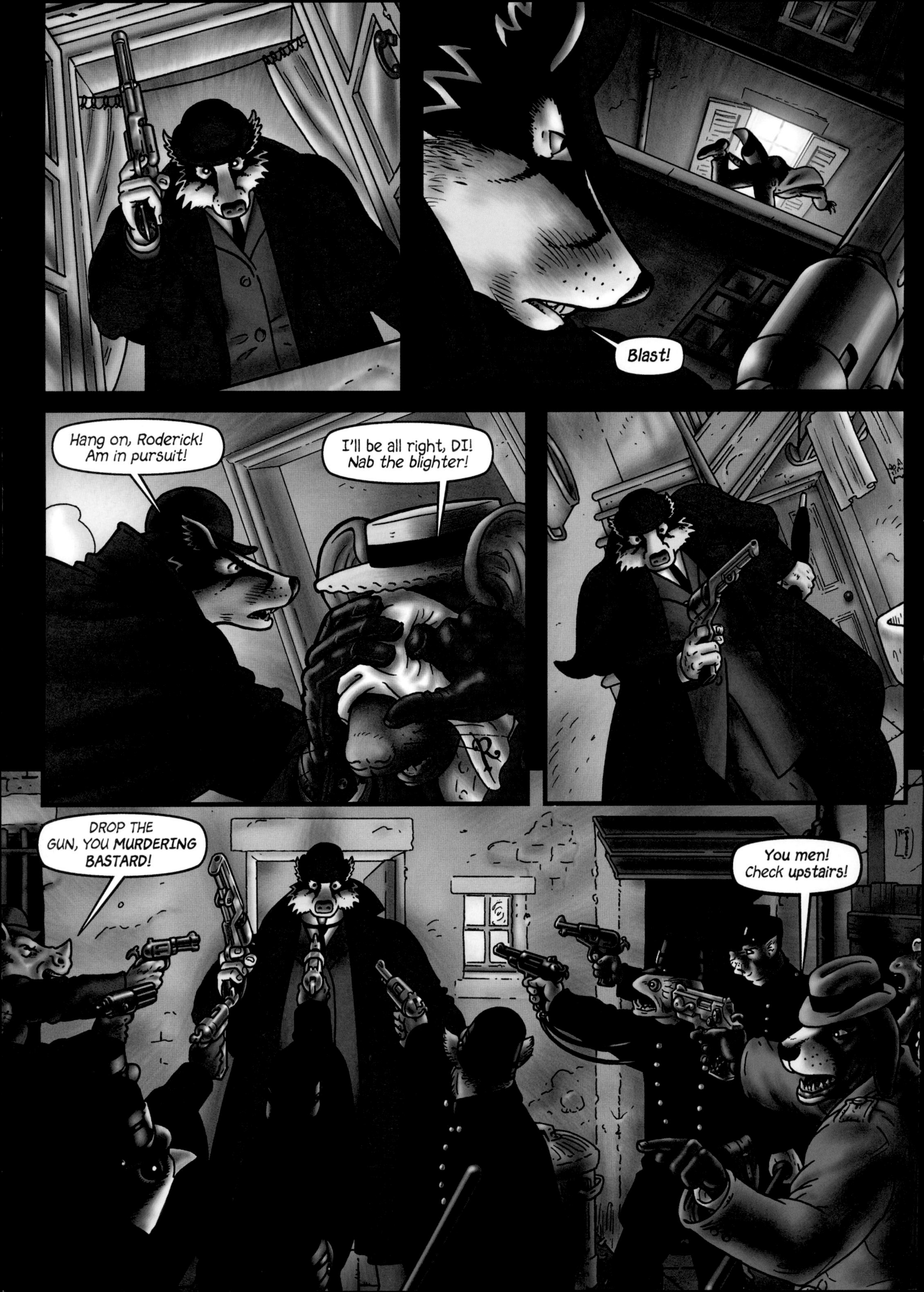
Blast!
Hang on, Roderick! Am in pursuit!
I'll be all right, DI! Nab the blighter!
DROP THE GUN, YOU MURDERING BASTARD!
You men! Check upstairs!

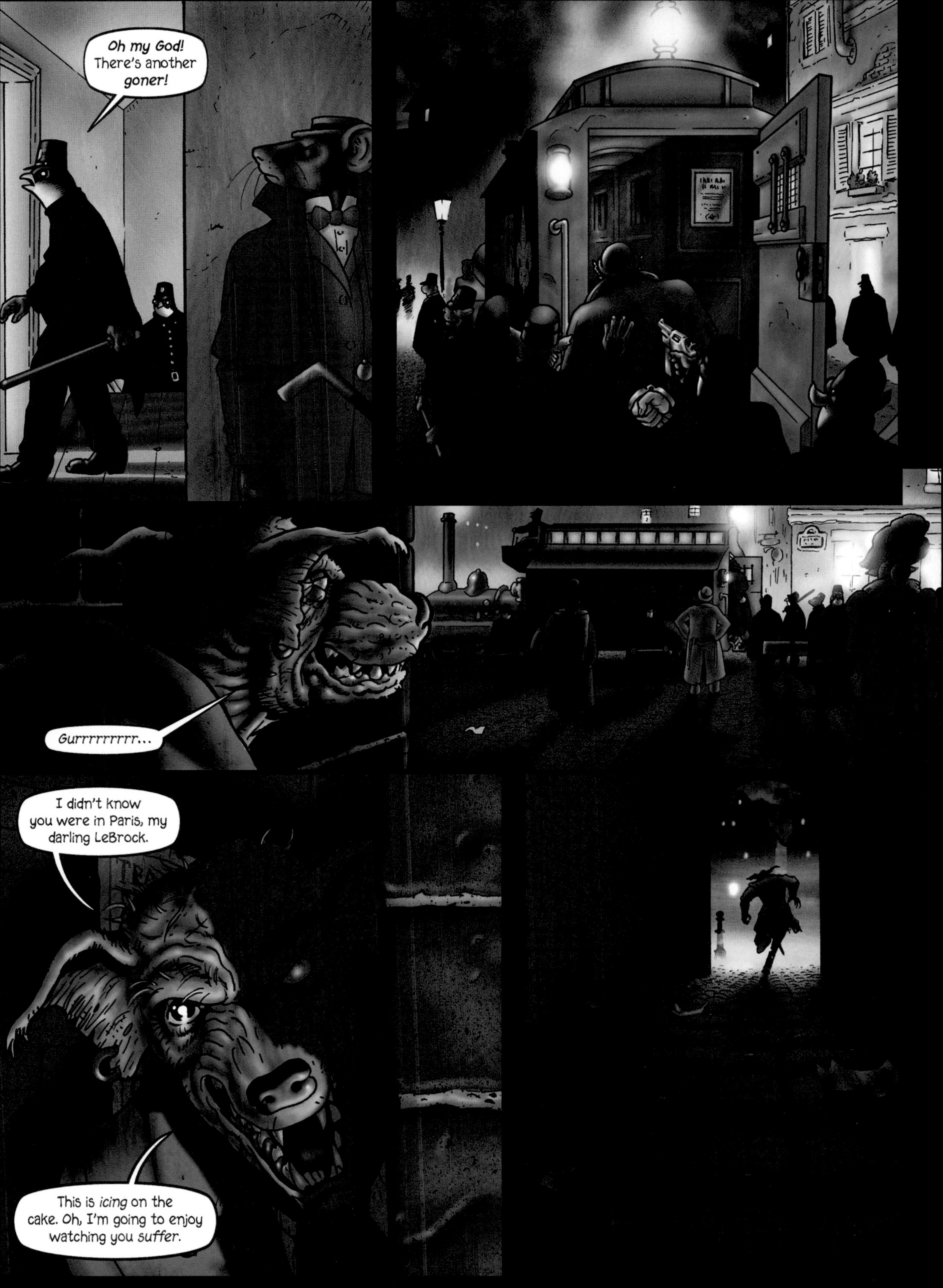

Oh my God! There's another *goner!*
Gurrrrrrrrrr...
I didn't know you were in Paris, my darling LeBrock.
This is *icing* on the cake. Oh, I'm going to enjoy watching you *suffer*.

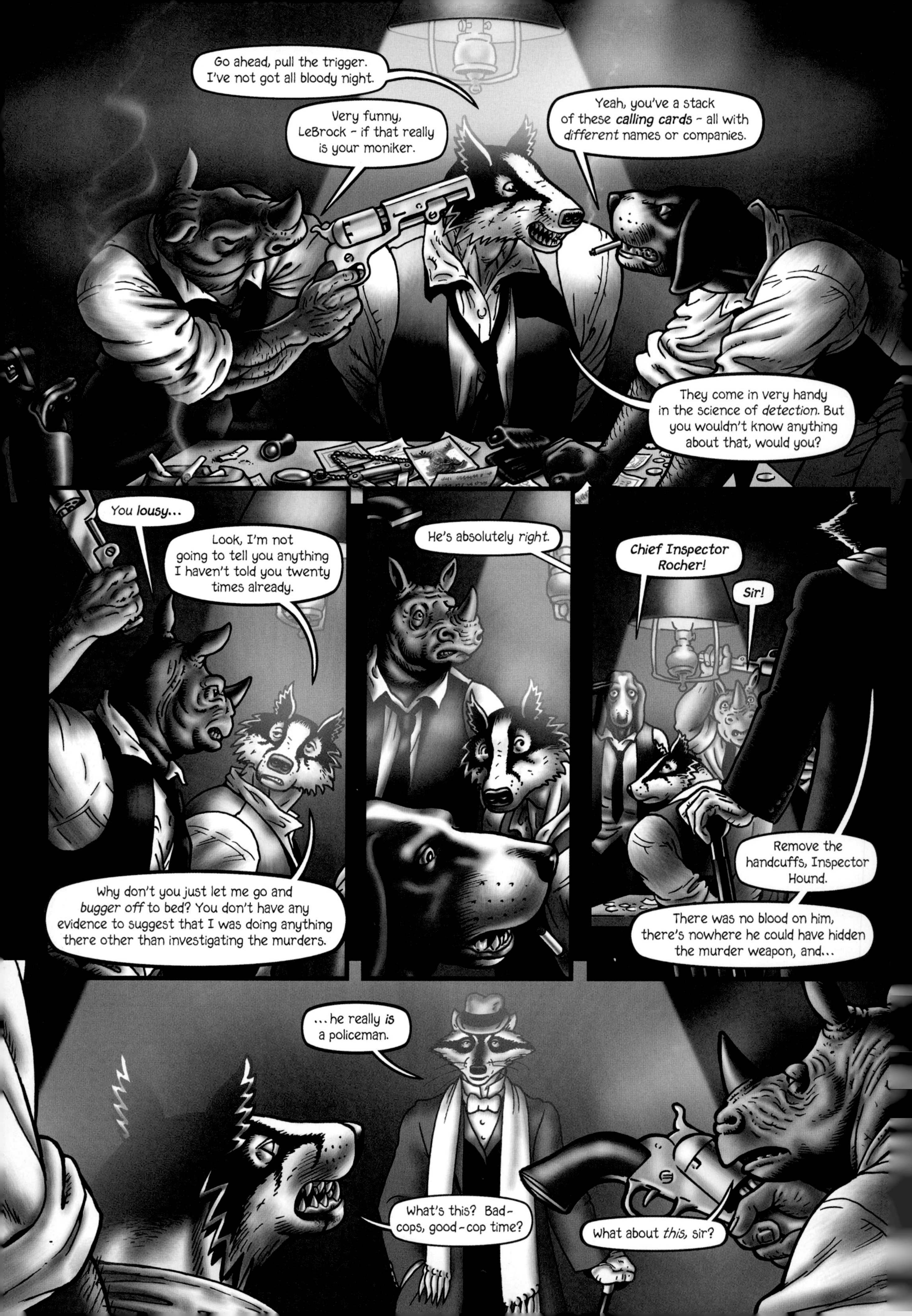

Go ahead, pull the trigger. I've not got all bloody night.
Very funny, LeBrock - if that really is your moniker.
Yeah, you've a stack of these *calling cards* - all with *different* names or companies.
They come in very handy in the science of *detection*. But you wouldn't know anything about that, would you?
You *lousy*...
Look, I'm not going to tell you anything I haven't told you twenty times already.
Why don't you just let me go and *bugger off* to bed? You don't have any evidence to suggest that I was doing anything there other than investigating the murders.
He's absolutely *right*.
Chief Inspector Rocher!
Sir!
Remove the handcuffs, Inspector Hound.
There was no blood on him, there's nowhere he could have hidden the murder weapon, and...
...he really *is* a policeman.
What's this? Bad-cops, good-cop time?
What about *this*, sir?

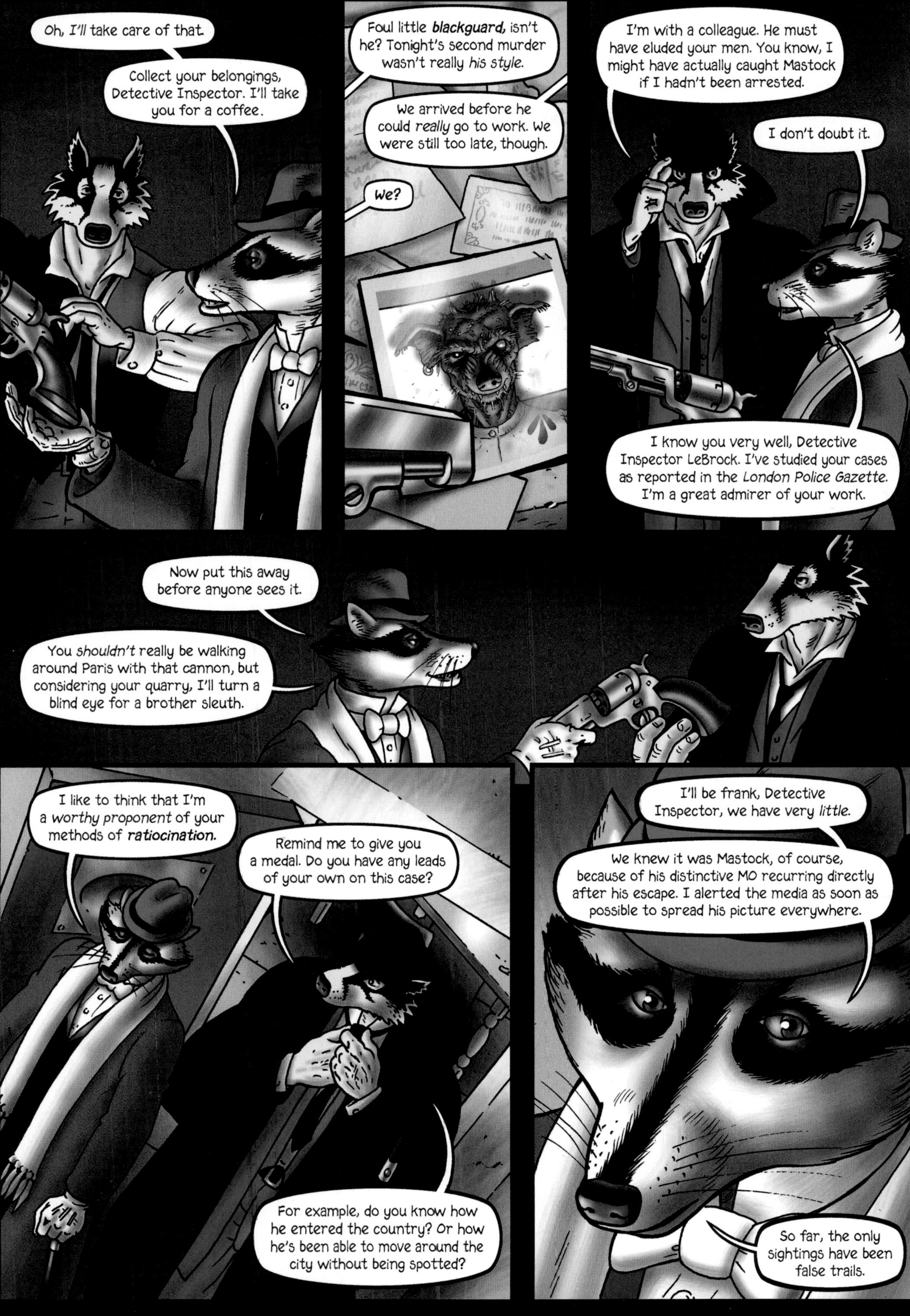
Oh, *I'll* take care of that.
Collect your belongings, Detective Inspector. I'll take you for a coffee.
Foul little **blackguard,** isn't he? Tonight's second murder wasn't really *his style.*
We arrived before he could *really* go to work. We were still too late, though.
We?
I'm with a colleague. He must have eluded your men. You know, I might have actually caught Mastock if I hadn't been arrested.
I don't doubt it.
I know you very well, Detective Inspector LeBrock. I've studied your cases as reported in the *London Police Gazette.* I'm a great admirer of your work.
Now put this away before anyone sees it.
You *shouldn't* really be walking around Paris with that cannon, but considering your quarry, I'll turn a blind eye for a brother sleuth.
I like to think that I'm a *worthy proponent* of your methods of ***ratiocination.***
Remind me to give you a medal. Do you have any leads of your own on this case?
For example, do you know how he entered the country? Or how he's been able to move around the city without being spotted?
I'll be frank, Detective Inspector, we have very *little.*
We knew it was Mastock, of course, because of his distinctive MO recurring directly after his escape. I alerted the media as soon as possible to spread his picture everywhere.
So far, the only sightings have been false trails.

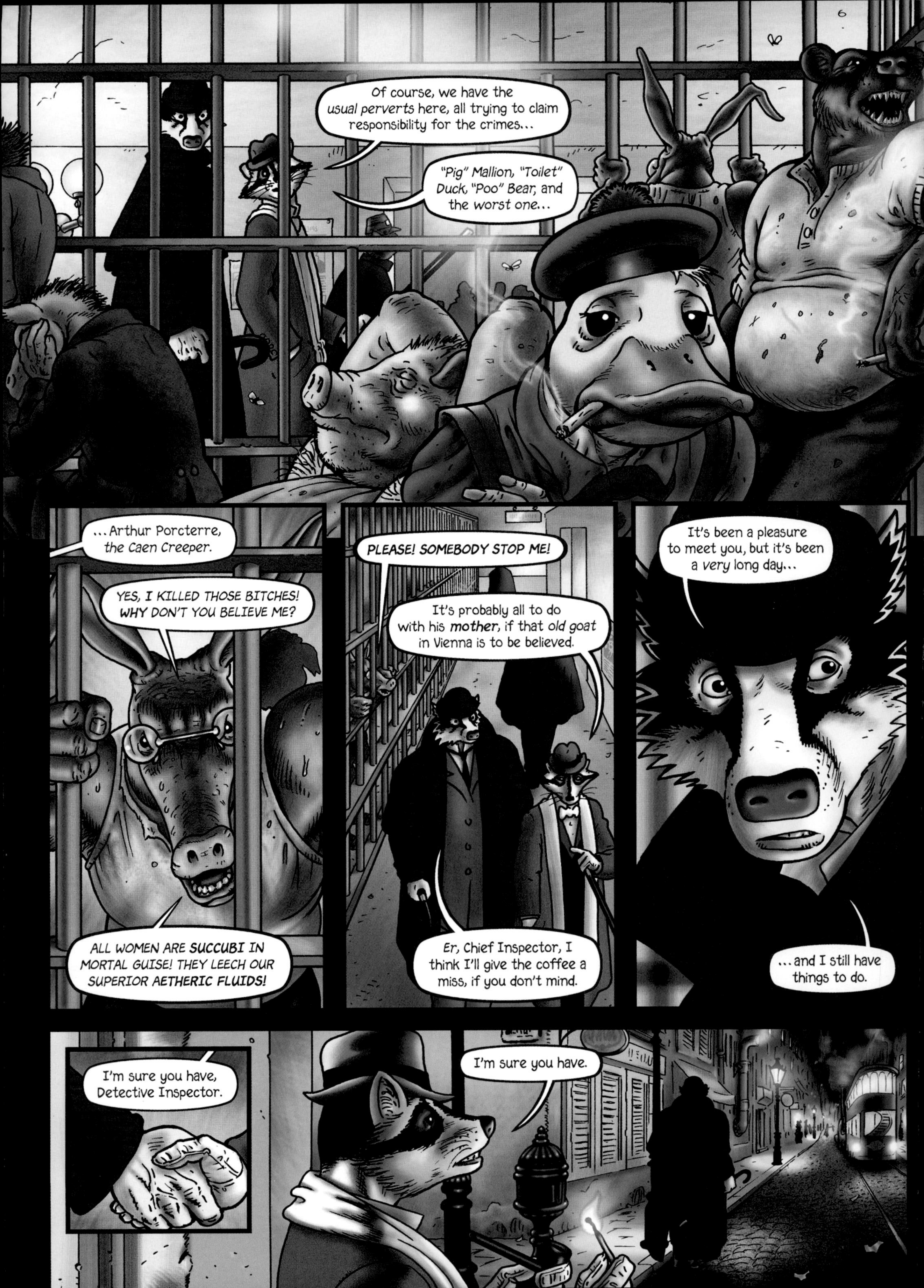

Of course, we have the usual perverts here, all trying to claim responsibility for the crimes...
"Pig" Mallion, "Toilet" Duck, "Poo" Bear, and the worst one...
...Arthur Porcterre, the Caen Creeper.
YES, I KILLED THOSE BITCHES! WHY DON'T YOU BELIEVE ME?
ALL WOMEN ARE SUCCUBI IN MORTAL GUISE! THEY LEECH OUR SUPERIOR AETHERIC FLUIDS!
PLEASE! SOMEBODY STOP ME!
It's probably all to do with his mother, if that old goat in Vienna is to be believed.
Er, Chief Inspector, I think I'll give the coffee a miss, if you don't mind.
It's been a pleasure to meet you, but it's been a very long day...
...and I still have things to do.
I'm sure you have, Detective Inspector.
I'm sure you have.

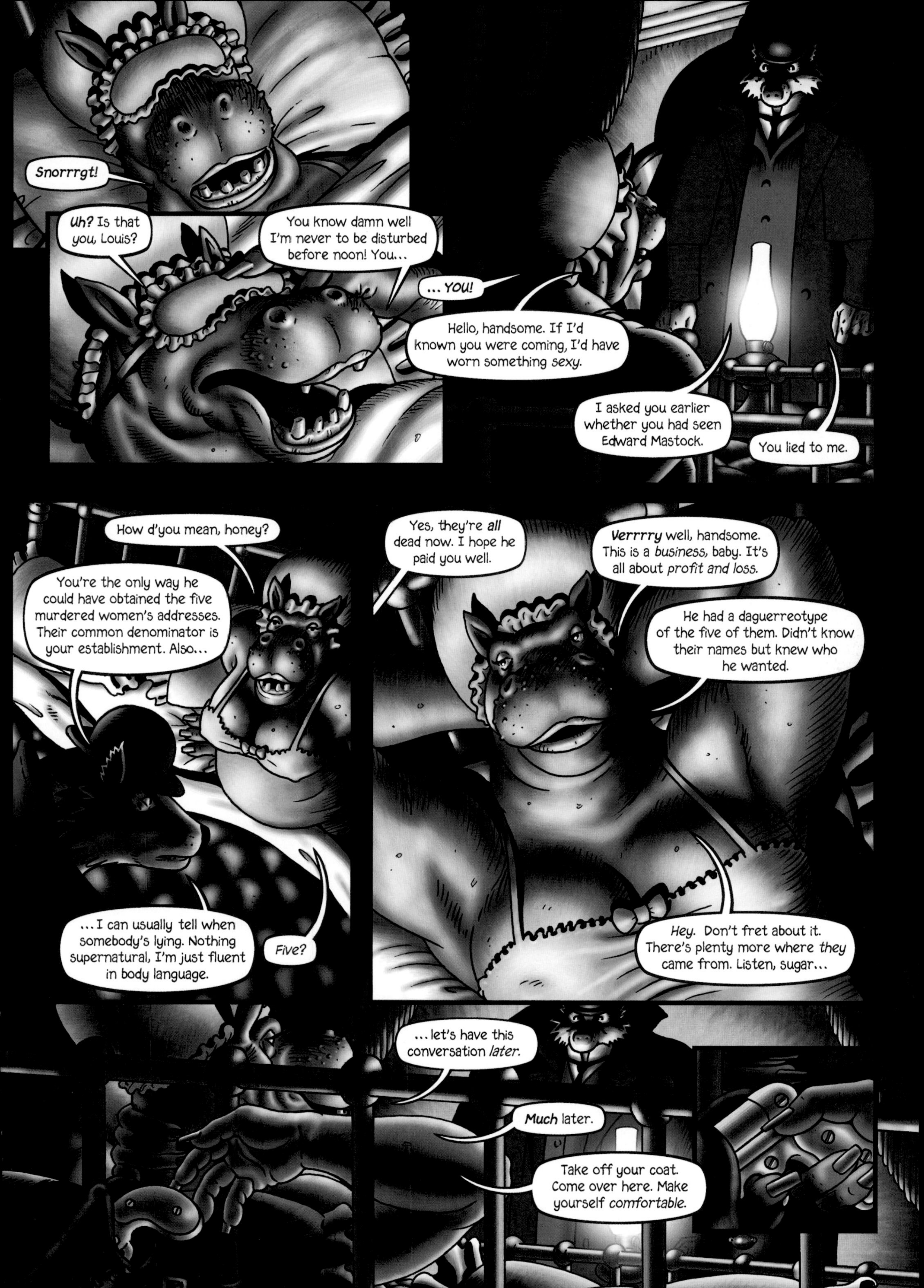
Snorrrgt!
Uh? Is that you, Louis?
You know damn well I'm never to be disturbed before noon! You...
... YOU!
Hello, handsome. If I'd known you were coming, I'd have worn something sexy.
I asked you earlier whether you had seen Edward Mastock.
You lied to me.
How d'you mean, honey?
You're the only way he could have obtained the five murdered women's addresses. Their common denominator is your establishment. Also...
...I can usually tell when somebody's lying. Nothing supernatural, I'm just fluent in body language.
Five?
Yes, they're all dead now. I hope he paid you well.
Verrrry well, handsome. This is a business, baby. It's all about profit and loss.
He had a daguerreotype of the five of them. Didn't know their names but knew who he wanted.
Hey. Don't fret about it. There's plenty more where they came from. Listen, sugar...
...let's have this conversation later.
Much later.
Take off your coat. Come over here. Make yourself comfortable.

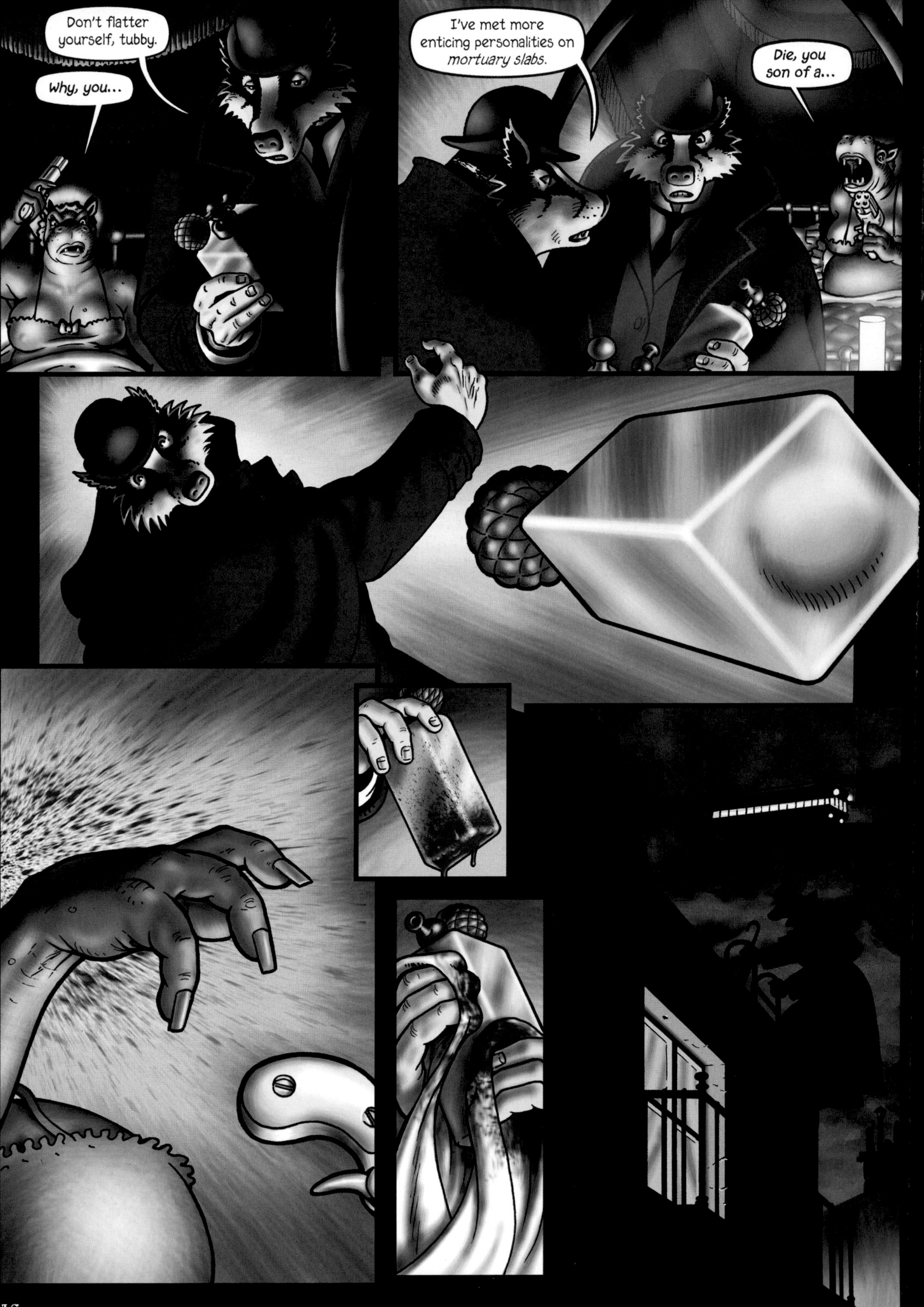
Why, you...
Don't flatter yourself, tubby.
I've met more enticing personalities on *mortuary slabs.*
Die, you son of a...

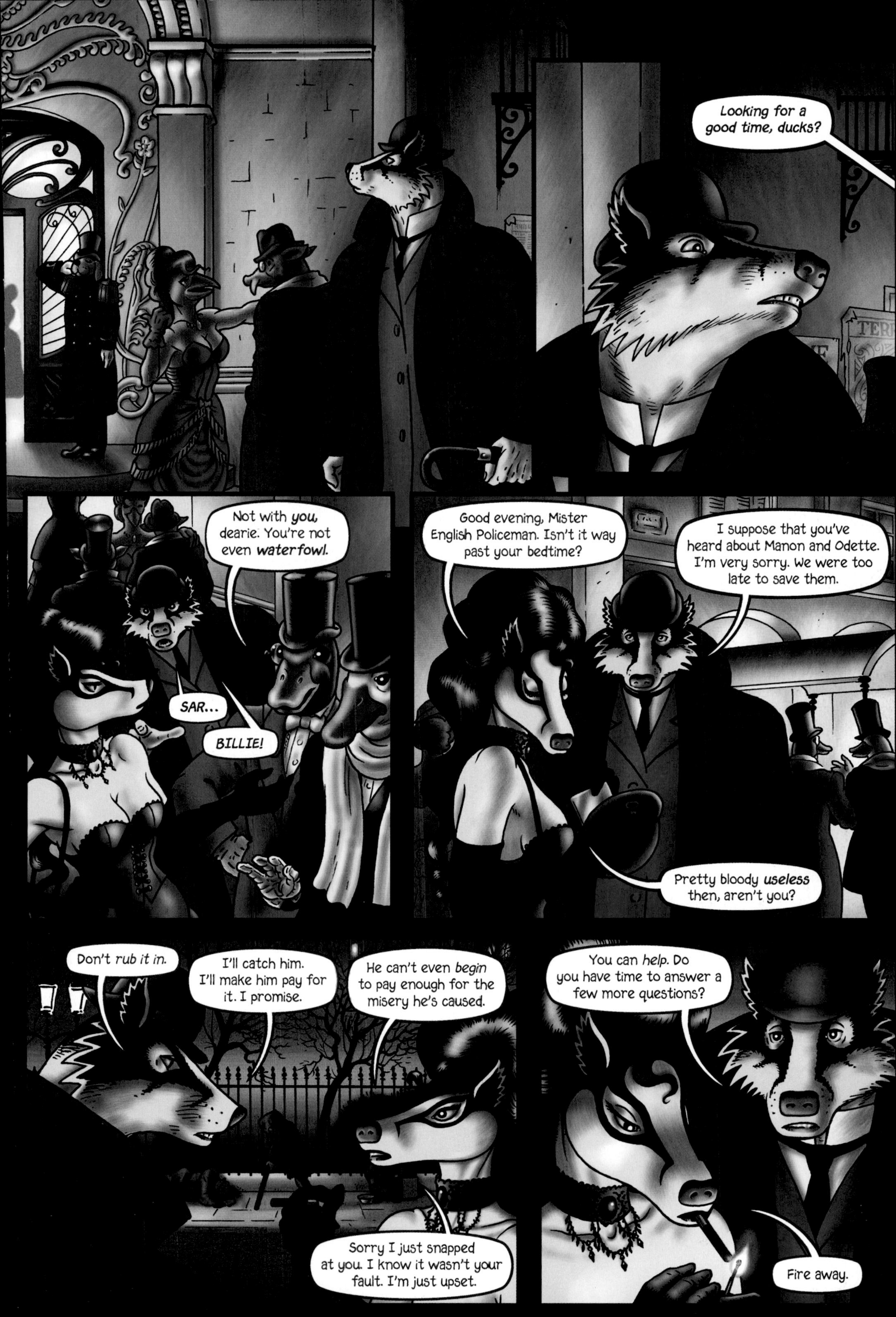
Looking for a good time, ducks?
Not with *you,* dearie. You're not even ***waterfowl!***
SAR...
BILLIE!
Good evening, Mister English Policeman. Isn't it way past your bedtime?
I suppose that you've heard about Manon and Odette. I'm very sorry. We were too late to save them.
Pretty bloody ***useless*** then, aren't you?
Don't *rub it in.*
I'll catch him. I'll make him pay for it. I promise.
He can't even *begin* to pay enough for the misery he's caused.
Sorry I just snapped at you. I know it wasn't your fault. I'm just upset.
You can *help*. Do you have time to answer a few more questions?
Fire away.

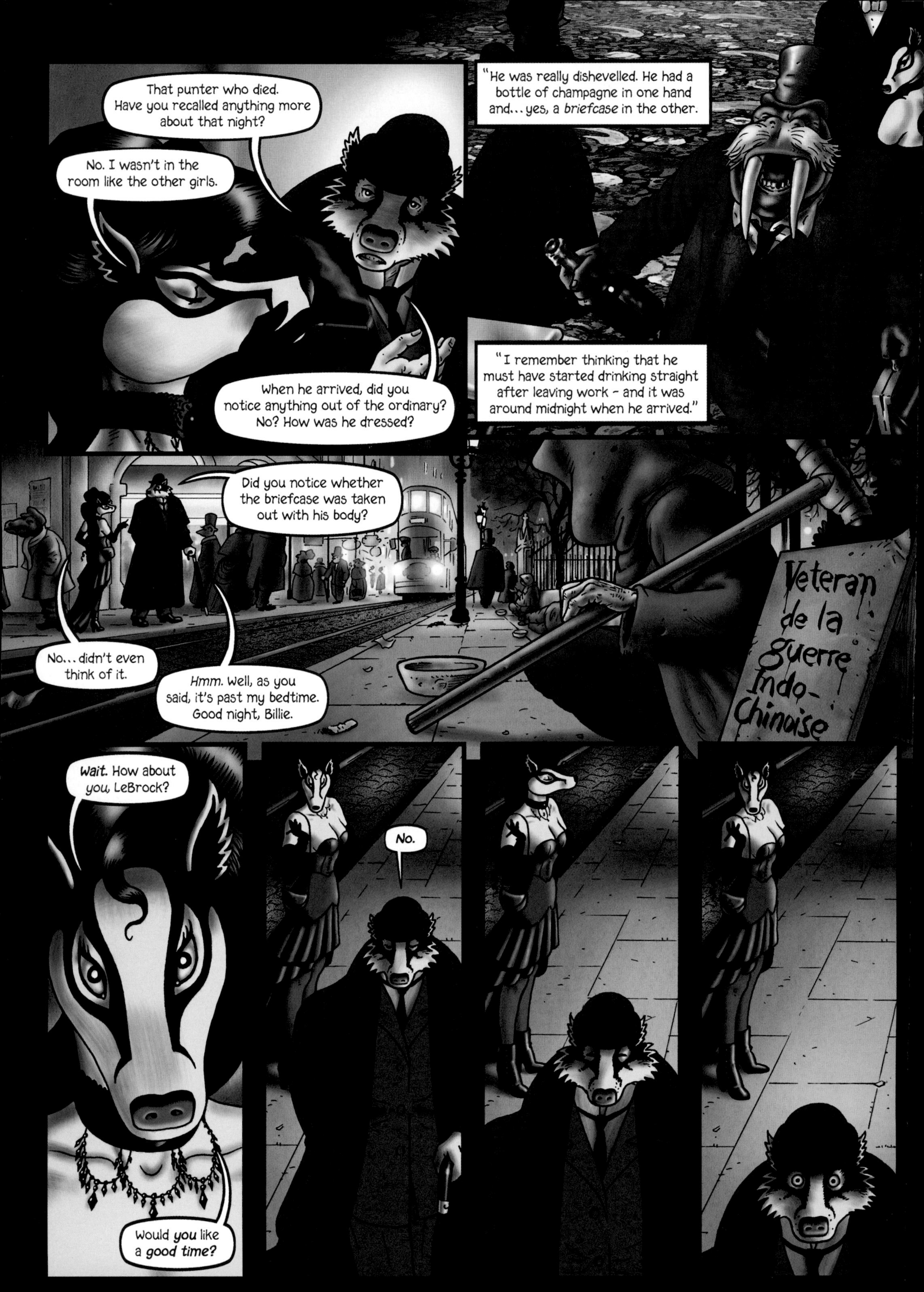
That punter who died. Have you recalled anything more about that night?
No. I wasn't in the room like the other girls.
When he arrived, did you notice anything out of the ordinary? No? How was he dressed?
"He was really dishevelled. He had a bottle of champagne in one hand and... yes, a *briefcase* in the other.
"I remember thinking that he must have started drinking straight after leaving work - and it was around midnight when he arrived."
Did you notice whether the briefcase was taken out with his body?
No... didn't even think of it.
Hmm. Well, as you said, it's past my bedtime. Good night, Billie.
Veteran de la guerre Indo-Chinoise
Wait. How about you, LeBrock?
Would *you* like a *good time?*
No.

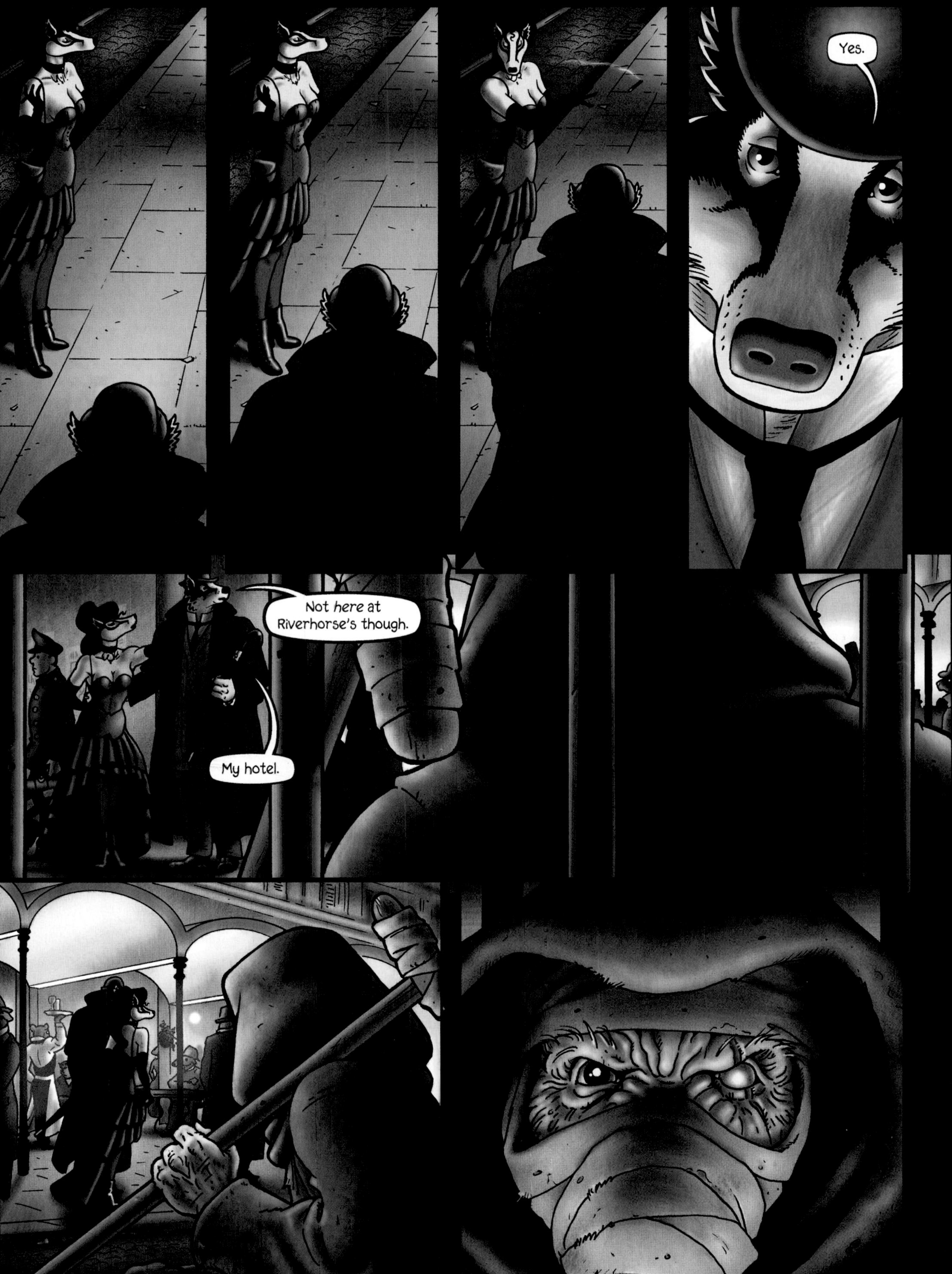
Yes.
Not *here* at Riverhorse's though.
My hotel.

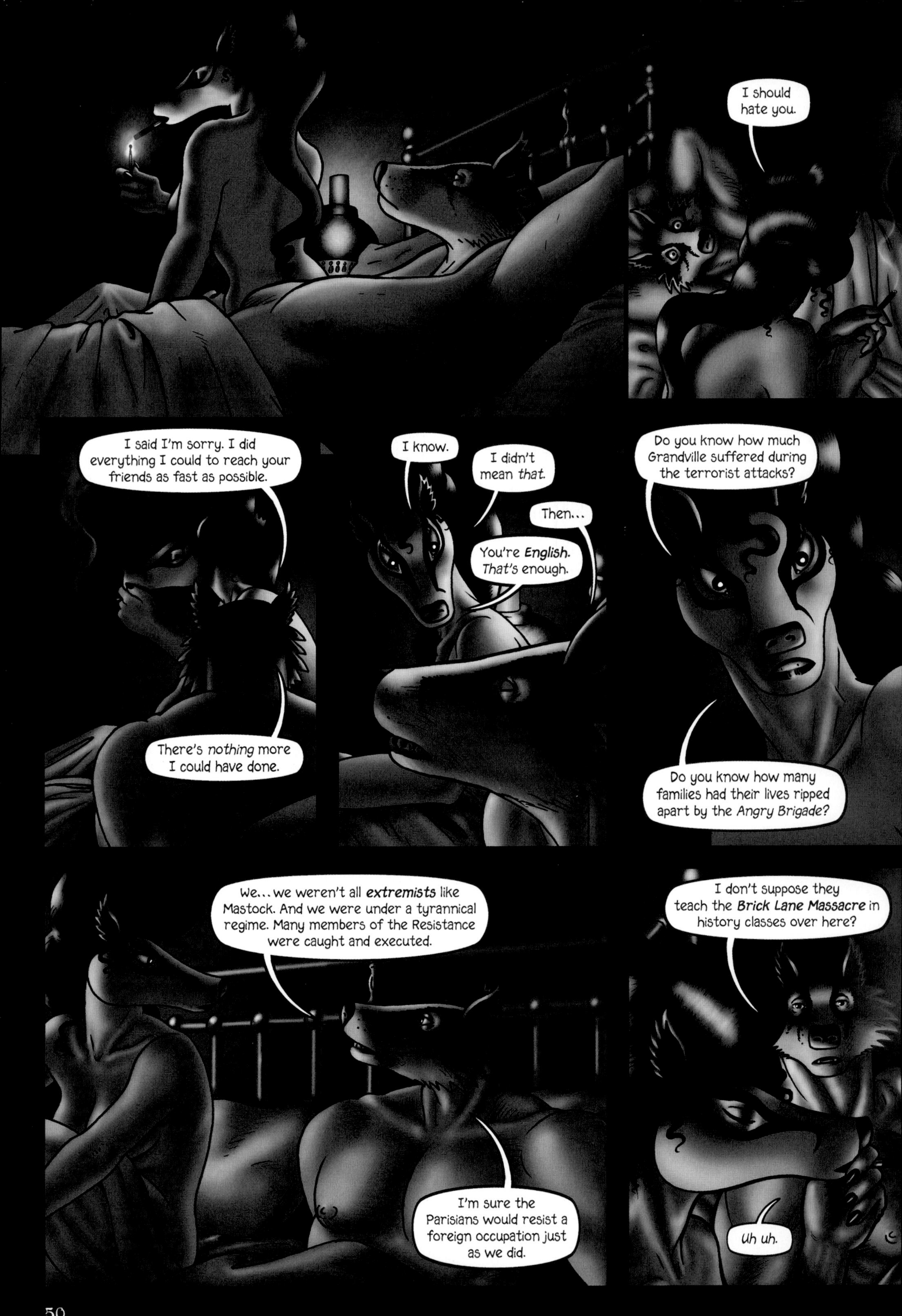
I should hate you.
I said I'm sorry. I did everything I could to reach your friends as fast as possible.
There's *nothing* more I could have done.
I know.
I didn't mean *that*.
Then...
You're **English**. *That's* enough.
Do you know how much Grandville suffered during the terrorist attacks?
Do you know how many families had their lives ripped apart by the *Angry Brigade*?
We... we weren't all **extremists** like Mastock. And we were under a tyrannical regime. Many members of the Resistance were caught and executed.
I'm sure the Parisians would resist a foreign occupation just as we did.
I don't suppose they teach the **Brick Lane Massacre** in history classes over here?
Uh uh.

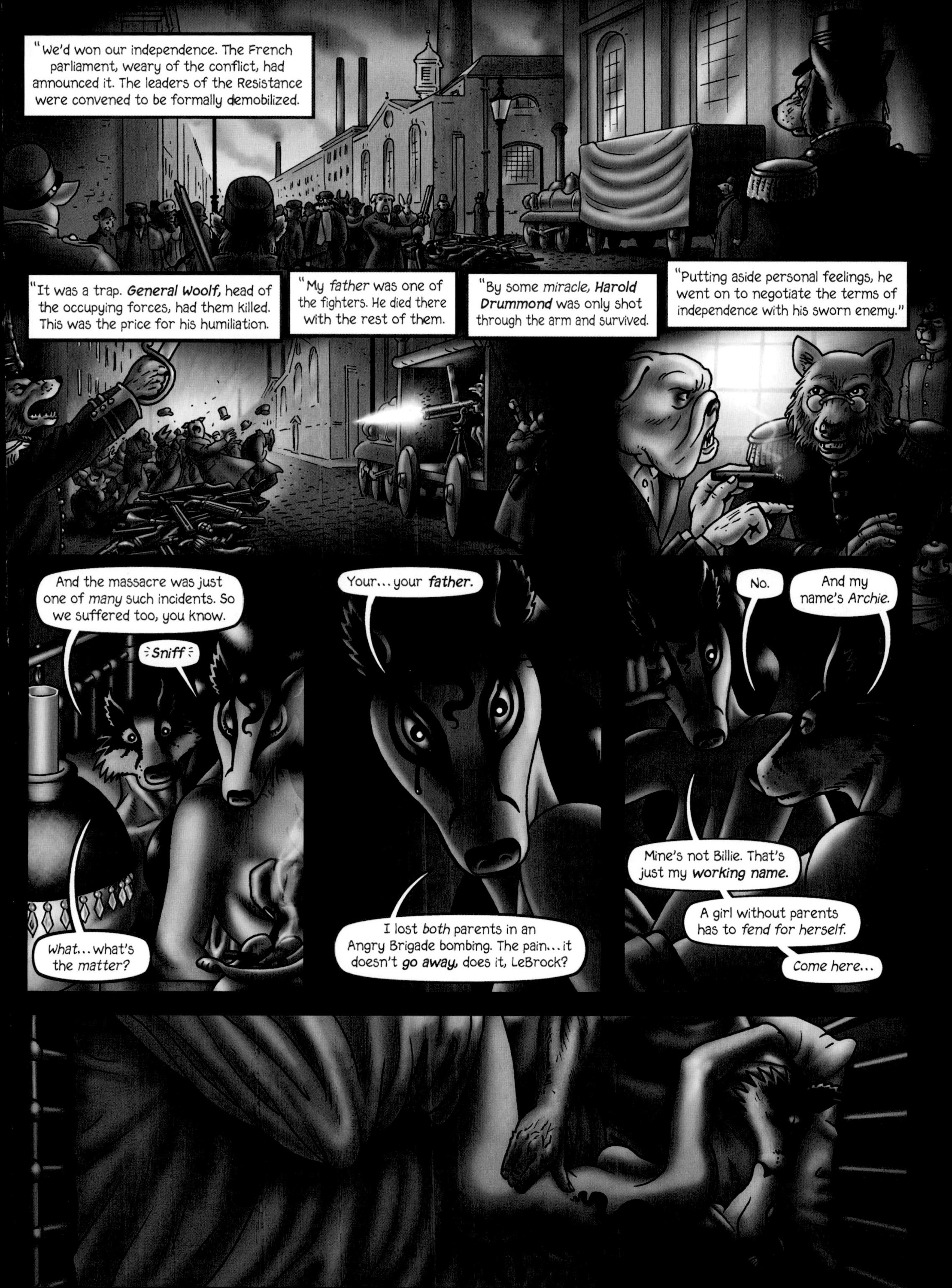

"We'd won our independence. The French parliament, weary of the conflict, had announced it. The leaders of the Resistance were convened to be formally demobilized.
"It was a trap. **General Woolf,** head of the occupying forces, had them killed. This was the price for his humiliation.
"My *father* was one of the fighters. He died there with the rest of them.
"By some *miracle,* **Harold Drummond** was only shot through the arm and survived.
"Putting aside personal feelings, he went on to negotiate the terms of independence with his sworn enemy."
And the massacre was just one of *many* such incidents. So we suffered too, you know.
Sniff
What... what's the *matter?*
Your... your **father.**
I lost *both* parents in an Angry Brigade bombing. The pain... it doesn't **go away,** does it, LeBrock?
No.
And my name's *Archie.*
Mine's not Billie. That's just my **working name.**
A girl without parents has to *fend for herself.*
Come here...

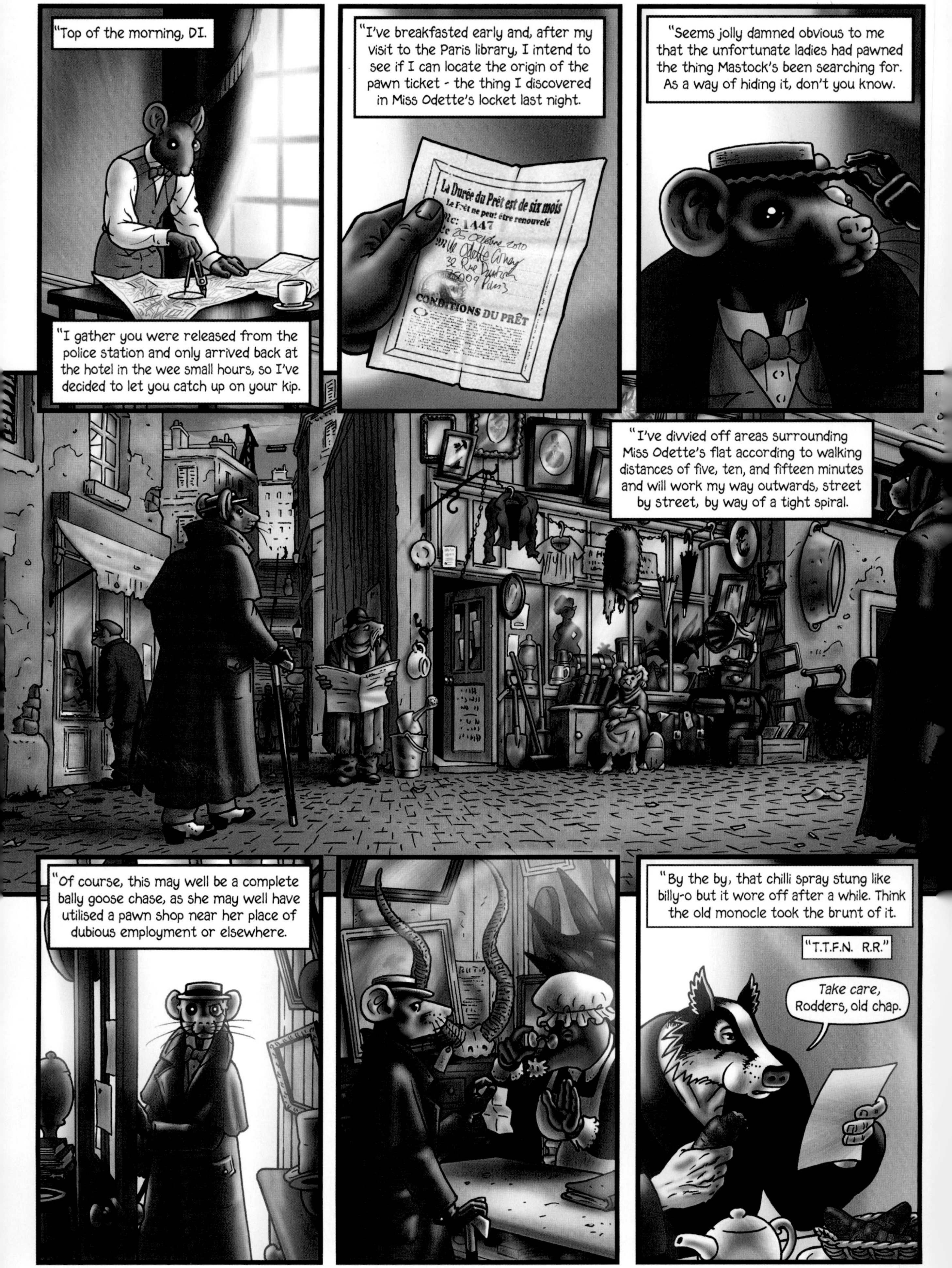
"Top of the morning, DI.
"I gather you were released from the police station and only arrived back at the hotel in the wee small hours, so I've decided to let you catch up on your kip.
"I've breakfasted early and, after my visit to the Paris library, I intend to see if I can locate the origin of the pawn ticket - the thing I discovered in Miss Odette's locket last night.
La Durée du Prêt est de six mois
Le Prêt ne peut être renouvelé
1447
CONDITIONS DU PRÊT
"Seems jolly damned obvious to me that the unfortunate ladies had pawned the thing Mastock's been searching for. As a way of hiding it, don't you know.
"I've divvied off areas surrounding Miss Odette's flat according to walking distances of five, ten, and fifteen minutes and will work my way outwards, street by street, by way of a tight spiral.
"Of course, this may well be a complete bally goose chase, as she may well have utilised a pawn shop near her place of dubious employment or elsewhere.
"By the by, that chilli spray stung like billy-o but it wore off after a while. Think the old monocle took the brunt of it.
"T.T.F.N. R.R."
Take care, Rodders, old chap.

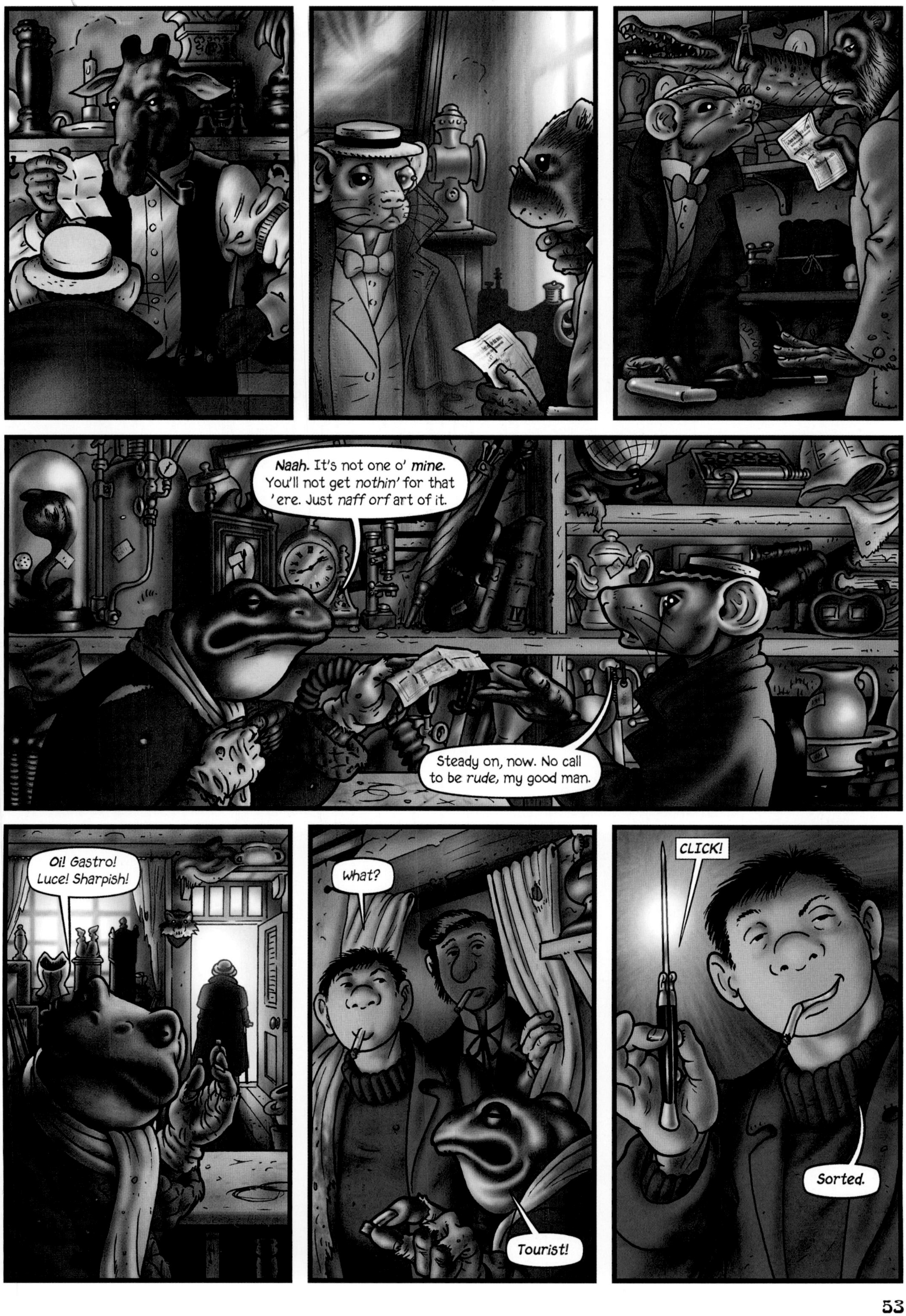
Naah. It's not one o' mine. You'll not get nothin' for that 'ere. Just naff orf art of it.
Steady on, now. No call to be rude, my good man.
Oi! Gastro! Luce! Sharpish!
What?
Tourist!
CLICK!
Sorted.

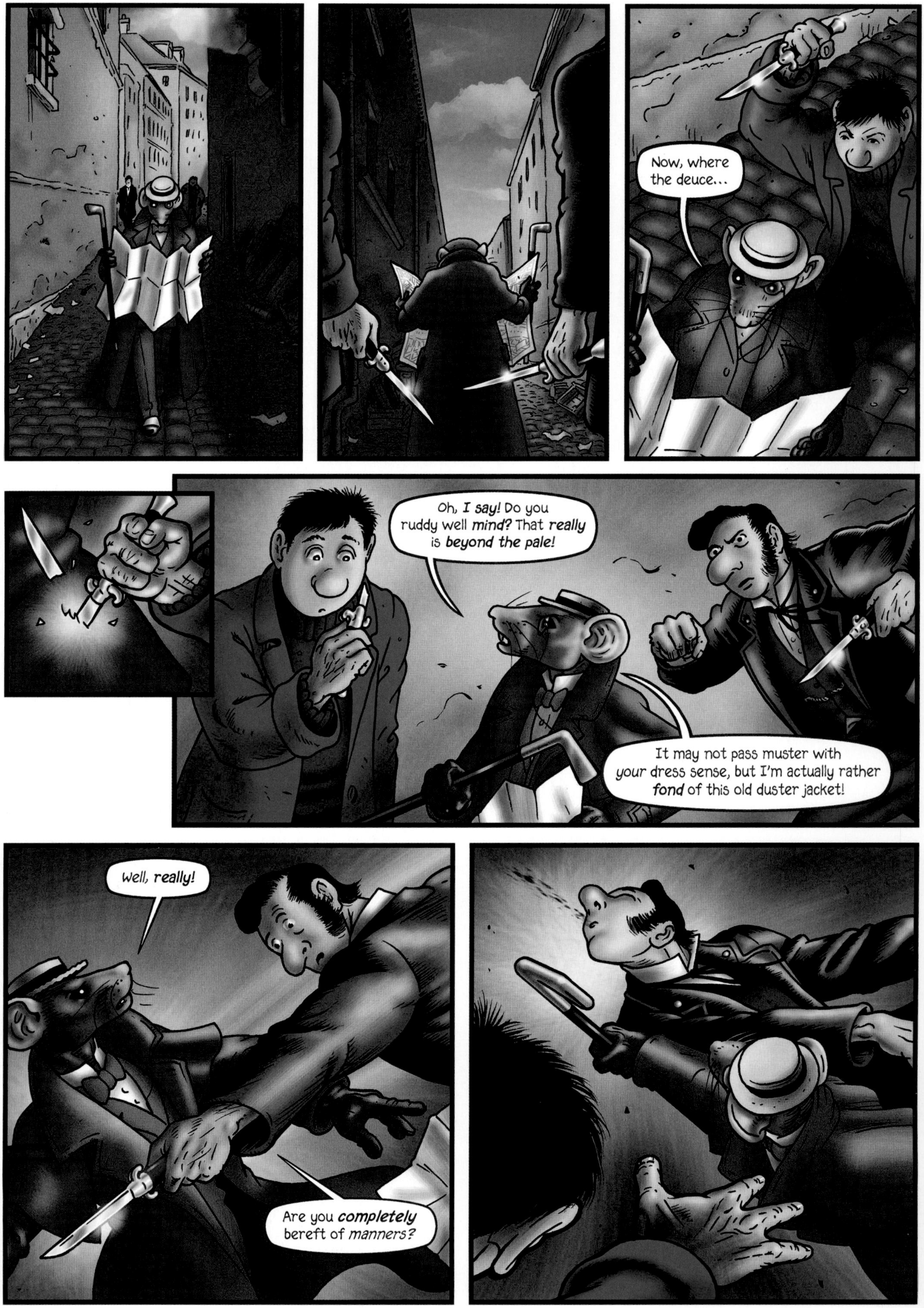
Now, where the deuce...
Oh, I say! Do you ruddy well mind? That really is beyond the pale!
It may not pass muster with your dress sense, but I'm actually rather fond of this old duster jacket!
Well, really!
Are you completely bereft of manners?

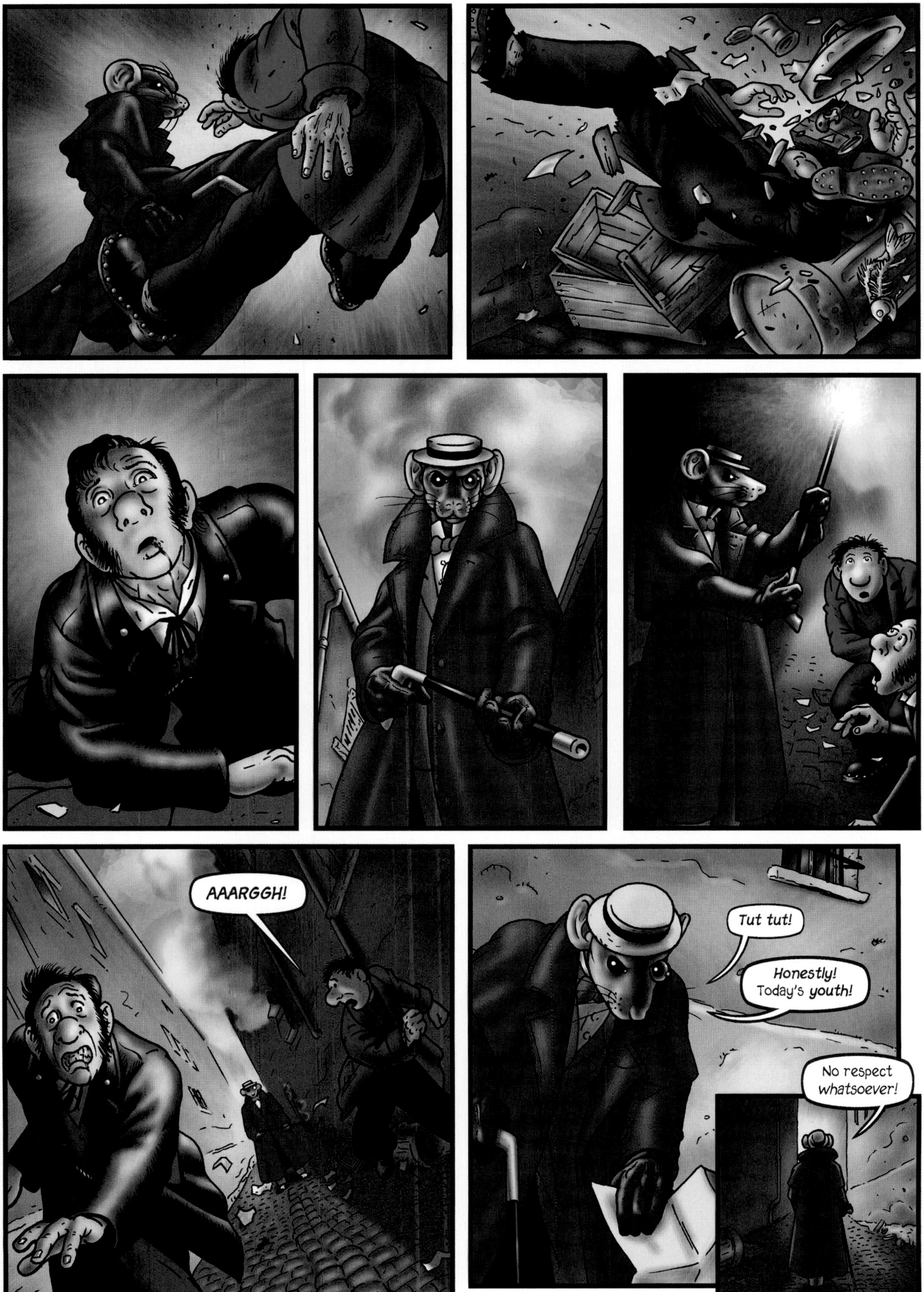
AAARGGH!
Tut tut!
Honestly! Today's youth!
No respect whatsoever!

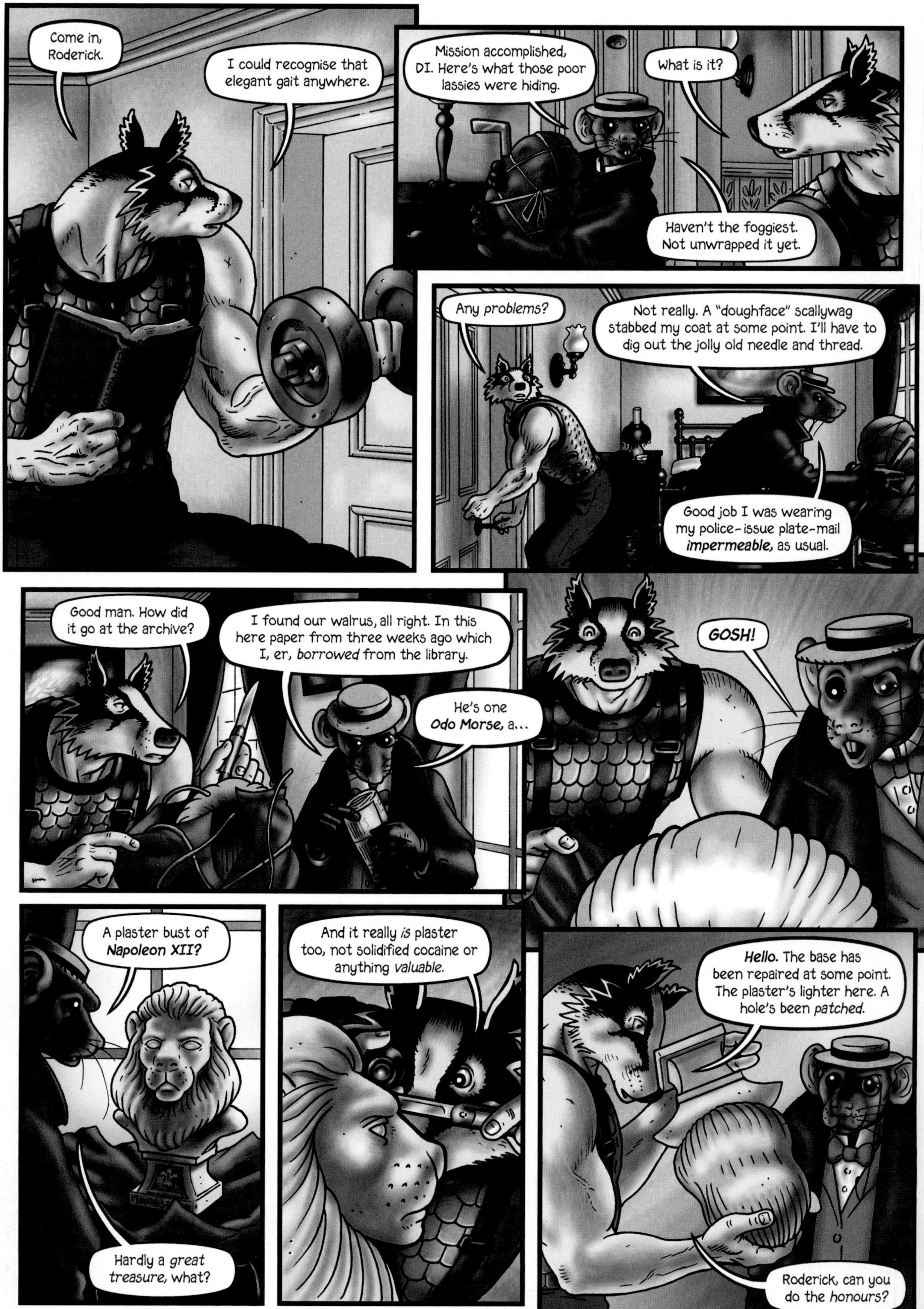
Come in, Roderick.
I could recognise that elegant gait anywhere.
Mission accomplished, DI. Here's what those poor lassies were hiding.
What is it?
Haven't the foggiest. Not unwrapped it yet.
Any *problems?*
Not really. A "doughface" scallywag stabbed my coat at some point. I'll have to dig out the jolly old needle and thread.
Good job I was wearing my police-issue plate-mail ***impermeable,*** as usual.
Good man. How did it go at the archive?
I found our walrus, all right. In this here paper from three weeks ago which I, er, *borrowed* from the library.
He's one **Odo Morse,** a...
GOSH!
A plaster bust of **Napoleon XII?**
Hardly a *great treasure,* what?
And it really *is* plaster too, not solidified cocaine or anything *valuable.*
Hello. The base has been repaired at some point. The plaster's lighter here. A hole's been *patched.*
Roderick, can you do the *honours?*

Certainly nothing *large* hidden in there.

Here we go.

A small key.

Hmm. What's *this*?

S.N.C.F!

The French *railway system*. It's the key to a station *left-luggage locker*. What were you saying about the walrus?

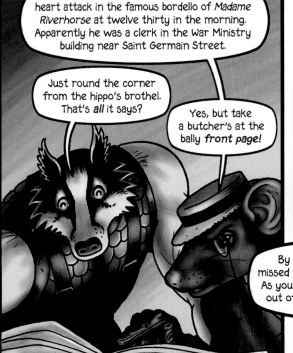

Here. A Mister *Odo Morse* died of a heart attack in the famous bordello of *Madame Riverhorse* at twelve thirty in the morning. Apparently he was a clerk in the War Ministry building near Saint Germain Street.

Just round the corner from the hippo's brothel. That's *all* it says?

Yes, but take a butcher's at the bally *front page!*

By *God!* Woolf dead! I'd missed this news back in Blighty. As you know, I've been a bit... out of circulation, as it were.

La Gazette de Fran...

LE GENERAL PIERRE WOOLF PERIT DANS UN INCENDIE!

This is the man who killed my *father!* The architect of the *Brick Lane Massacre!* The erstwhile dictator of Britain! Let's see...

"...His office and most of the third floor of the Ministry of War were gutted by a fire that started at approximately nine o'clock last night."

"Fortunately most of the building was *empty*."

Excellent work, Roderick. *Right.* Let's hit the stations.

We'll start with the *D'Orsay.* It's practically *spitting* distance from the brothel.

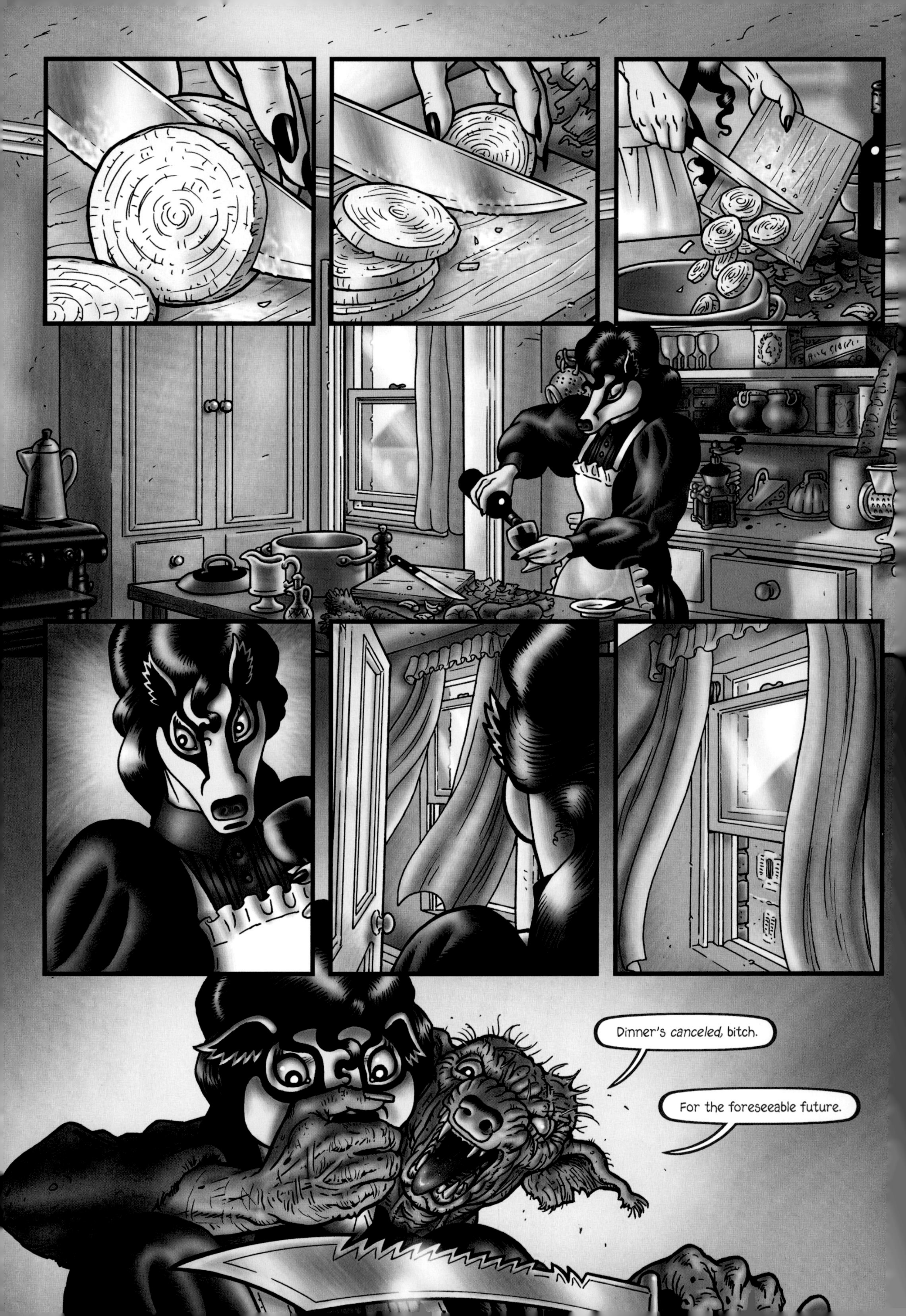

Dinner's *canceled,* bitch.
For the foreseeable future.

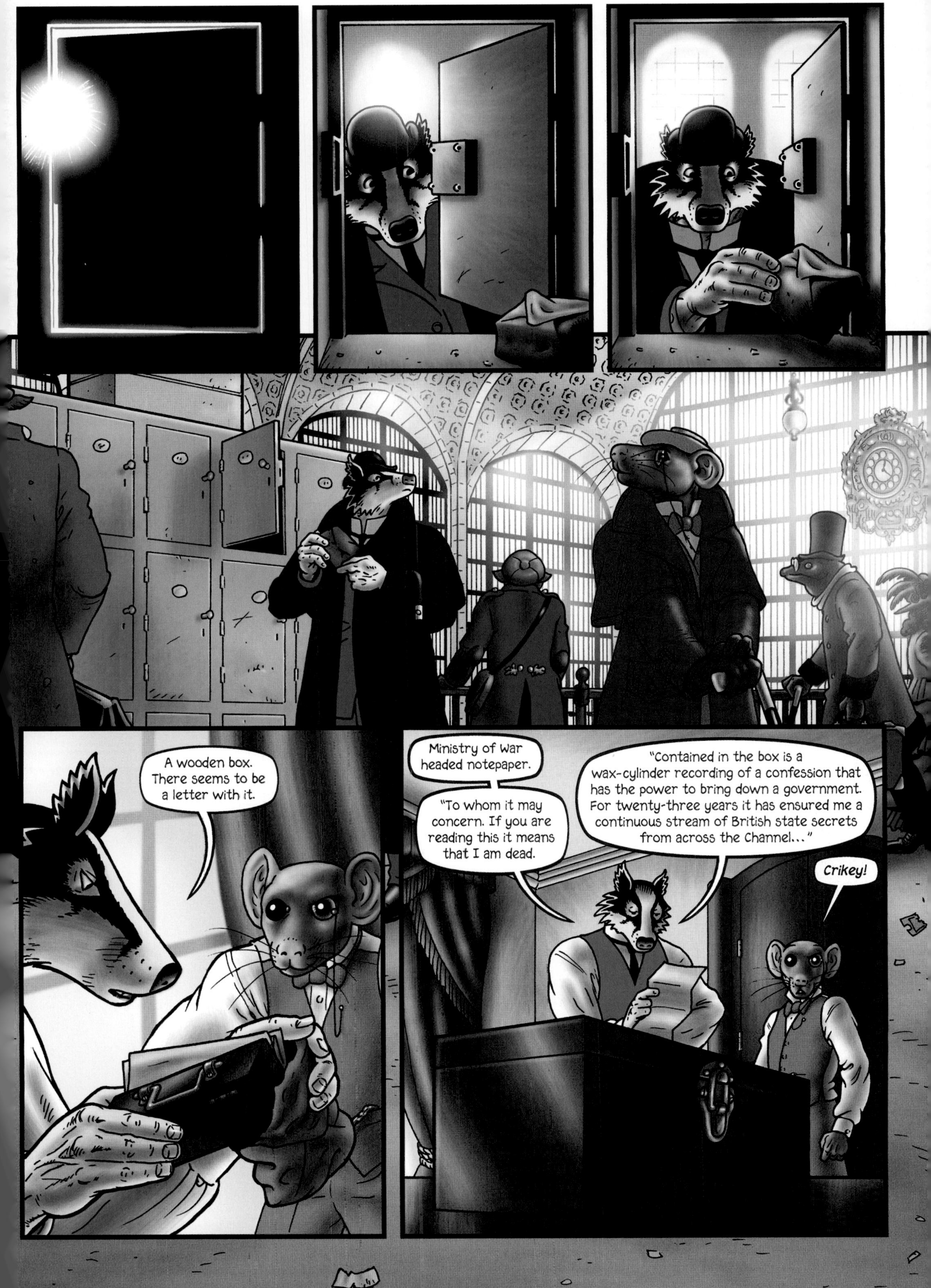
A wooden box. There seems to be a letter with it.
Ministry of War headed notepaper.
"To whom it may concern. If you are reading this it means that I am dead.
"Contained in the box is a wax-cylinder recording of a confession that has the power to bring down a government. For twenty-three years it has ensured me a continuous stream of British state secrets from across the Channel..."
Crikey!

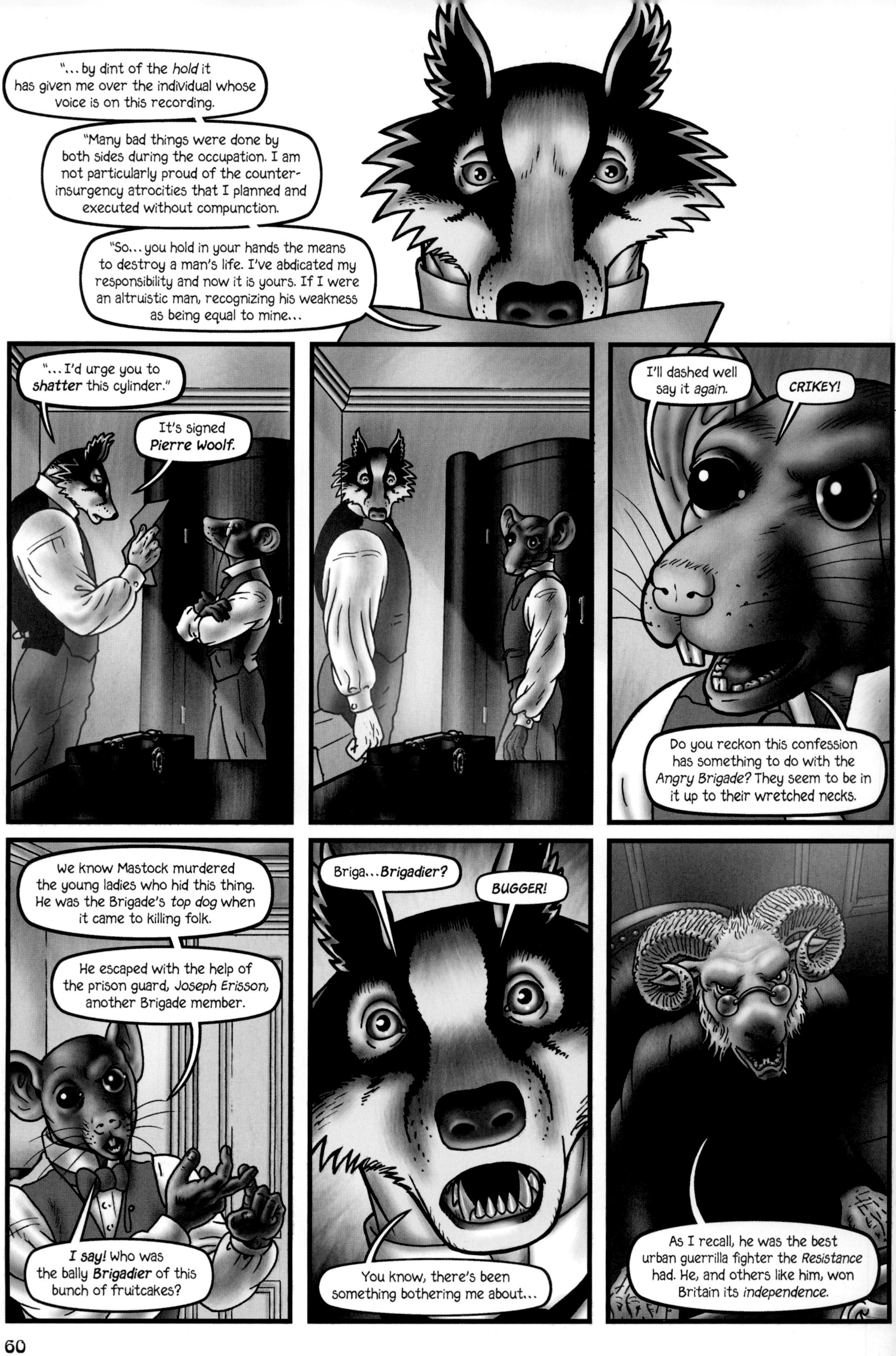
"...by dint of the *hold* it has given me over the individual whose voice is on this recording.
"Many bad things were done by both sides during the occupation. I am not particularly proud of the counter-insurgency atrocities that I planned and executed without compunction.
"So...you hold in your hands the means to destroy a man's life. I've abdicated my responsibility and now it is yours. If I were an altruistic man, recognizing his weakness as being equal to mine...
"...I'd urge you to **shatter** this cylinder."
It's signed **Pierre Woolf.**
I'll dashed well say it *again.*
CRIKEY!
Do you reckon this confession has something to do with the *Angry Brigade?* They seem to be in it up to their wretched necks.
We know Mastock murdered the young ladies who hid this thing. He was the Brigade's *top dog* when it came to killing folk.
He escaped with the help of the prison guard, *Joseph Erisson,* another Brigade member.
I say! Who was the bally ***Brigadier*** of this bunch of fruitcakes?
Briga...*Brigadier?*
BUGGER!
You know, there's been something bothering me about...
As I recall, he was the best urban guerrilla fighter the *Resistance* had. He, and others like him, won Britain its *independence.*

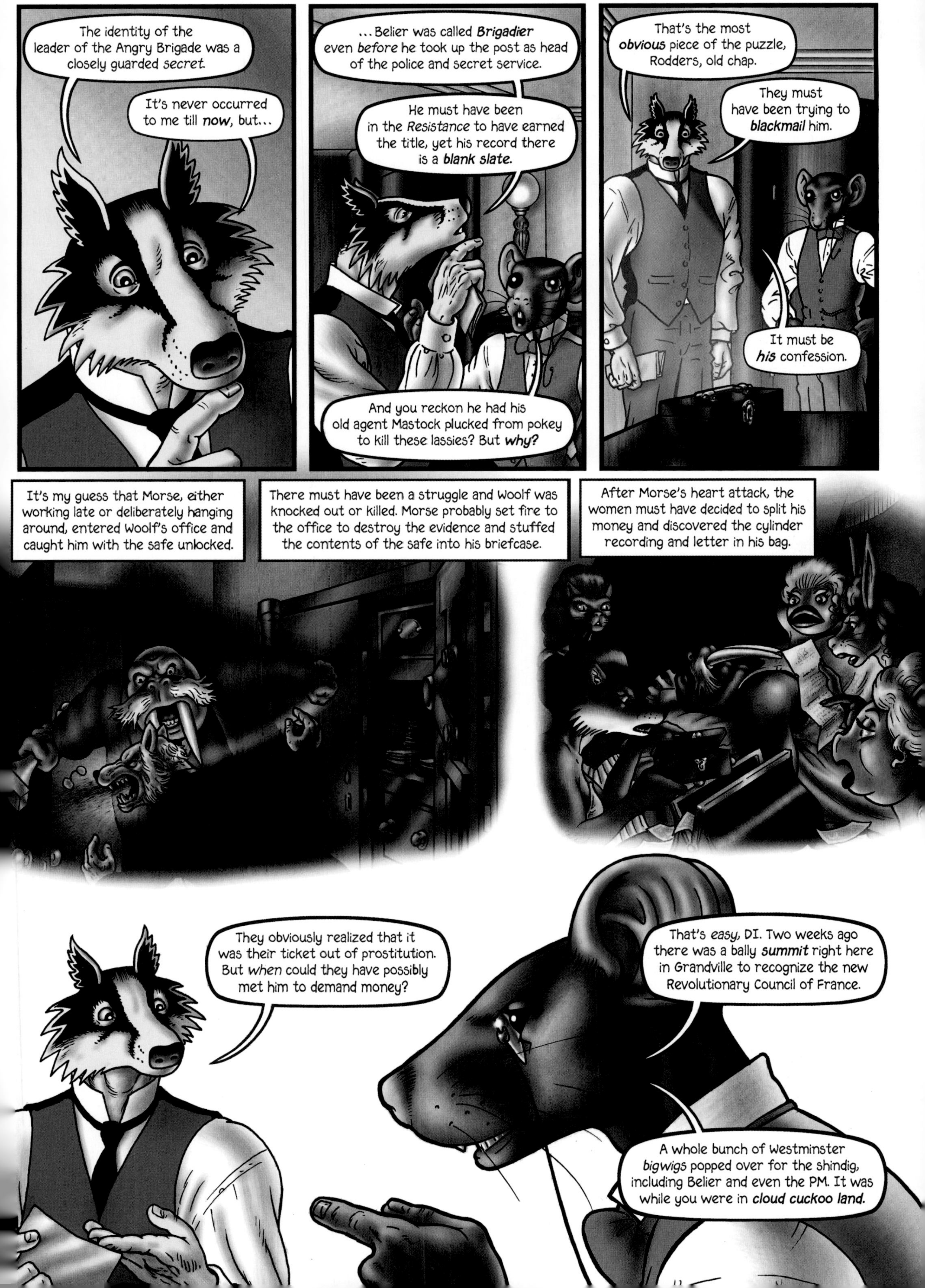
The identity of the leader of the Angry Brigade was a closely guarded *secret.*
It's never occurred to me till **now**, but...
...Belier was called **Brigadier** even *before* he took up the post as head of the police and secret service.
He must have been in the *Resistance* to have earned the title, yet his record there is a **blank slate.**
And you reckon he had his old agent Mastock plucked from pokey to kill these lassies? But **why?**
That's the most **obvious** piece of the puzzle, Rodders, old chap.
They must have been trying to **blackmail** him.
It must be **his** confession.
It's my guess that Morse, either working late or deliberately hanging around, entered Woolf's office and caught him with the safe unlocked.
There must have been a struggle and Woolf was knocked out or killed. Morse probably set fire to the office to destroy the evidence and stuffed the contents of the safe into his briefcase.
After Morse's heart attack, the women must have decided to split his money and discovered the cylinder recording and letter in his bag.
They obviously realized that it was their ticket out of prostitution. But *when* could they have possibly met him to demand money?
That's *easy,* DI. Two weeks ago there was a bally **summit** right here in Grandville to recognize the new Revolutionary Council of France.
A whole bunch of Westminster *bigwigs* popped over for the shindig, including Belier and even the PM. It was while you were in **cloud cuckoo land.**

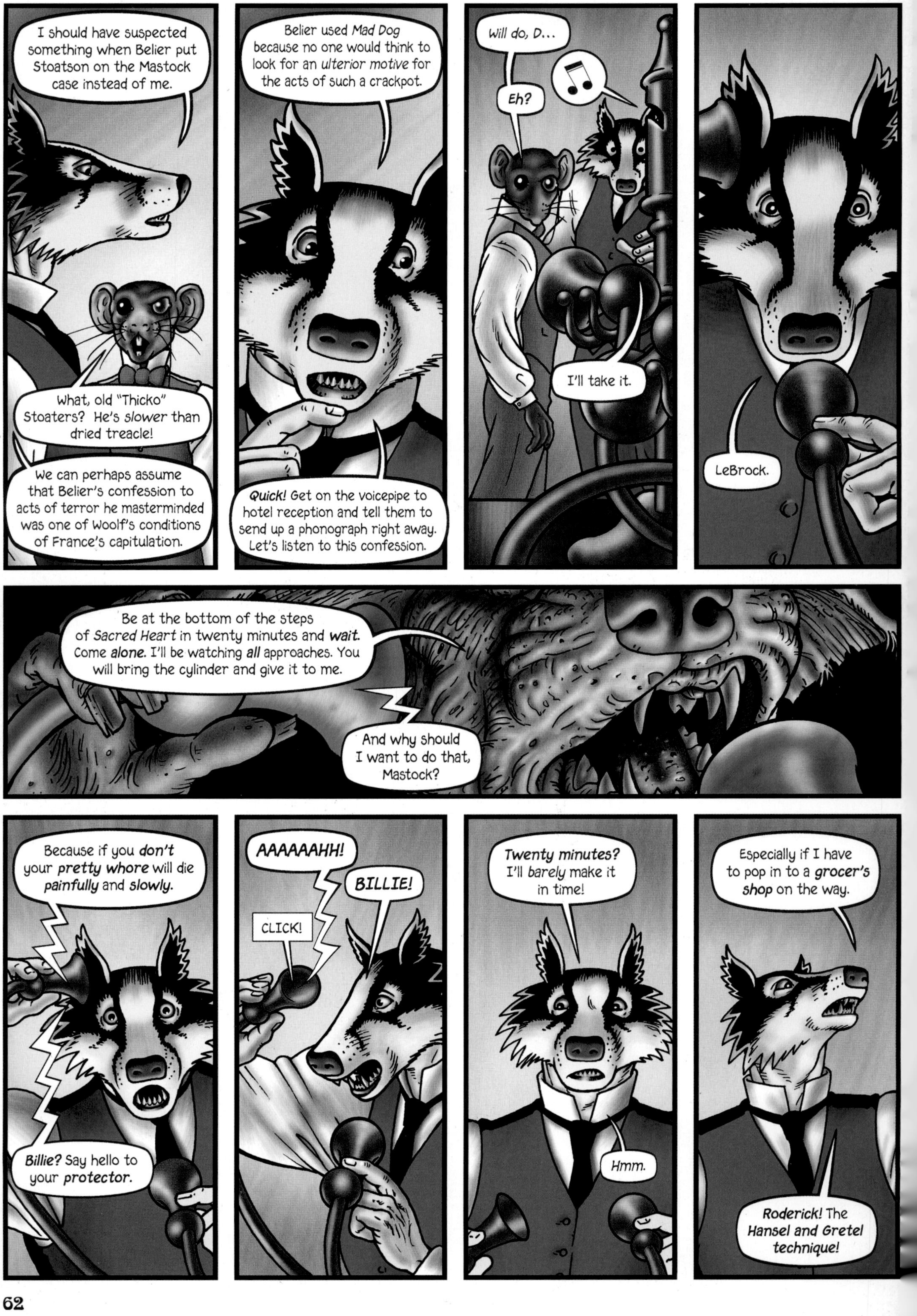

I should have suspected something when Belier put Stoatson on the Mastock case instead of me.
What, old "Thicko" Stoaters? He's *slower* than dried treacle!
We can perhaps assume that Belier's confession to acts of terror he masterminded was one of Woolf's conditions of France's capitulation.
Belier used *Mad Dog* because no one would think to look for an *ulterior motive* for the acts of such a crackpot.
Quick! Get on the voicepipe to hotel reception and tell them to send up a phonograph right away. Let's listen to this confession.
Will do, D...
Eh?
I'll take it.
LeBrock.
Be at the bottom of the steps of *Sacred Heart* in twenty minutes and ***wait***. Come ***alone***. I'll be watching ***all*** approaches. You will bring the cylinder and give it to me.
And why should I want to do that, Mastock?
Because if you ***don't*** your ***pretty whore*** will die ***painfully*** and ***slowly***.
Billie? Say hello to your ***protector***.
AAAAAAHH!
CLICK!
BILLIE!
Twenty minutes? I'll *barely* make it in time!
Hmm.
Especially if I have to pop in to a ***grocer's shop*** on the way.
Roderick! The ***Hansel and Gretel technique!***

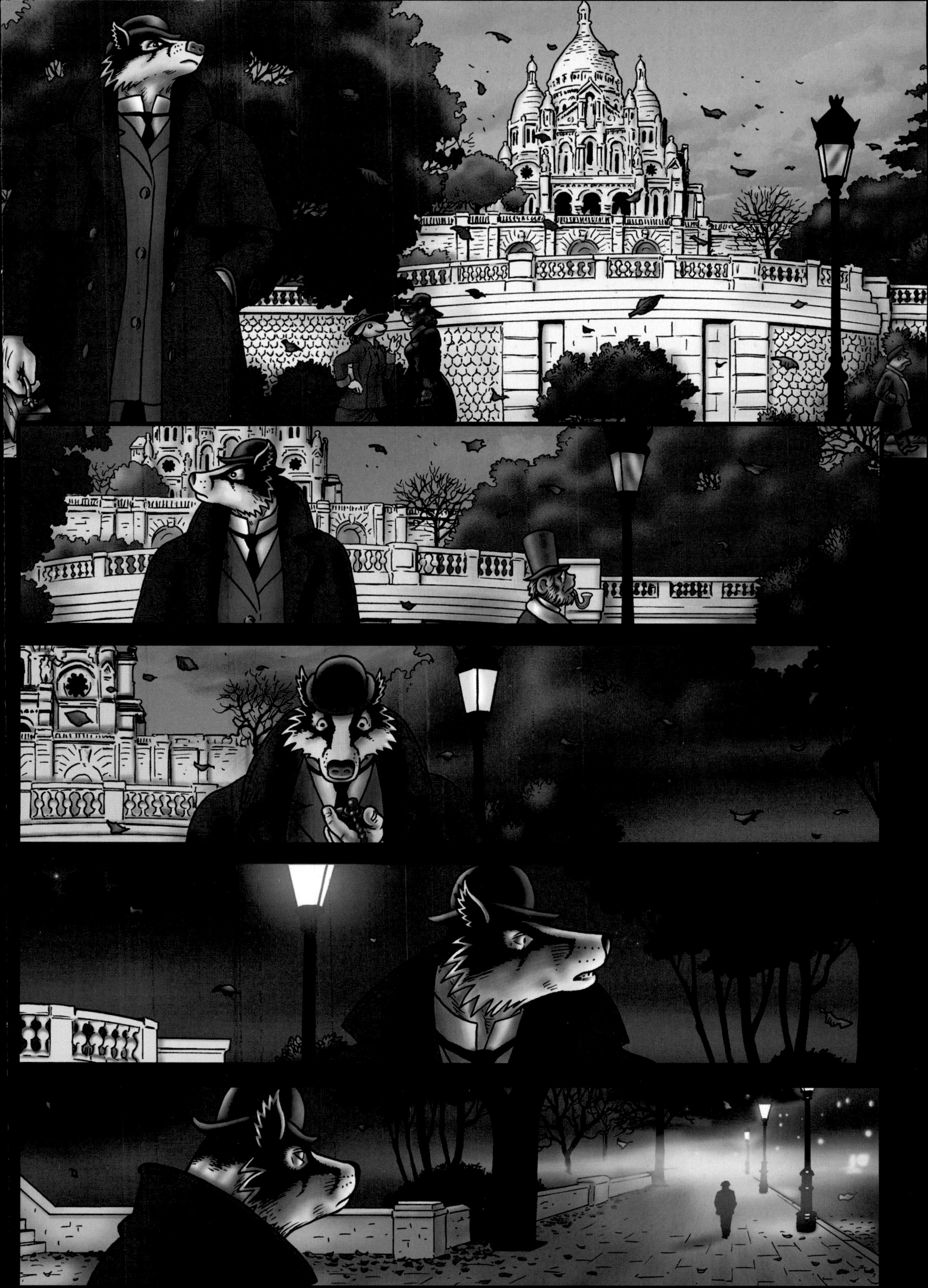

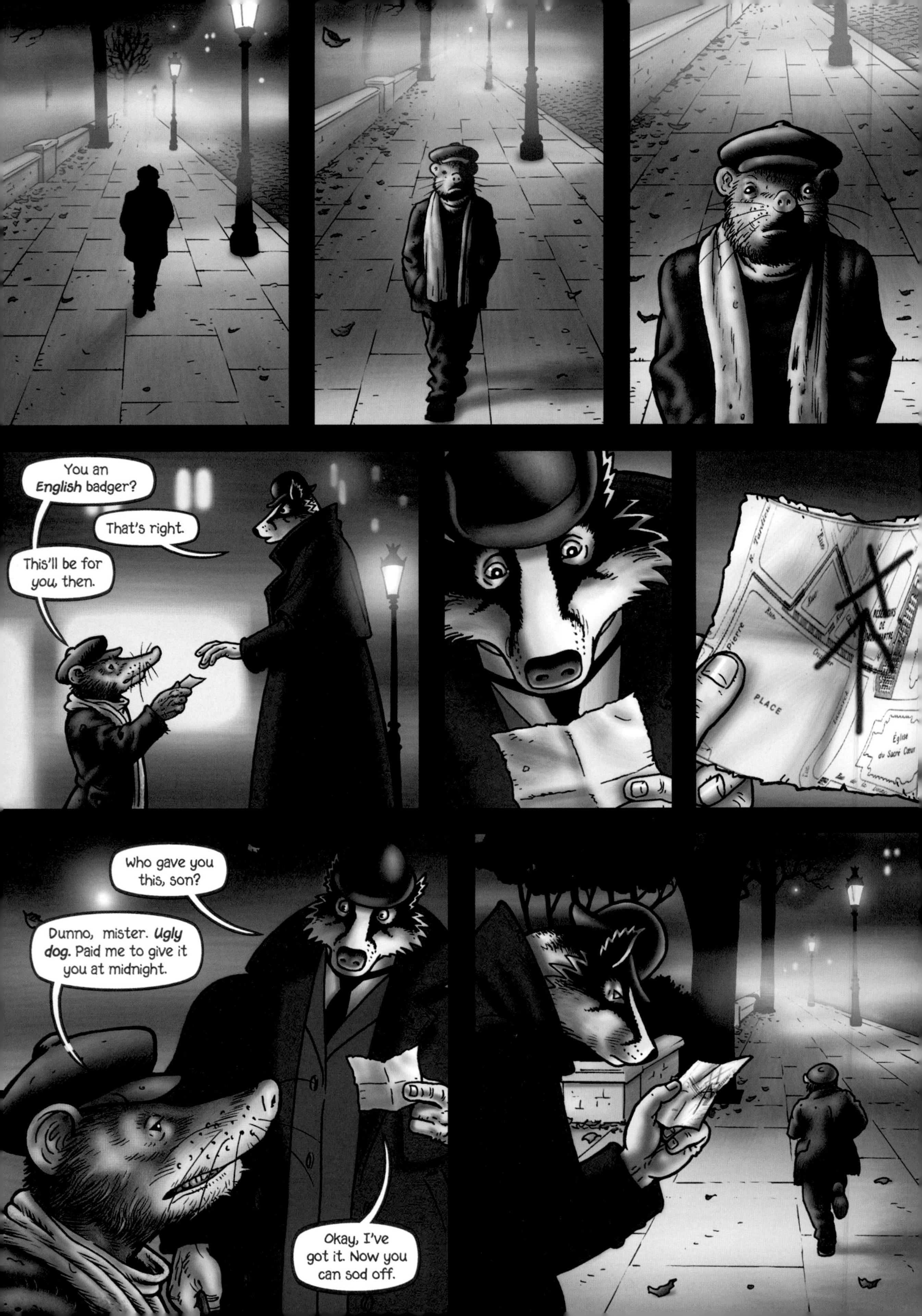
You an English badger?
That's right.
This'll be for you, then.
PLACE
Église du Sacré Cœur
Who gave you this, son?
Dunno, mister. Ugly dog. Paid me to give it you at midnight.
Okay, I've got it. Now you can sod off.

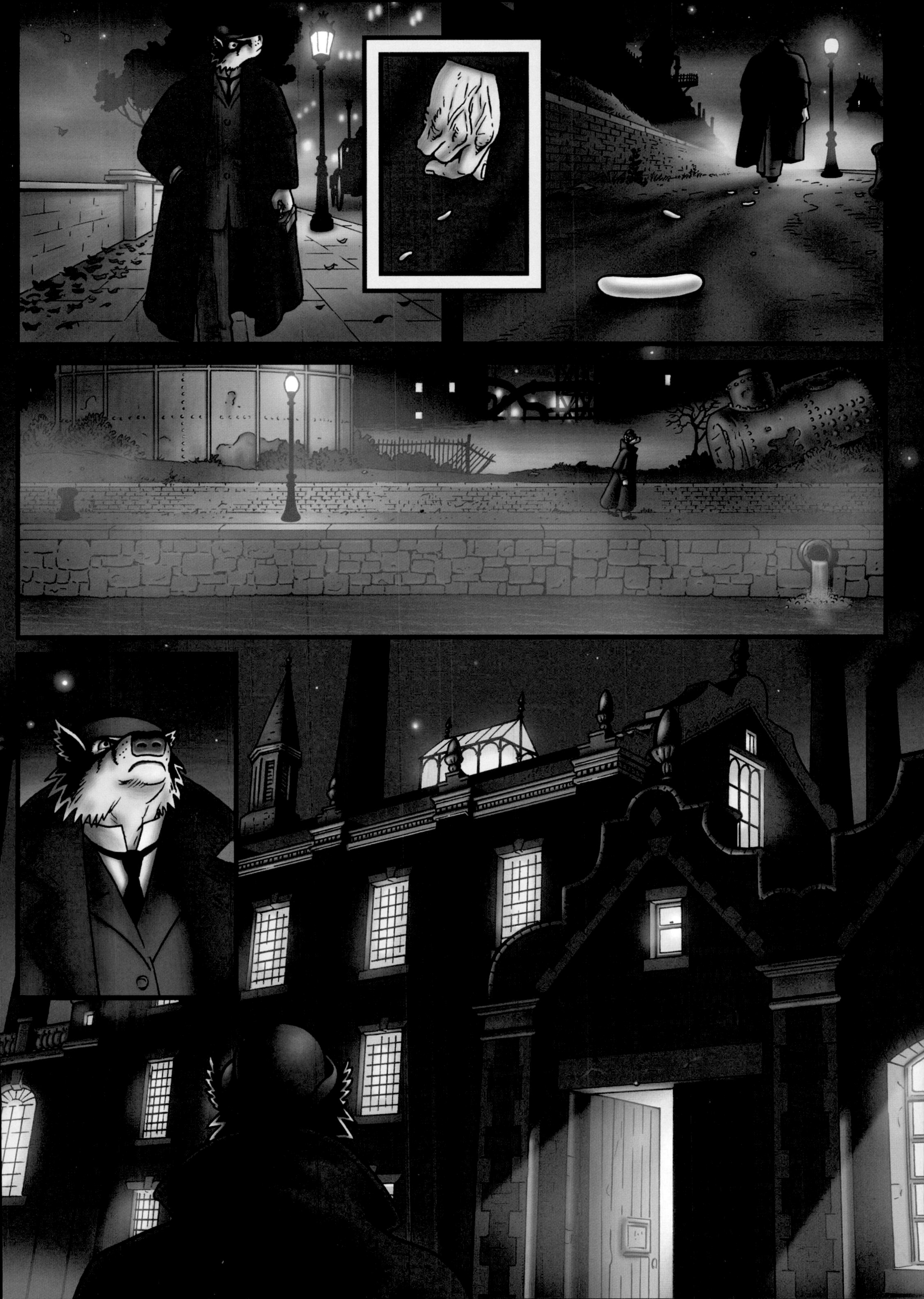

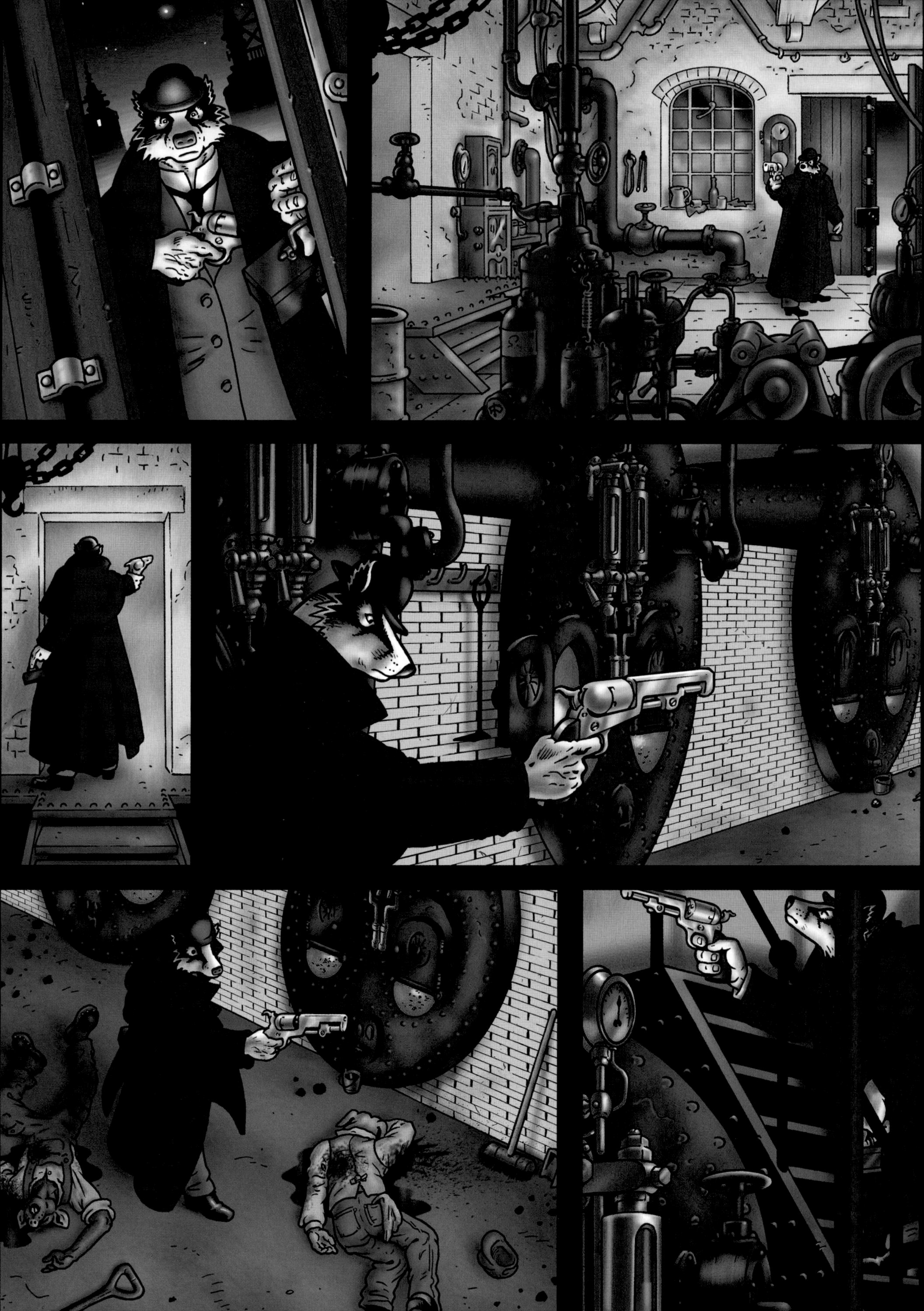

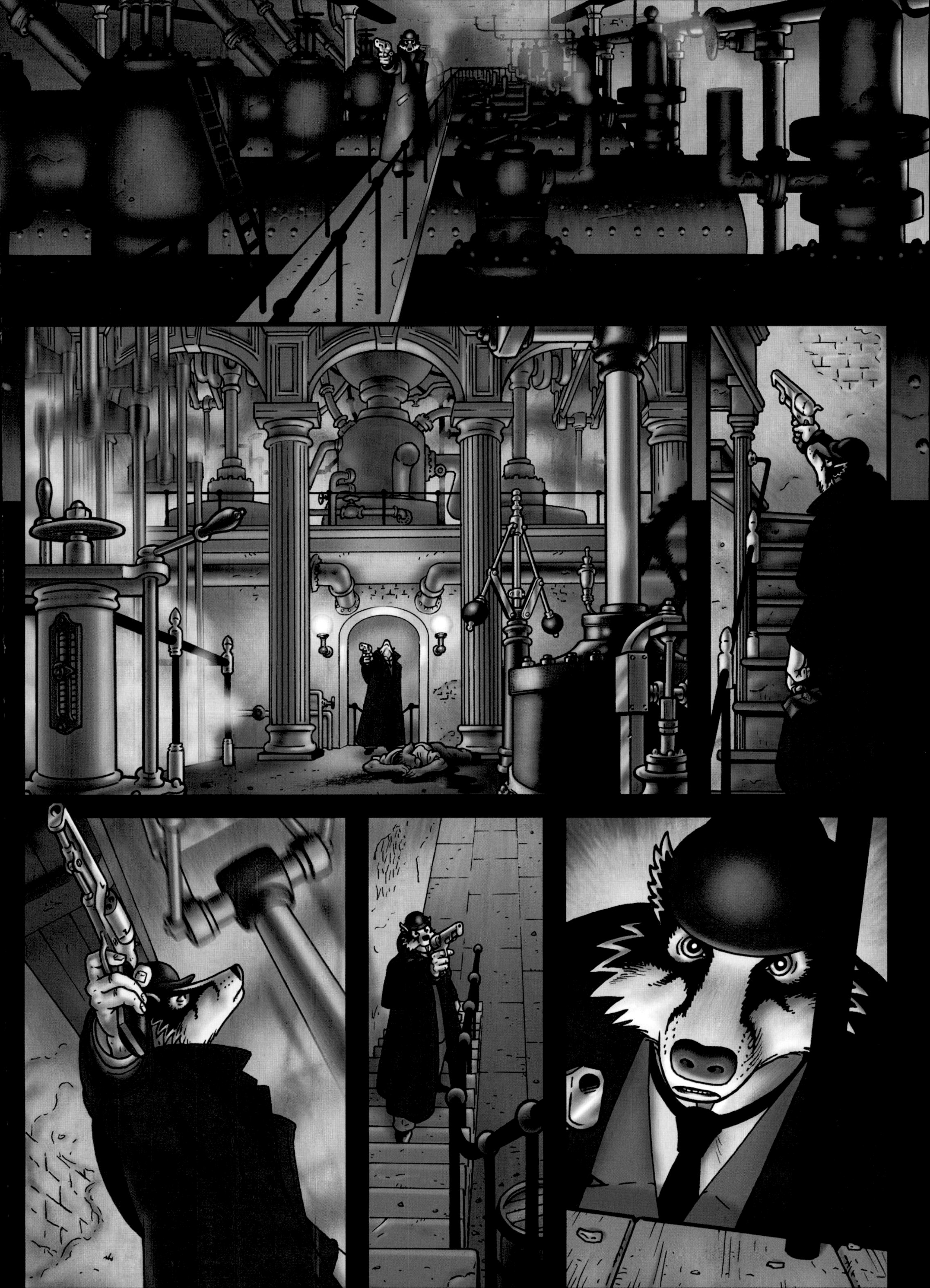

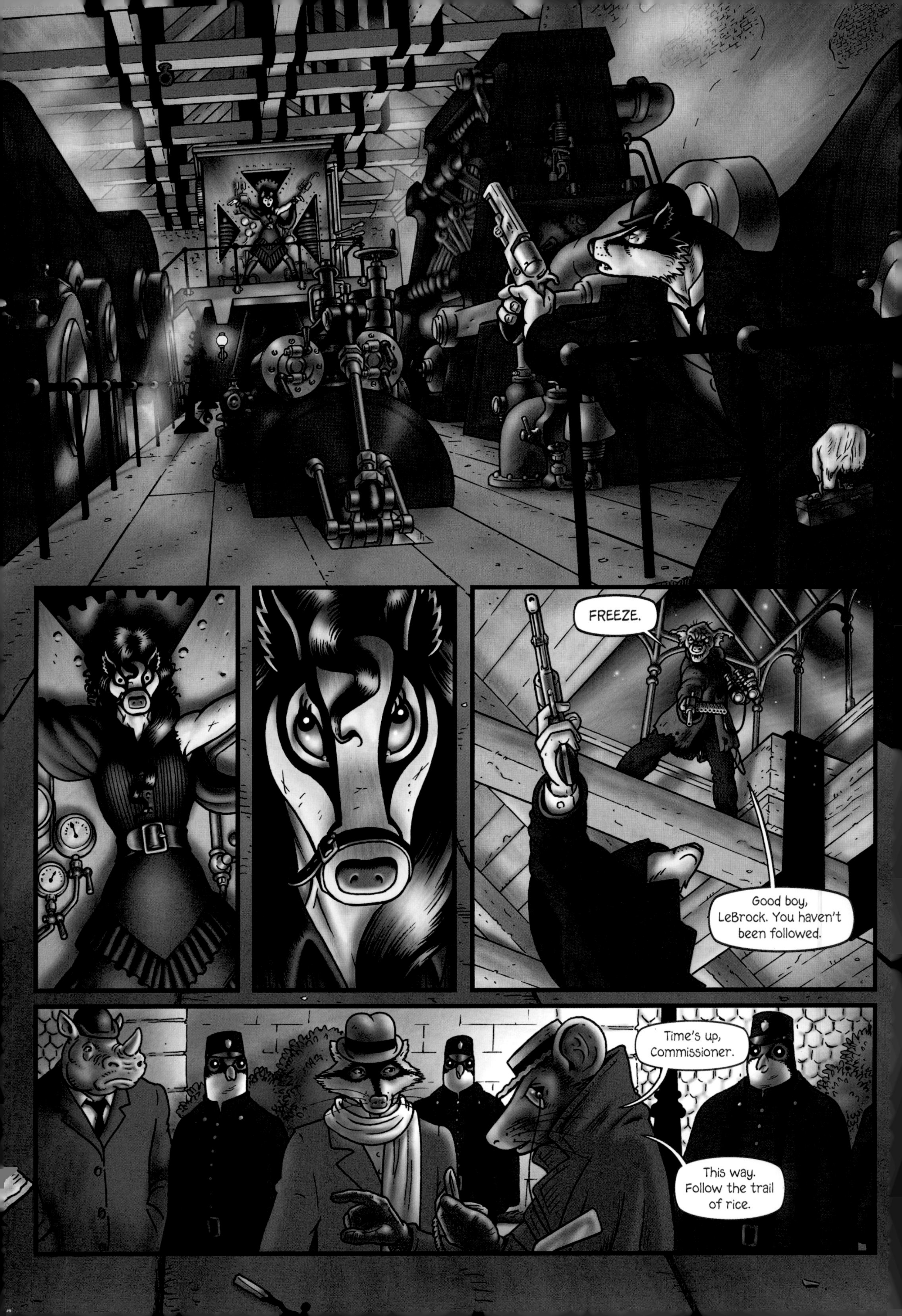

FREEZE.
Good boy, LeBrock. You haven't been followed.
Time's up, Commissioner.
This way. Follow the trail of rice.

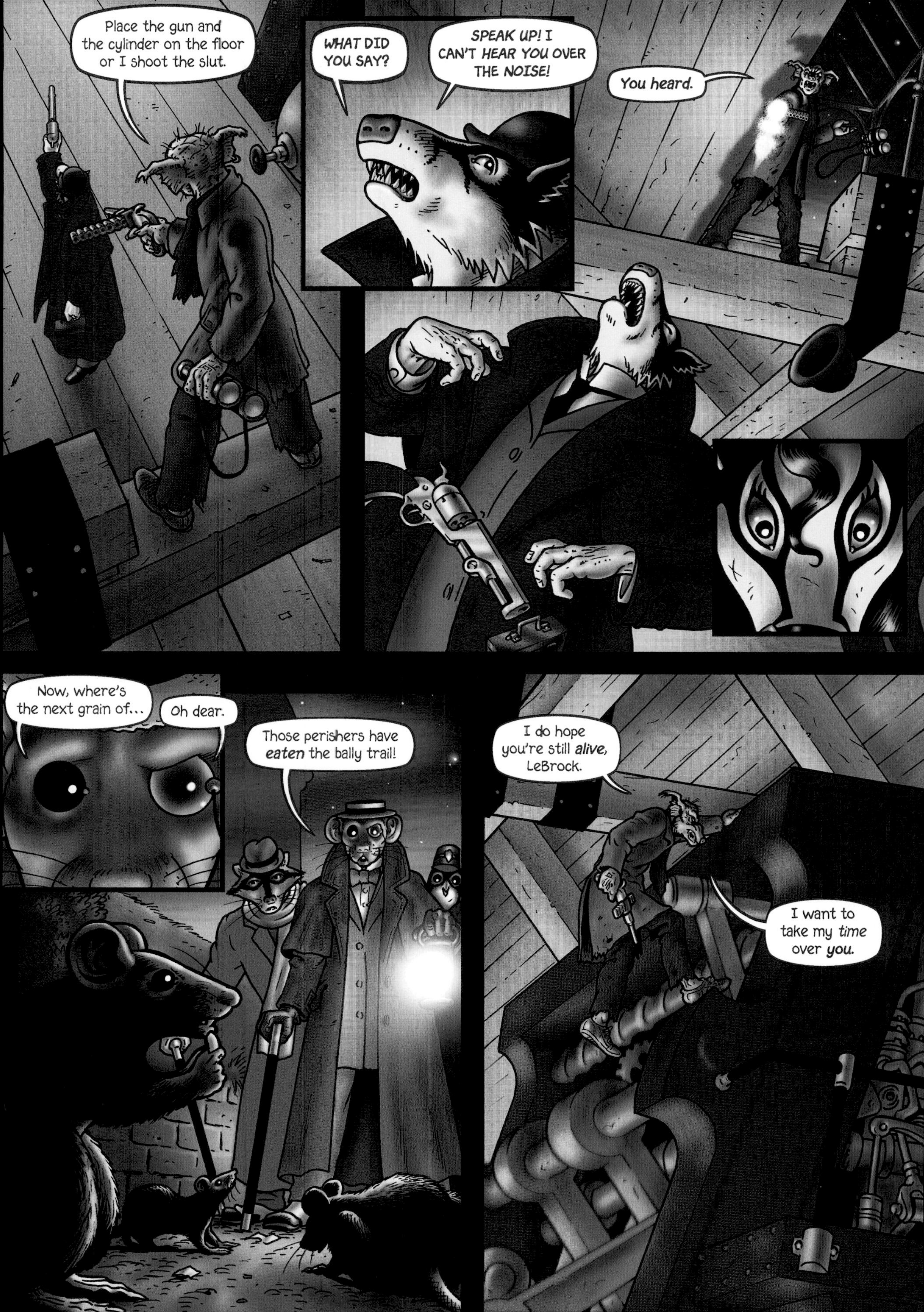
Place the gun and the cylinder on the floor or I shoot the slut.
WHAT DID YOU SAY?
SPEAK UP! I CAN'T HEAR YOU OVER THE NOISE!
You heard.
Now, where's the next grain of...
Oh dear.
Those perishers have eaten the bally trail!
I do hope you're still alive, LeBrock.
I want to take my time over you.

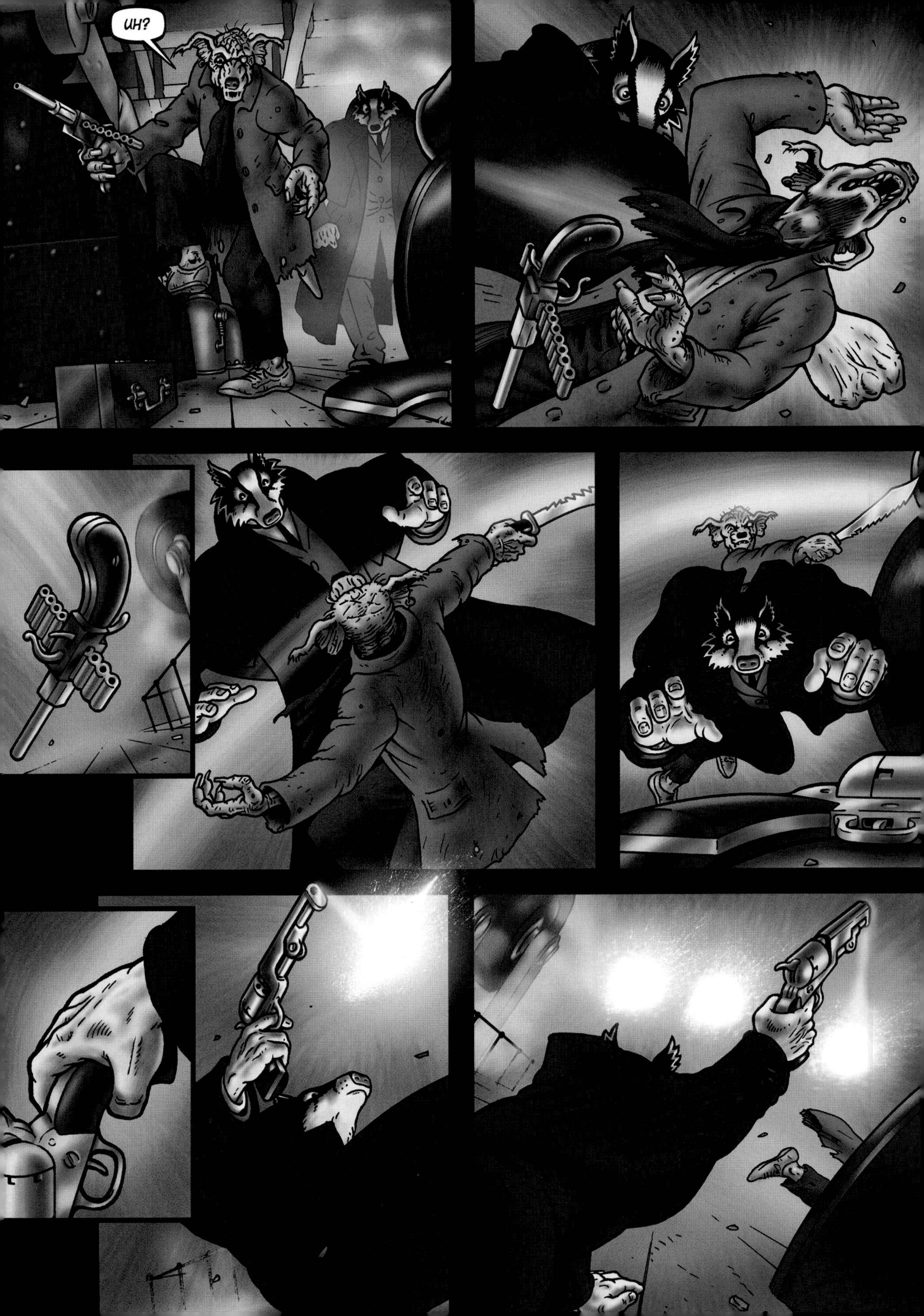
UH?

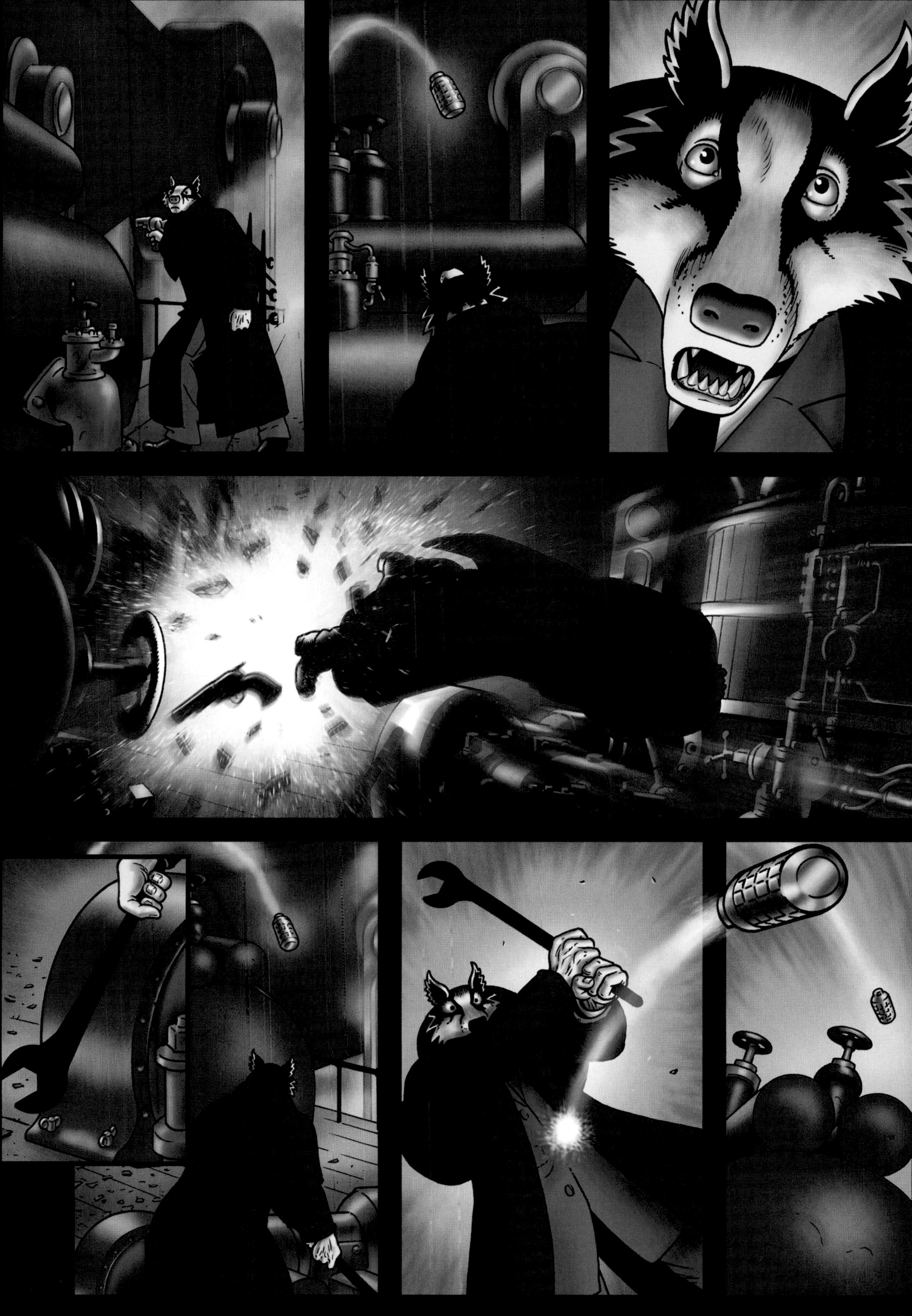

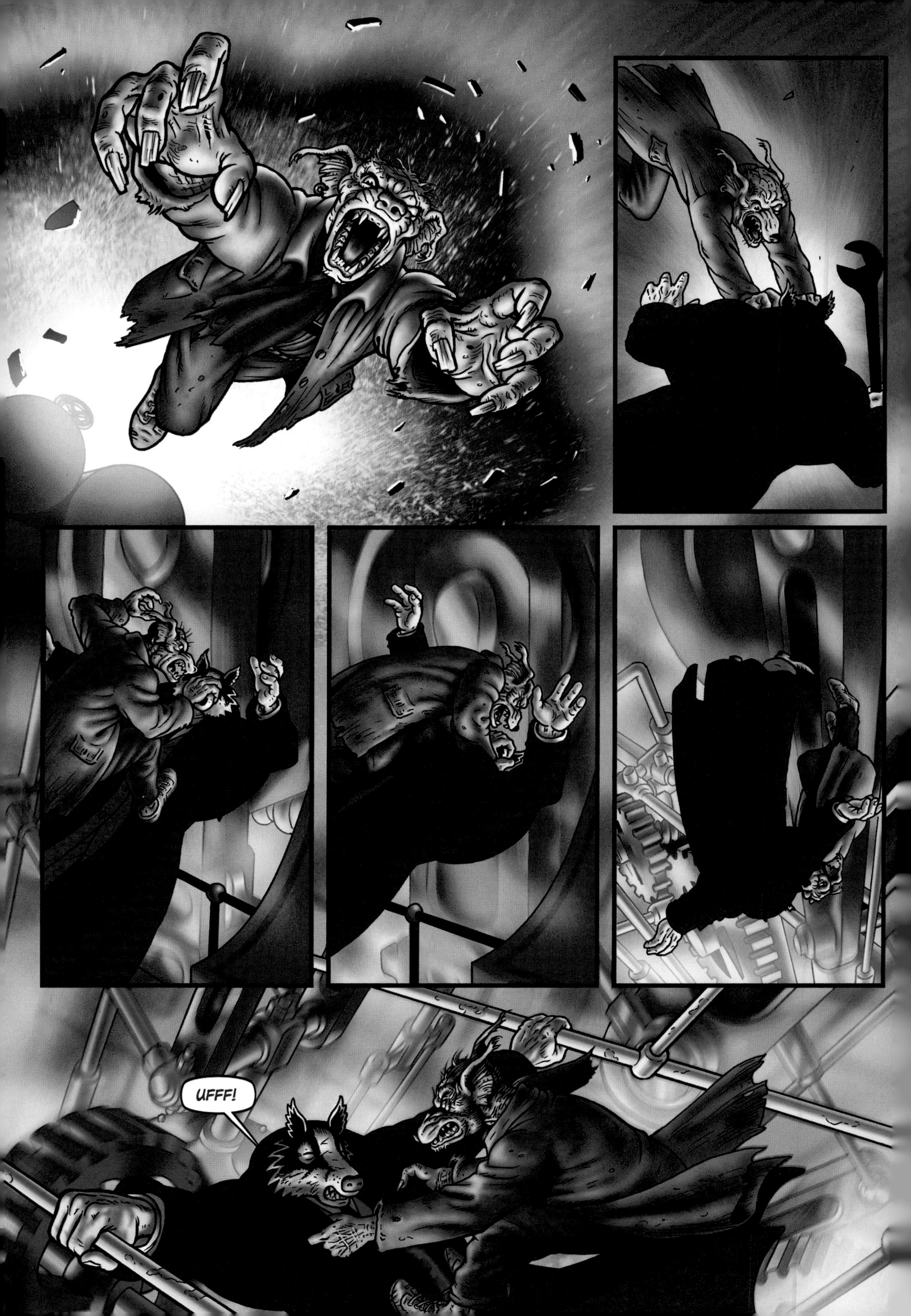
UFFF!

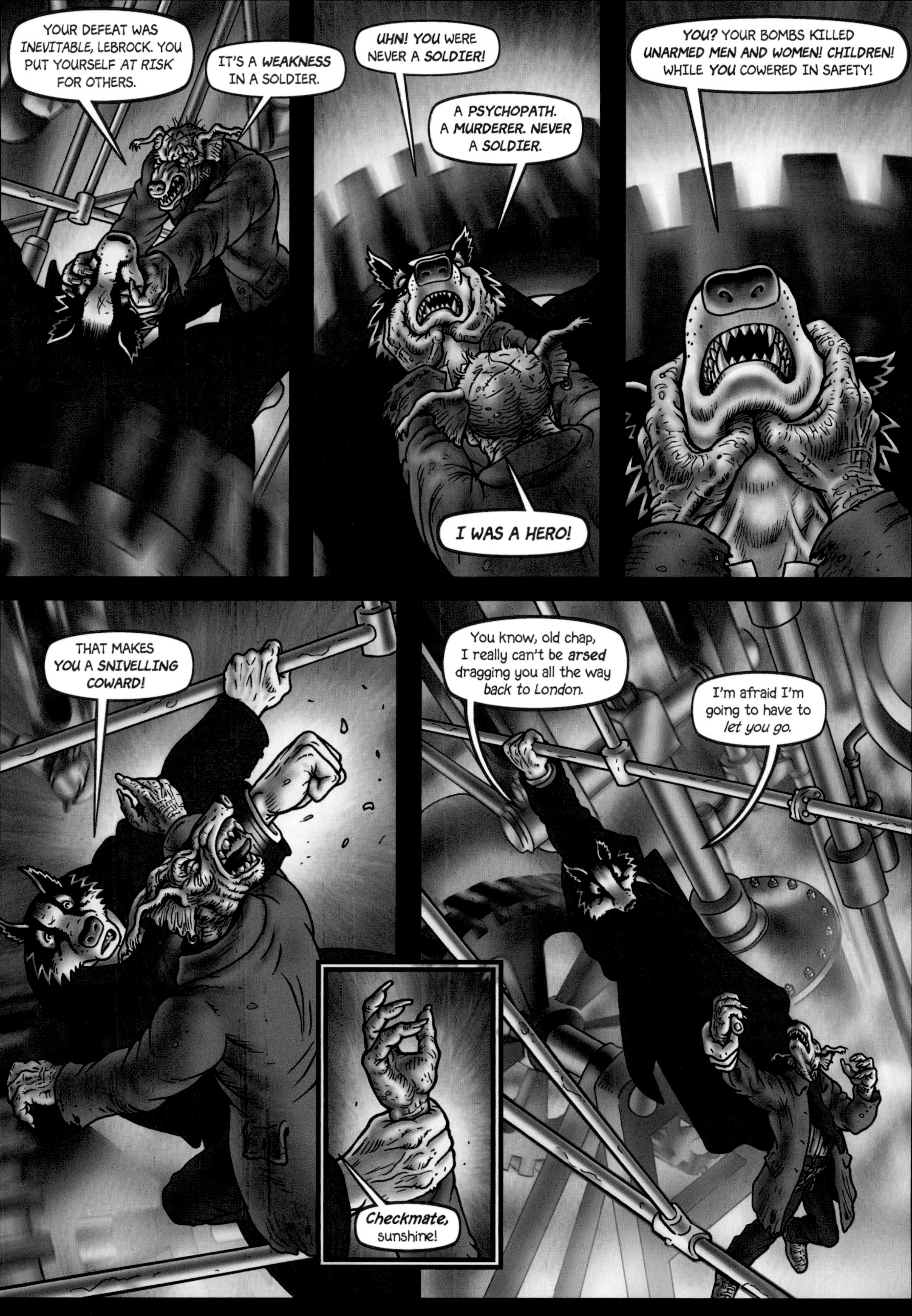

YOUR DEFEAT WAS INEVITABLE, LEBROCK. YOU PUT YOURSELF AT RISK FOR OTHERS.
IT'S A WEAKNESS IN A SOLDIER.
UHN! YOU WERE NEVER A SOLDIER!
A PSYCHOPATH. A MURDERER. NEVER A SOLDIER.
I WAS A HERO!
YOU? YOUR BOMBS KILLED UNARMED MEN AND WOMEN! CHILDREN! WHILE YOU COWERED IN SAFETY!
THAT MAKES YOU A SNIVELLING COWARD!
Checkmate, sunshine!
You know, old chap, I really can't be arsed dragging you all the way back to London.
I'm afraid I'm going to have to let you go.

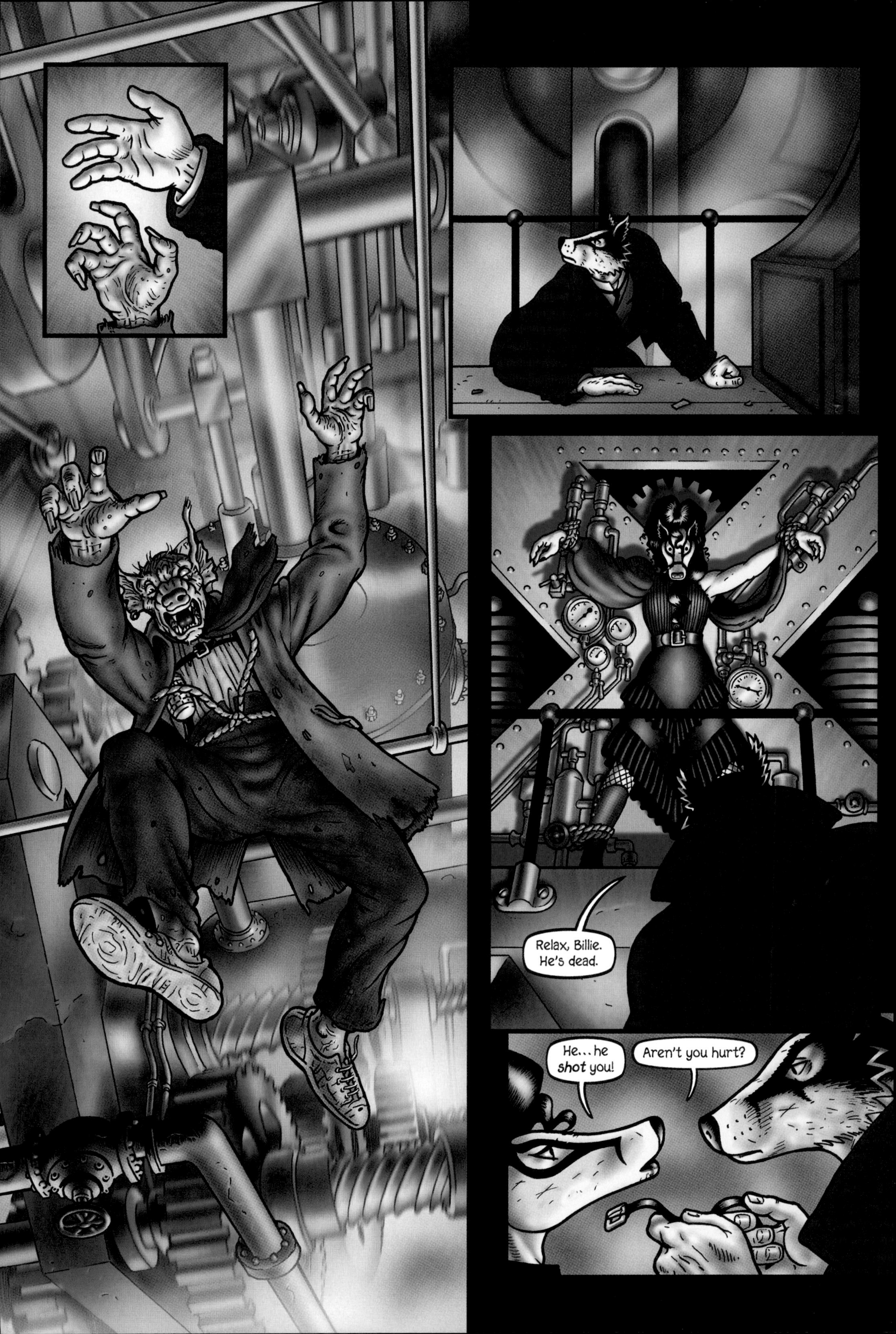

Relax, Billie. He's dead.
He... he *shot* you!
Aren't you hurt?

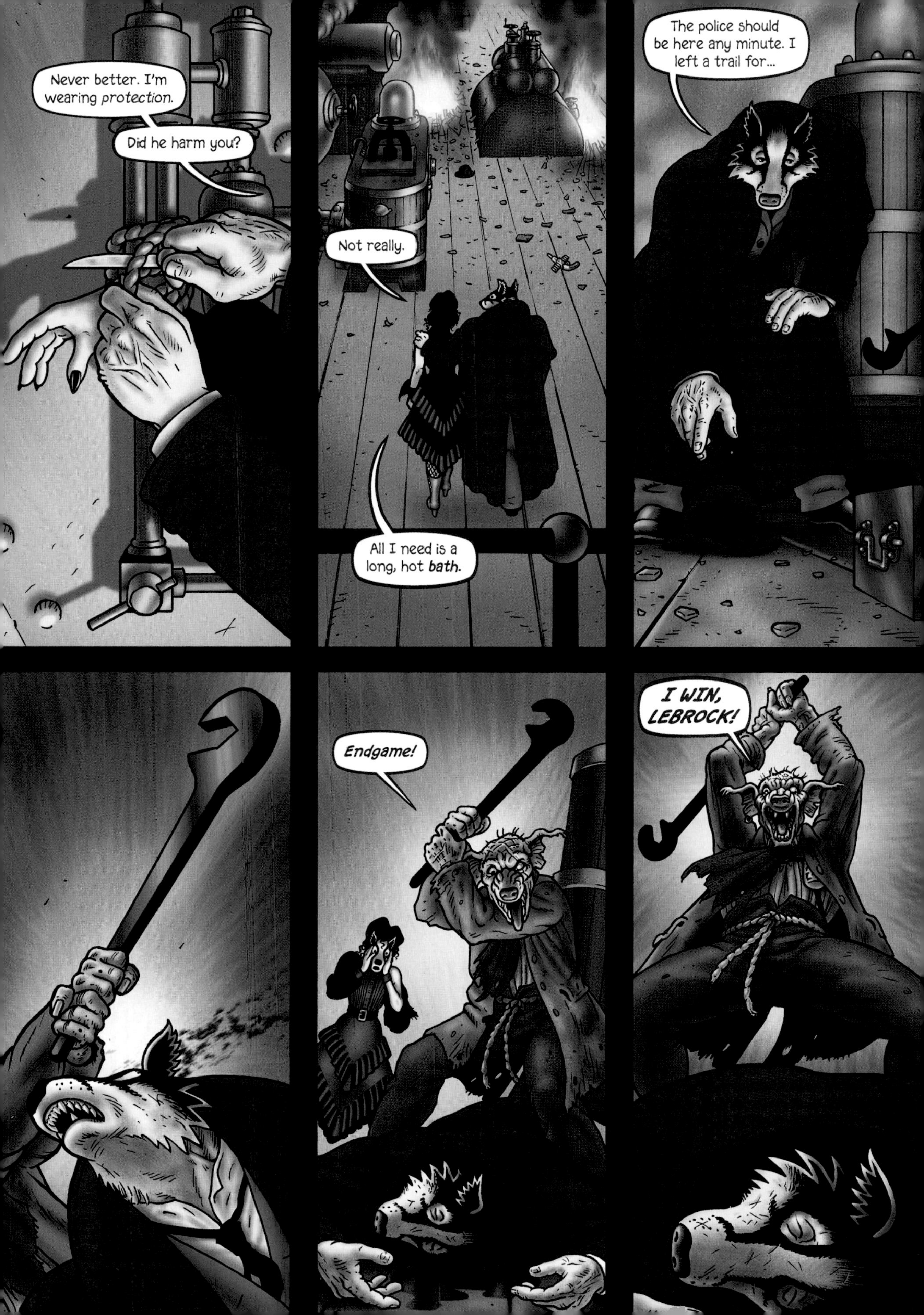
Never better. I'm wearing *protection*.
Did he harm you?
Not really.
All I need is a long, hot *bath*.
The police should be here any minute. I left a trail for...
Endgame!
I WIN, LEBROCK!

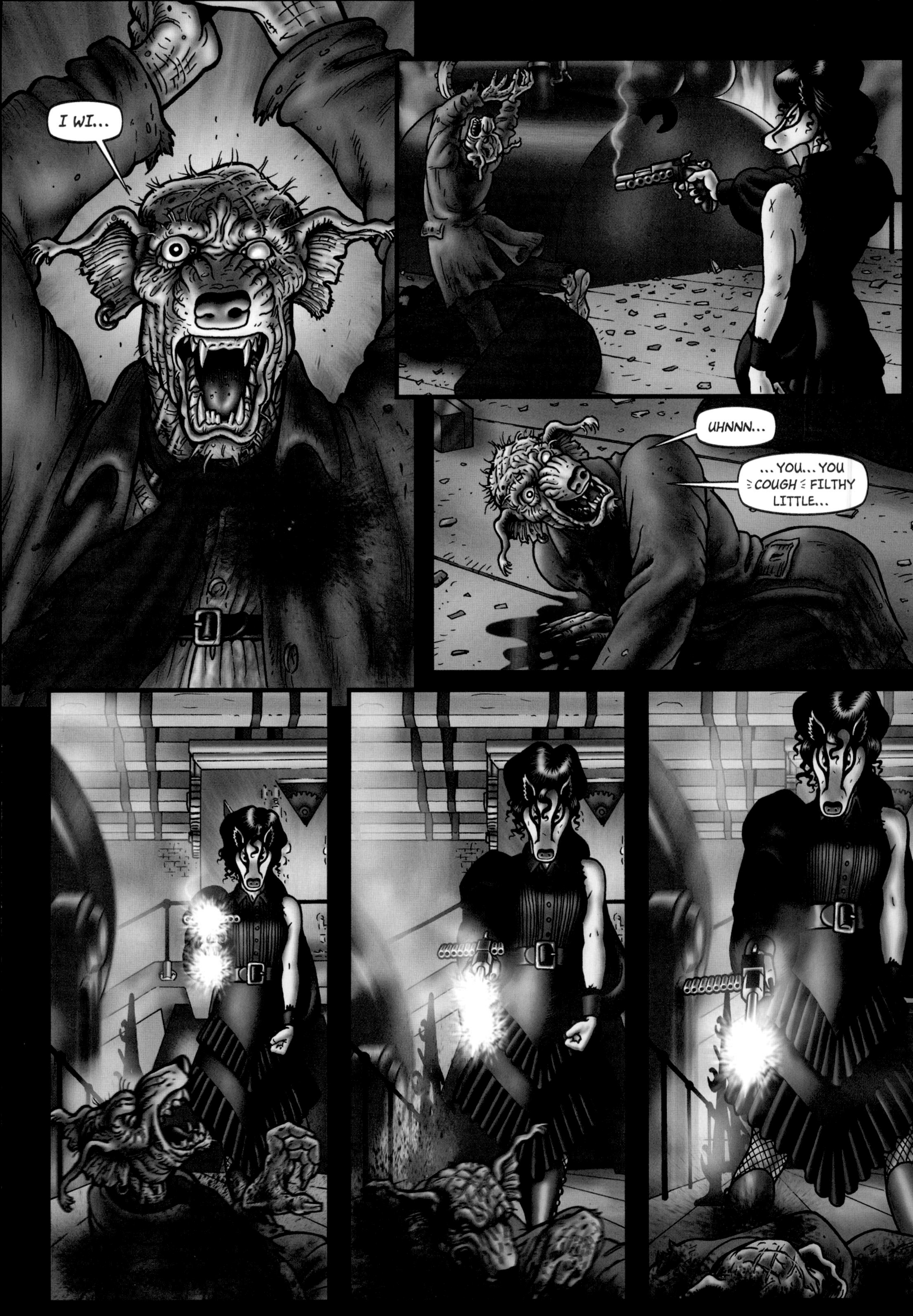
I WI...
UHNNN...
...YOU...YOU
COUGH FILTHY
LITTLE...

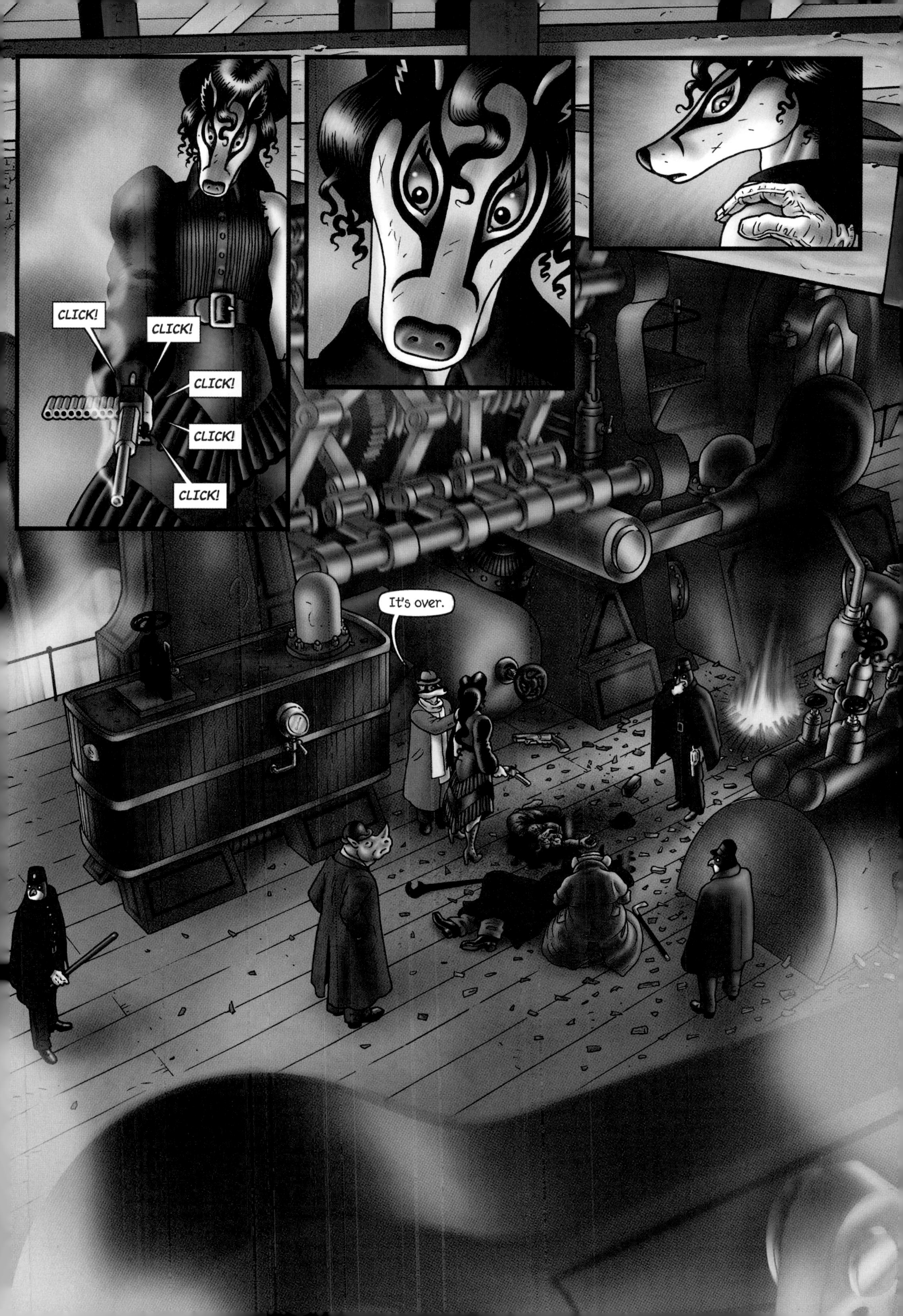

CLICK!
CLICK!
CLICK!
CLICK!
CLICK!
It's over.

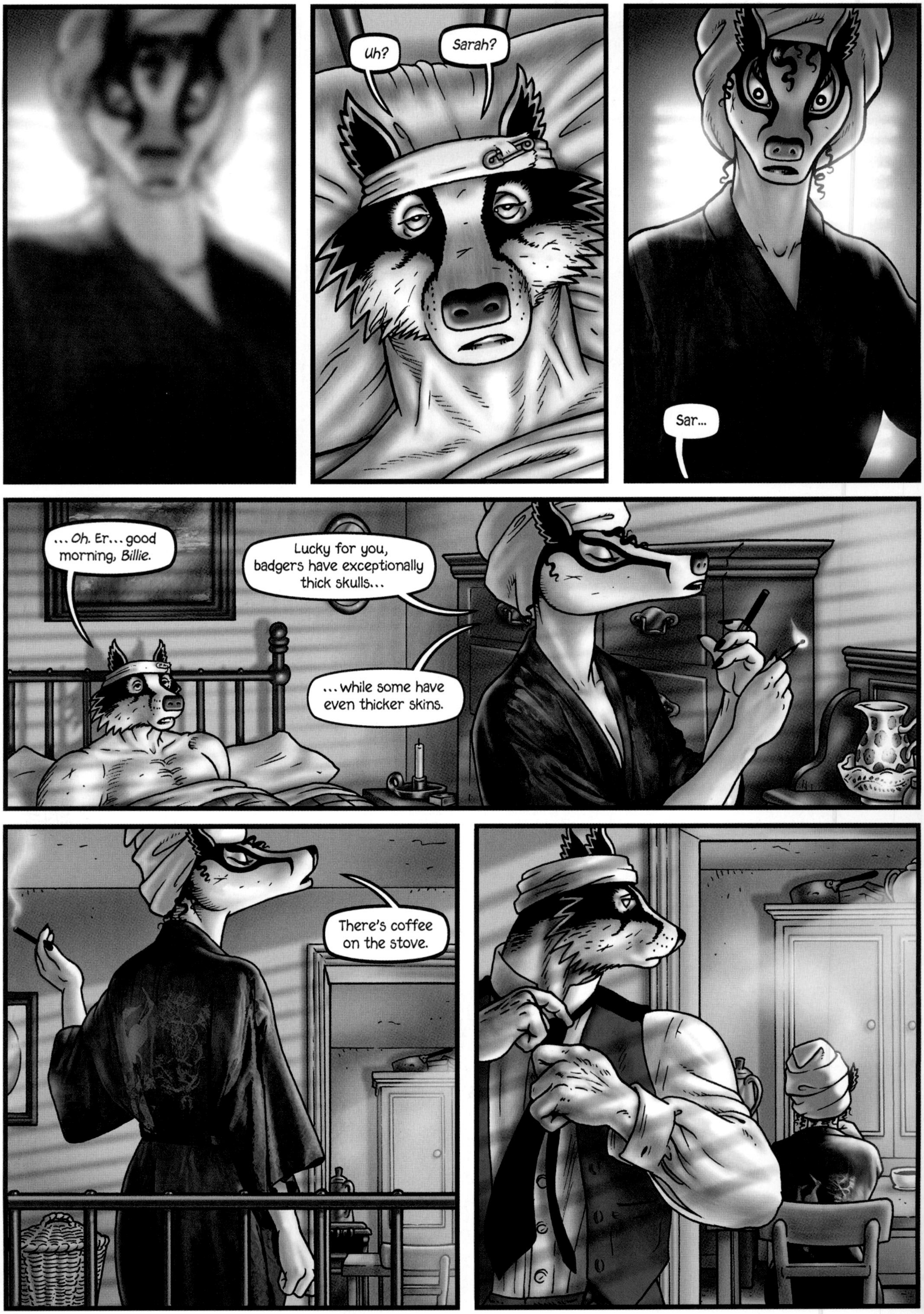
Uh?
Sarah?
Sar...
...Oh. Er...good morning, Billie.
Lucky for you, badgers have exceptionally thick skulls...
...while some have even thicker skins.
There's coffee on the stove.

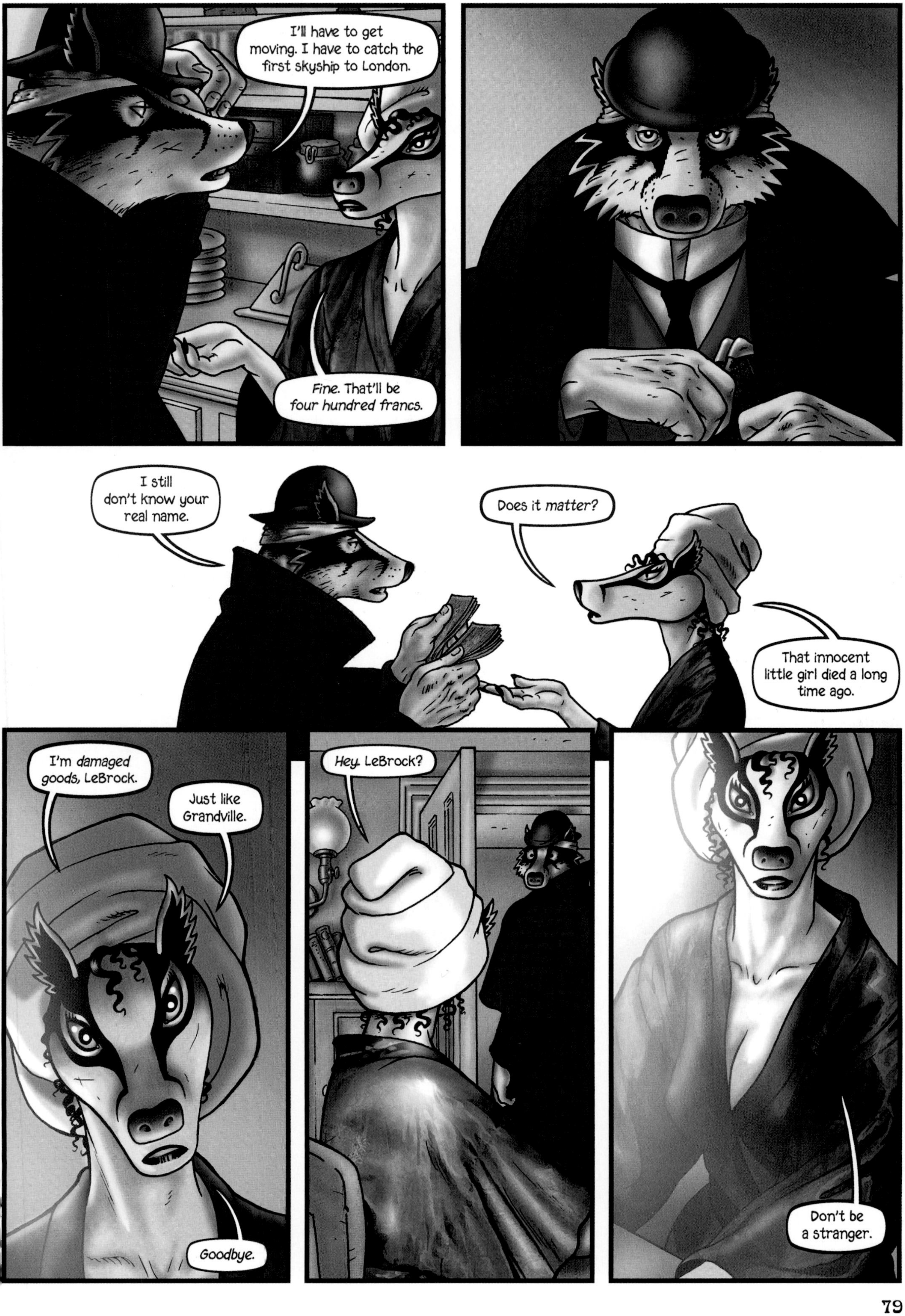
I'll have to get moving. I have to catch the first skyship to London.
Fine. That'll be four hundred francs.
I still don't know your real name.
Does it *matter?*
That innocent little girl died a long time ago.
I'm *damaged* goods, LeBrock.
Just like Grandville.
Goodbye.
Hey. LeBrock?
Don't be a stranger.

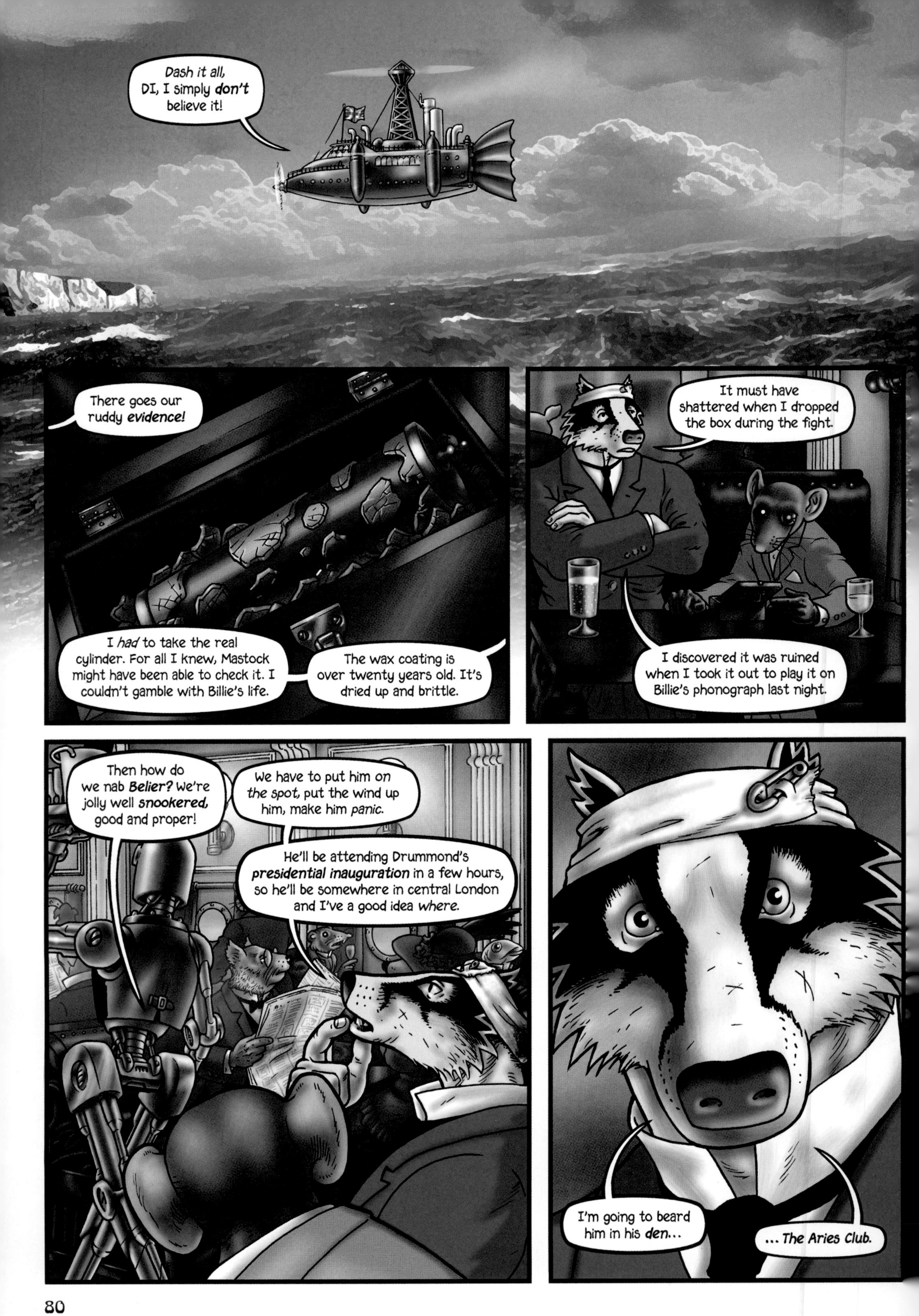

Dash it all, DI, I simply **don't** believe it!
There goes our ruddy **evidence!**
I *had* to take the real cylinder. For all I knew, Mastock might have been able to check it. I couldn't gamble with Billie's life.
The wax coating is over twenty years old. It's dried up and brittle.
It must have shattered when I dropped the box during the fight.
I discovered it was ruined when I took it out to play it on Billie's phonograph last night.
Then how do we nab **Belier?** We're jolly well **snookered,** good and proper!
We have to put him *on the spot*, put the wind up him, make him *panic*.
He'll be attending Drummond's **presidential inauguration** in a few hours, so he'll be somewhere in central London and I've a good idea *where*.
I'm going to beard him in his **den**...
... The Aries Club.

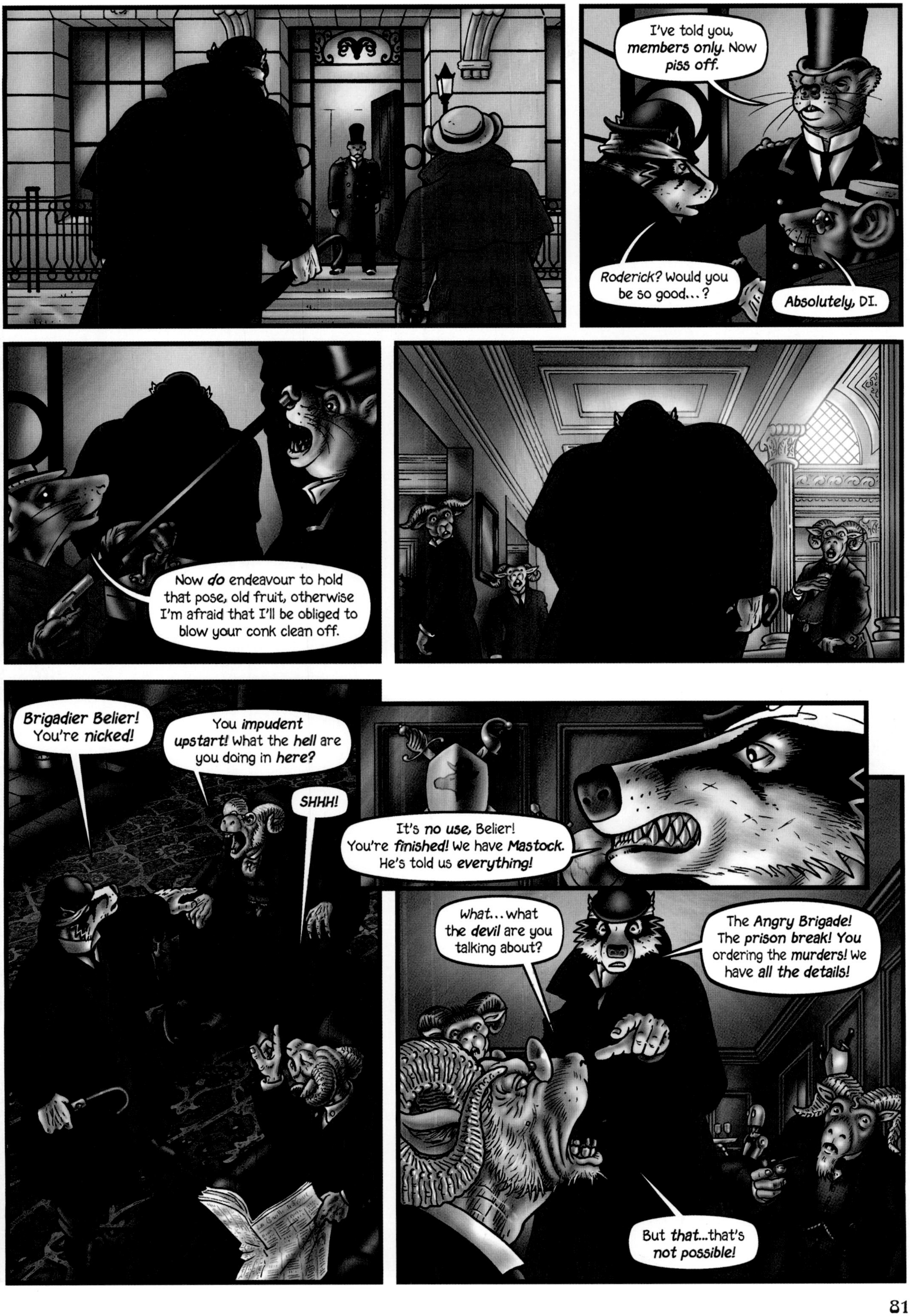
I've told you, members only. Now piss off.
Roderick? Would you be so good...?
Absolutely, DI.
Now do endeavour to hold that pose, old fruit, otherwise I'm afraid that I'll be obliged to blow your conk clean off.
Brigadier Belier! You're nicked!
You impudent upstart! What the hell are you doing in here?
SHHH!
It's no use, Belier! You're finished! We have Mastock. He's told us everything!
What...what the devil are you talking about?
The Angry Brigade! The prison break! You ordering the murders! We have all the details!
But that...that's not possible!

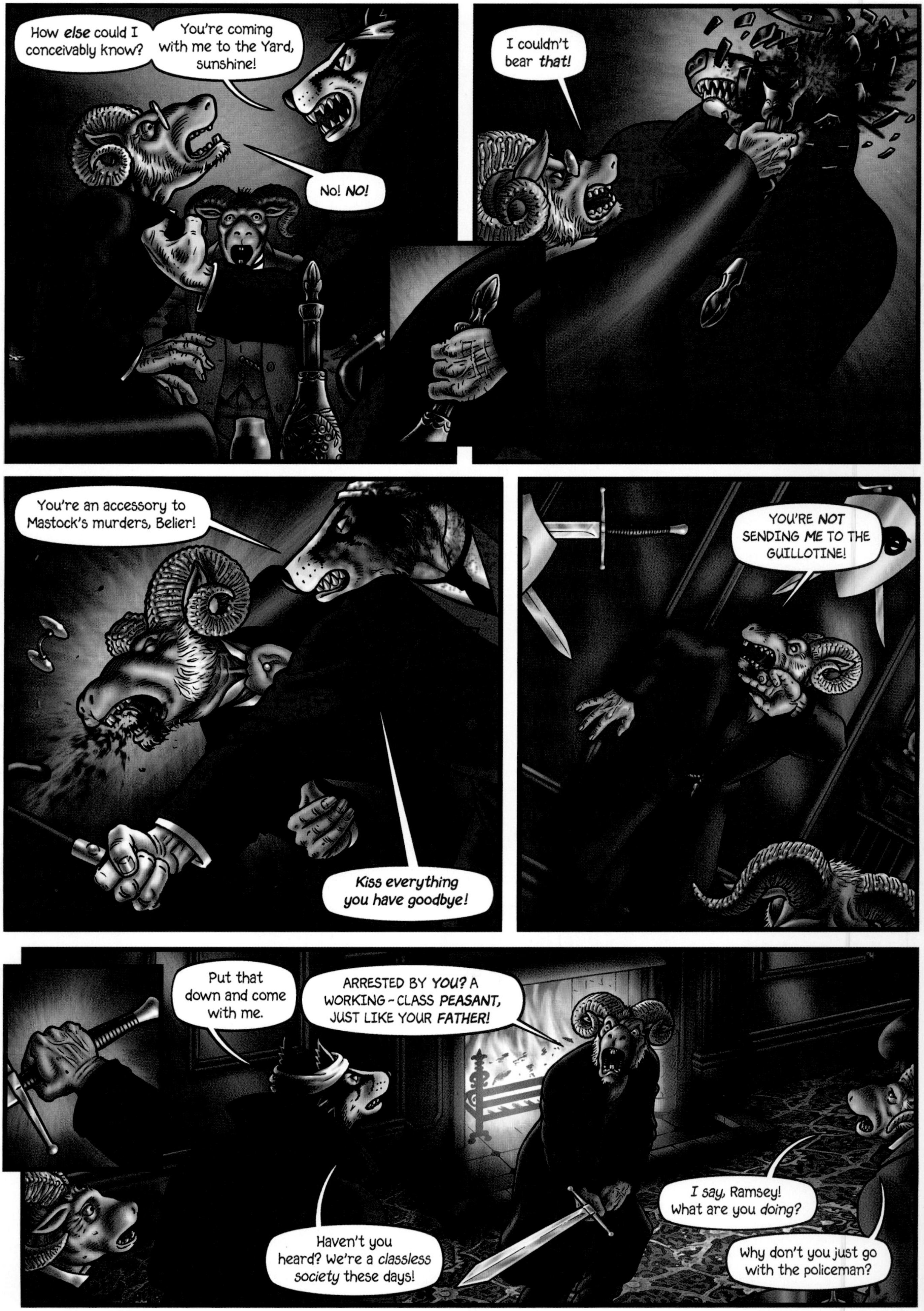
How *else* could I conceivably know?
You're coming with me to the Yard, sunshine!
No! ***NO!***
I couldn't bear ***that!***
You're an accessory to Mastock's murders, Belier!
Kiss everything you have goodbye!
YOU'RE **NOT** SENDING **ME** TO THE GUILLOTINE!
Put that down and come with me.
ARRESTED BY ***YOU?*** A WORKING-CLASS ***PEASANT,*** JUST LIKE YOUR ***FATHER!***
Haven't you heard? We're a *classless society* these days!
I say, Ramsey! What are you *doing?*
Why don't you just go with the policeman?

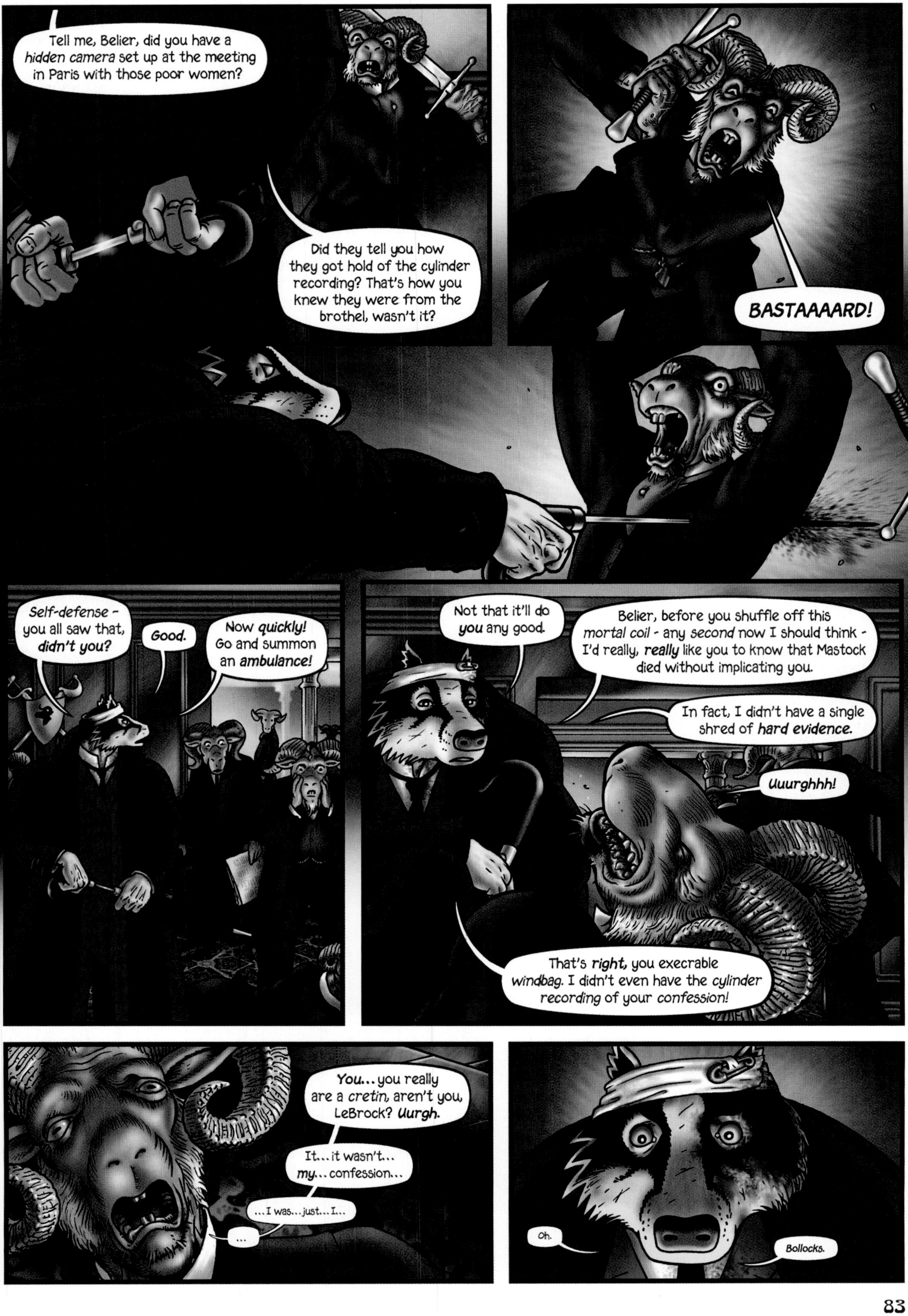
Tell me, Belier, did you have a *hidden camera* set up at the meeting in Paris with those poor women?
Did they tell you how they got hold of the cylinder recording? That's how you knew they were from the brothel, wasn't it?
BASTAAAARD!
Self-defense - you all saw that, ***didn't you?***
Good.
Now ***quickly!*** Go and summon an ***ambulance!***
Not that it'll do ***you*** any good.
Belier, before you shuffle off this *mortal coil* - any *second* now I should think - I'd really, ***really*** like you to know that Mastock died without implicating you.
In fact, I didn't have a single shred of ***hard evidence.***
Uuurghhh!
That's ***right,*** you execrable *windbag.* I didn't even have the *cylinder recording* of your *confession!*
You... you really are a *cretin,* aren't you, LeBrock? ***Uurgh.***
It... it wasn't... ***my...*** confession...
...I was... just... I...
...
Oh.
Bollocks.

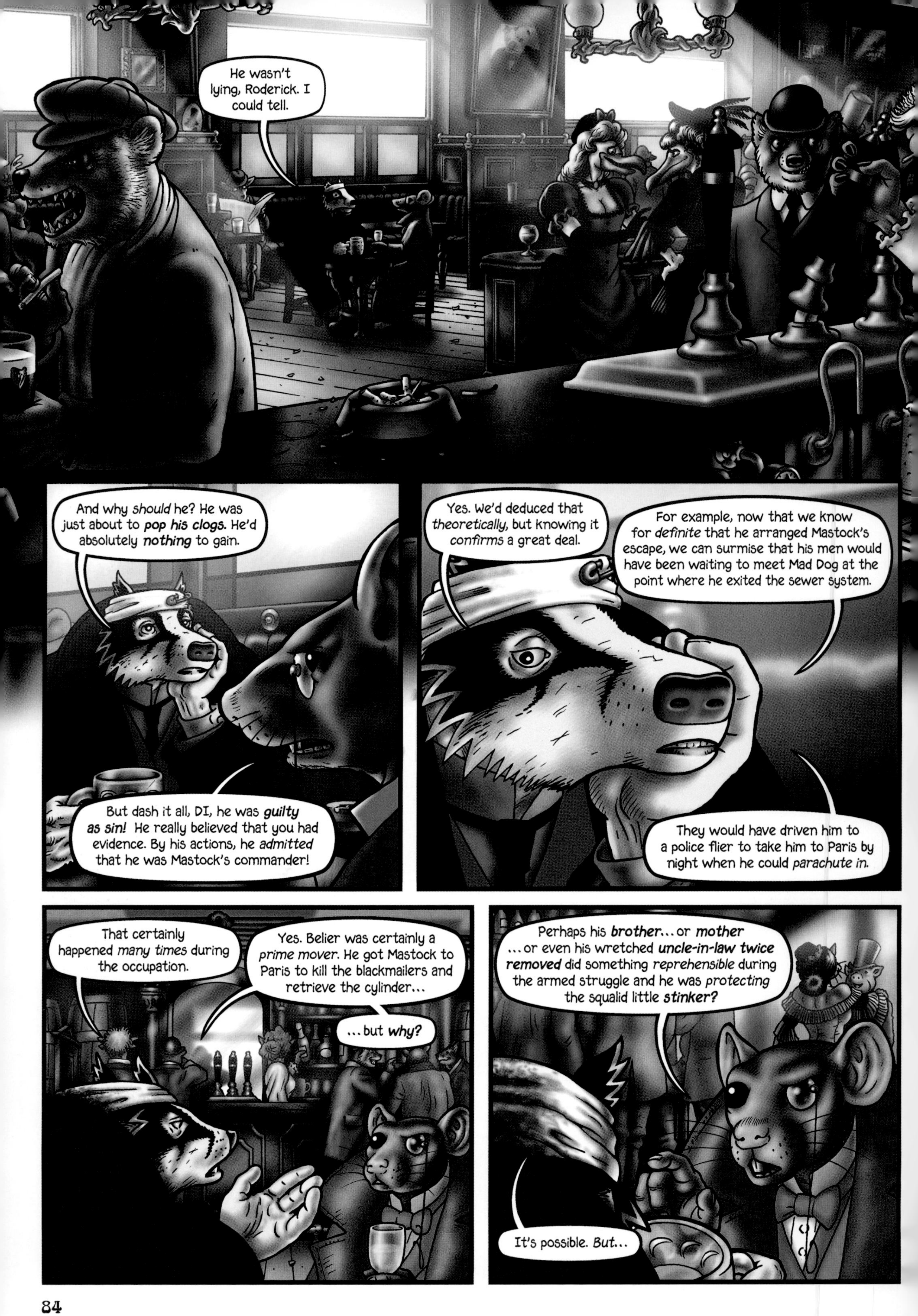
He wasn't lying, Roderick. I could tell.
And why *should* he? He was just about to ***pop his clogs.*** He'd absolutely ***nothing*** to gain.
But dash it all, DI, he was ***guilty as sin!*** He really believed that you had evidence. By his actions, he *admitted* that he was Mastock's commander!
Yes. We'd deduced that *theoretically,* but knowing it *confirms* a great deal.
For example, now that we know for *definite* that he arranged Mastock's escape, we can surmise that his men would have been waiting to meet Mad Dog at the point where he exited the sewer system.
They would have driven him to a police flier to take him to Paris by night when he could *parachute in.*
That certainly happened *many times* during the occupation.
Yes. Belier was certainly a *prime mover.* He got Mastock to Paris to kill the blackmailers and retrieve the cylinder...
...but ***why?***
Perhaps his ***brother***... or ***mother*** ...or even his wretched ***uncle-in-law twice removed*** did something *reprehensible* during the armed struggle and he was *protecting* the squalid little ***stinker?***
It's possible. *But...*

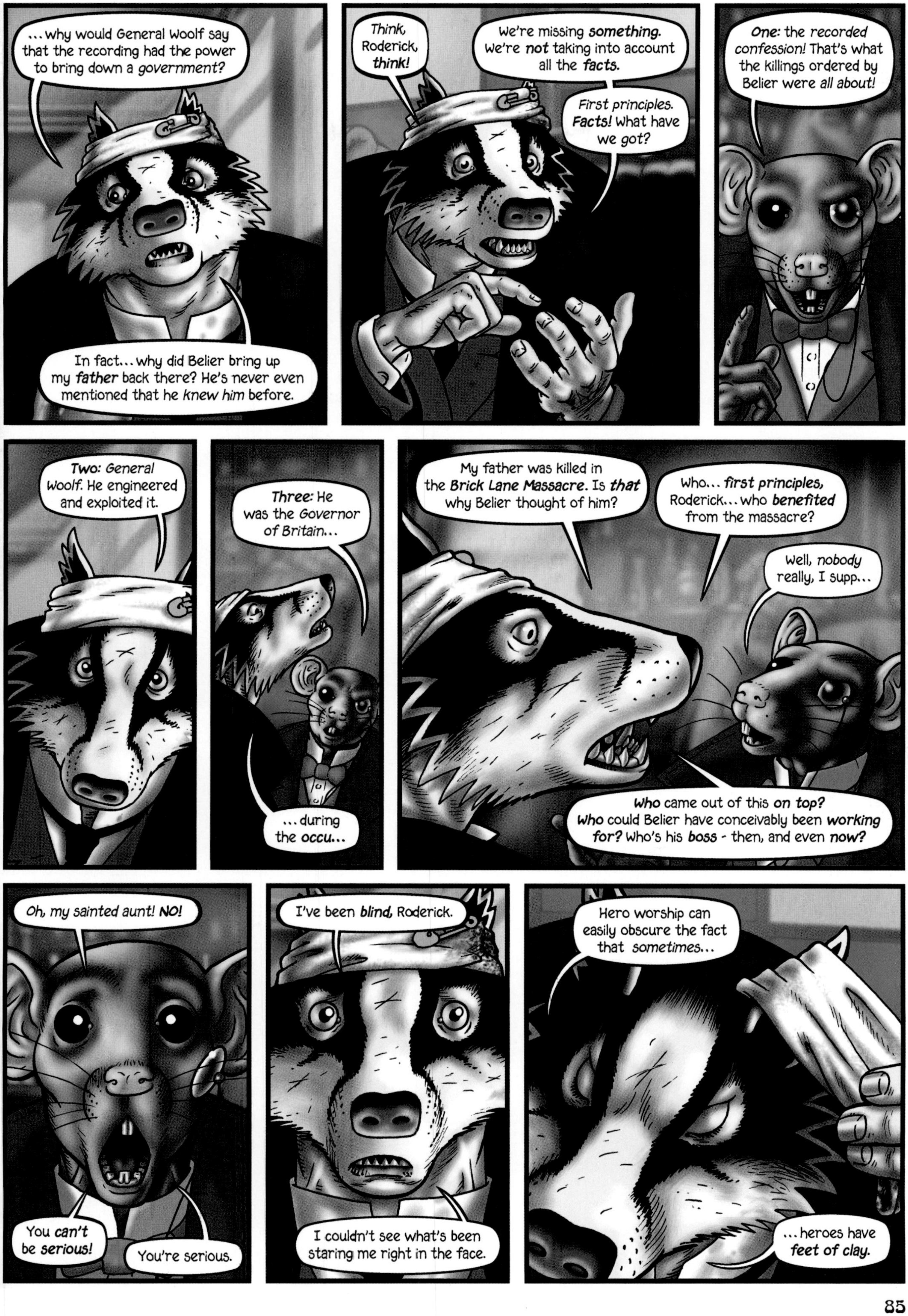
...why would General Woolf say that the recording had the power to bring down a *government*?
In fact... why did Belier bring up my *father* back there? He's never even mentioned that he *knew him* before.
Think, Roderick, think!
We're missing **something**. We're **not** taking into account all the **facts**.
First principles. **Facts!** What have we got?
One: *the recorded confession!* That's what the killings ordered by Belier were *all about!*
Two: *General Woolf.* He engineered and exploited it.
Three: *He was the Governor of Britain...*
...during the **occu...**
My father was killed in the **Brick Lane Massacre**. Is **that** why Belier thought of him?
Who... **first principles,** Roderick... who **benefited** from the massacre?
Well, *nobody* really, I supp...
Who came out of this **on top?** **Who** could Belier have conceivably been **working for?** Who's his **boss** - then, and even **now?**
Oh, my sainted aunt! **NO!**
You **can't** be **serious!**
You're serious.
I've been **blind,** Roderick.
I couldn't see what's been staring me right in the face.
Hero worship can easily obscure the fact that *sometimes...*
...heroes have **feet of clay.**

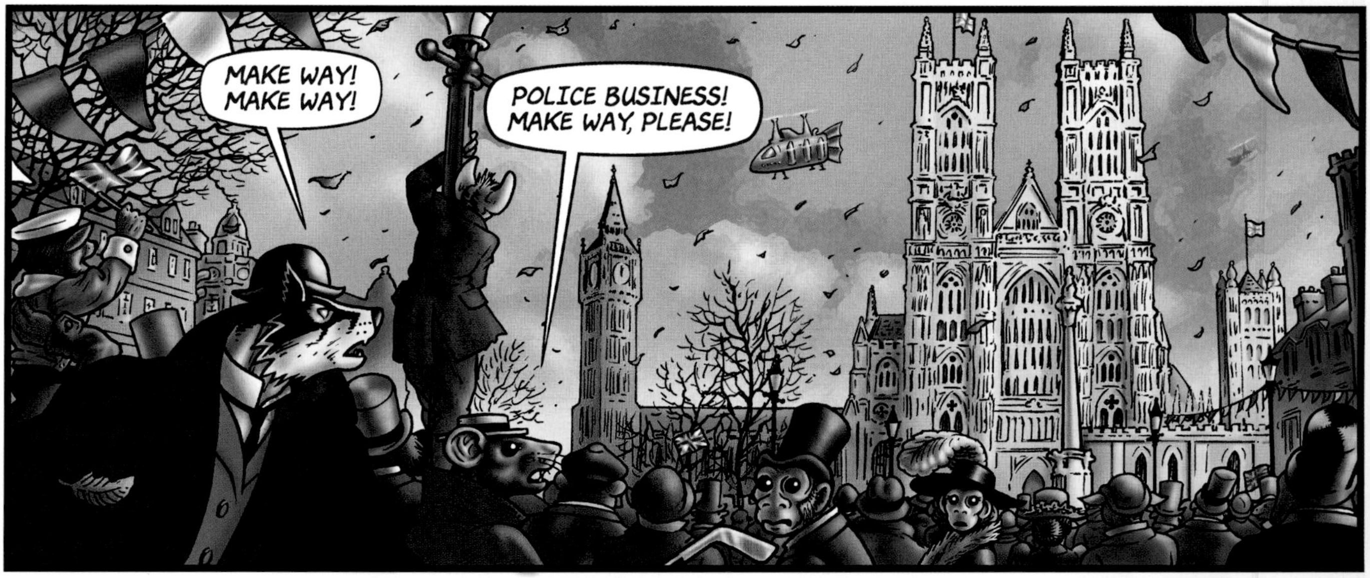
MAKE WAY! MAKE WAY!
POLICE BUSINESS! MAKE WAY, PLEASE!

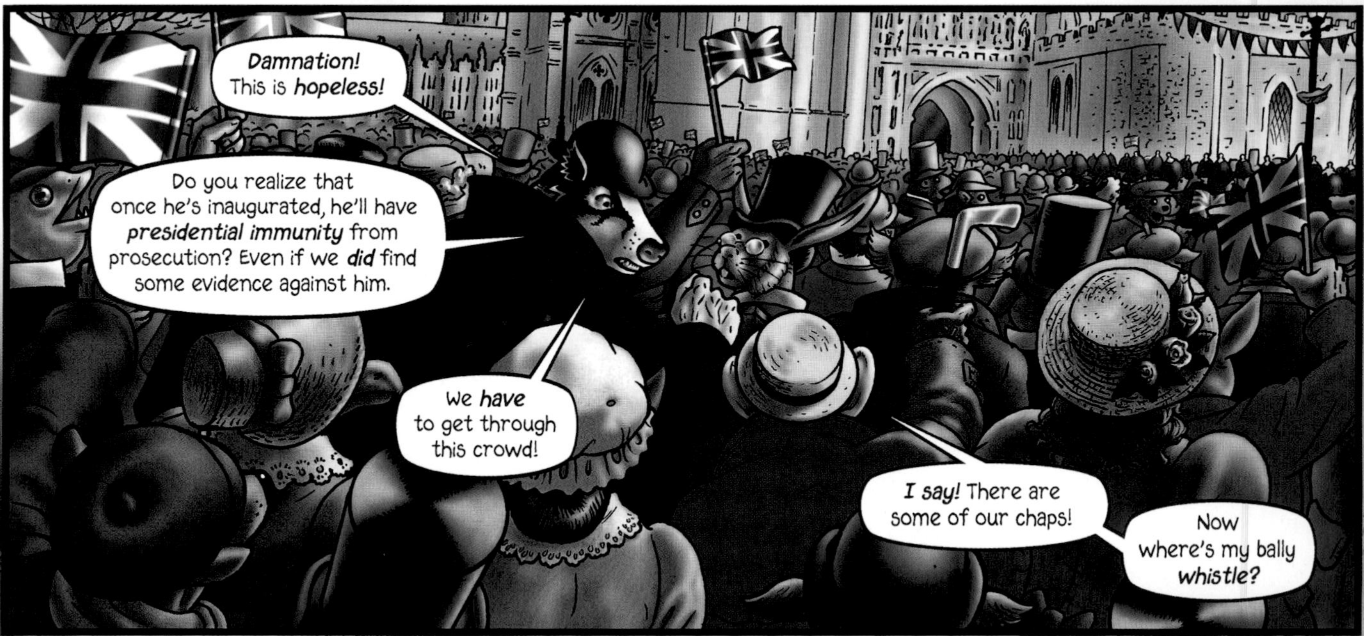
Damnation! This is ***hopeless!***
Do you realize that once he's inaugurated, he'll have ***presidential immunity*** from prosecution? Even if we ***did*** find some evidence against him.
We ***have*** to get through this crowd!
I say! There are some of our chaps!
Now where's my bally ***whistle?***

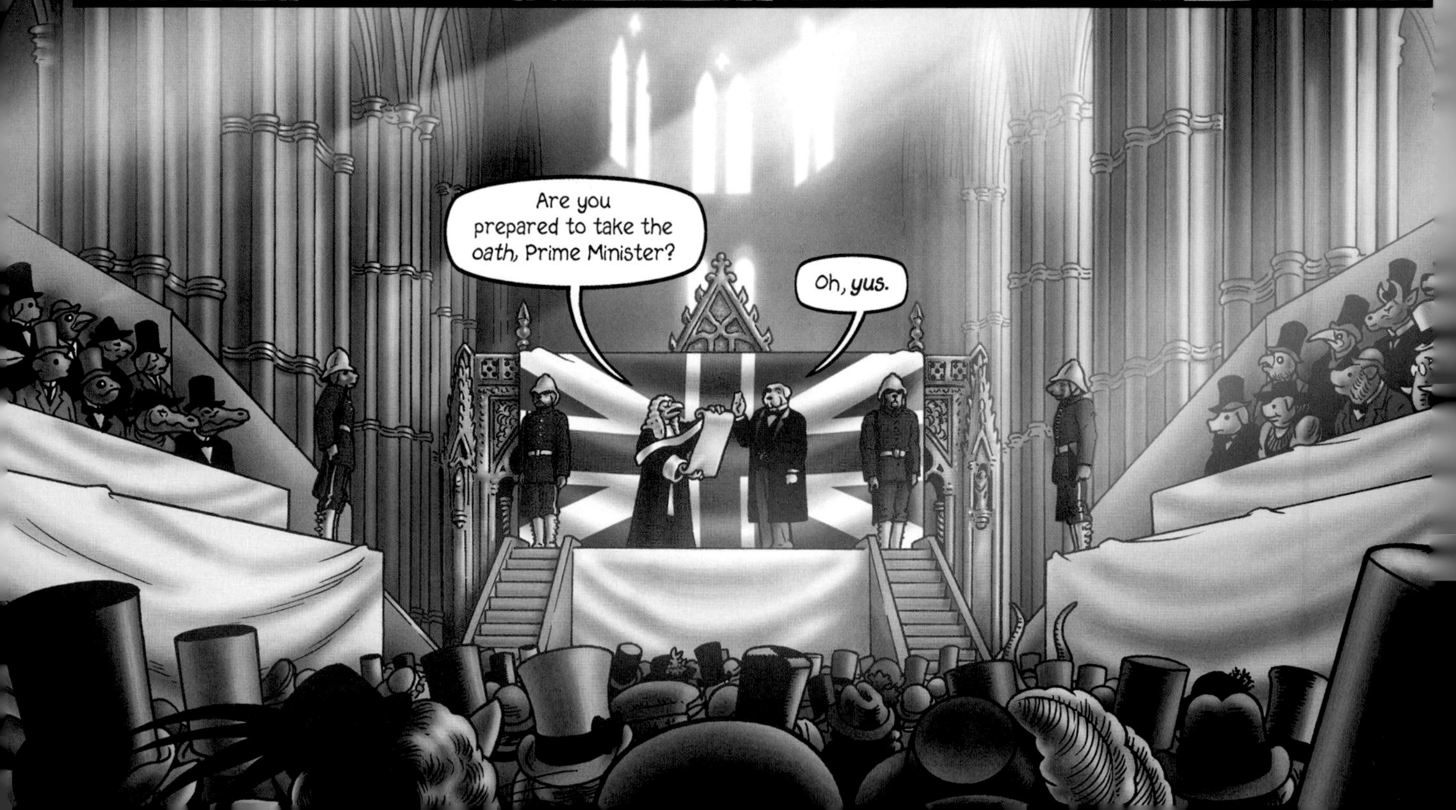
Are you prepared to take the *oath,* Prime Minister?
Oh, ***yus.***

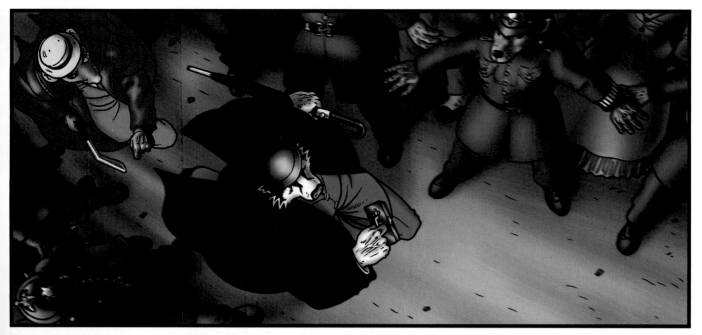

Repeat after me:

I, Harold Neville Drummond, do solemnly swear...

I, Harold Neville Drummond, do solemnly swear...

...that I will execute the office of the President of the Socialist Republic of Britain faithfully...

...that I will execute the office of the President of the Socialist Republic of Britain faithfully...

...and will, to the best of my ability...

...and will, to the best of my ability...

...preserve, protect, and defend the constitution of the Socialist Republic of Britain.

...preserve, protect, and defend the constitution of the Socialist Republic of Britain.

I now pronounce you...

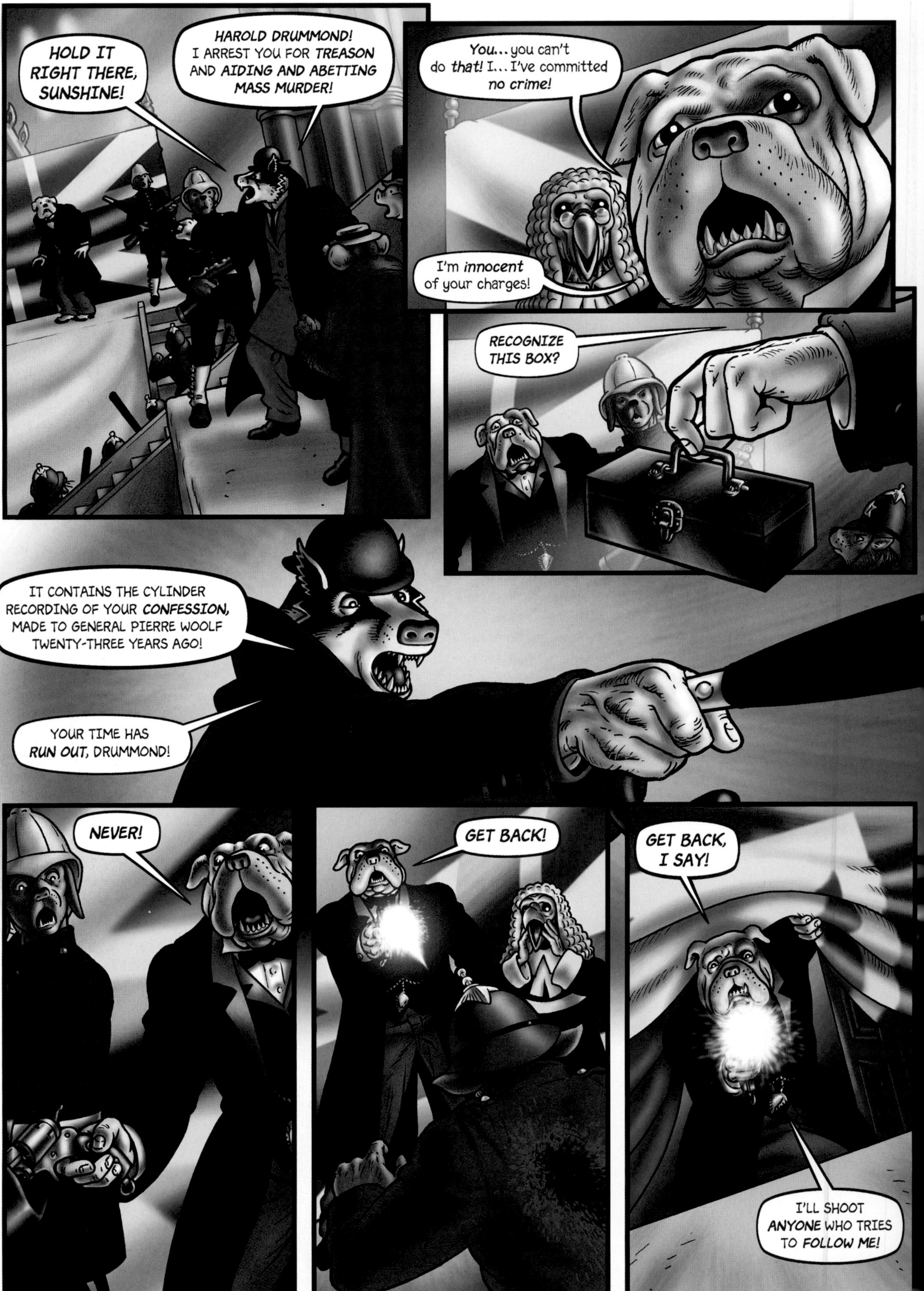
HOLD IT RIGHT THERE, SUNSHINE!
HAROLD DRUMMOND! I ARREST YOU FOR TREASON AND AIDING AND ABETTING MASS MURDER!
You... you can't do that! I... I've committed no crime!
I'm innocent of your charges!
RECOGNIZE THIS BOX?
IT CONTAINS THE CYLINDER RECORDING OF YOUR CONFESSION, MADE TO GENERAL PIERRE WOOLF TWENTY-THREE YEARS AGO!
YOUR TIME HAS RUN OUT, DRUMMOND!
NEVER!
GET BACK!
GET BACK, I SAY!
I'LL SHOOT ANYONE WHO TRIES TO FOLLOW ME!

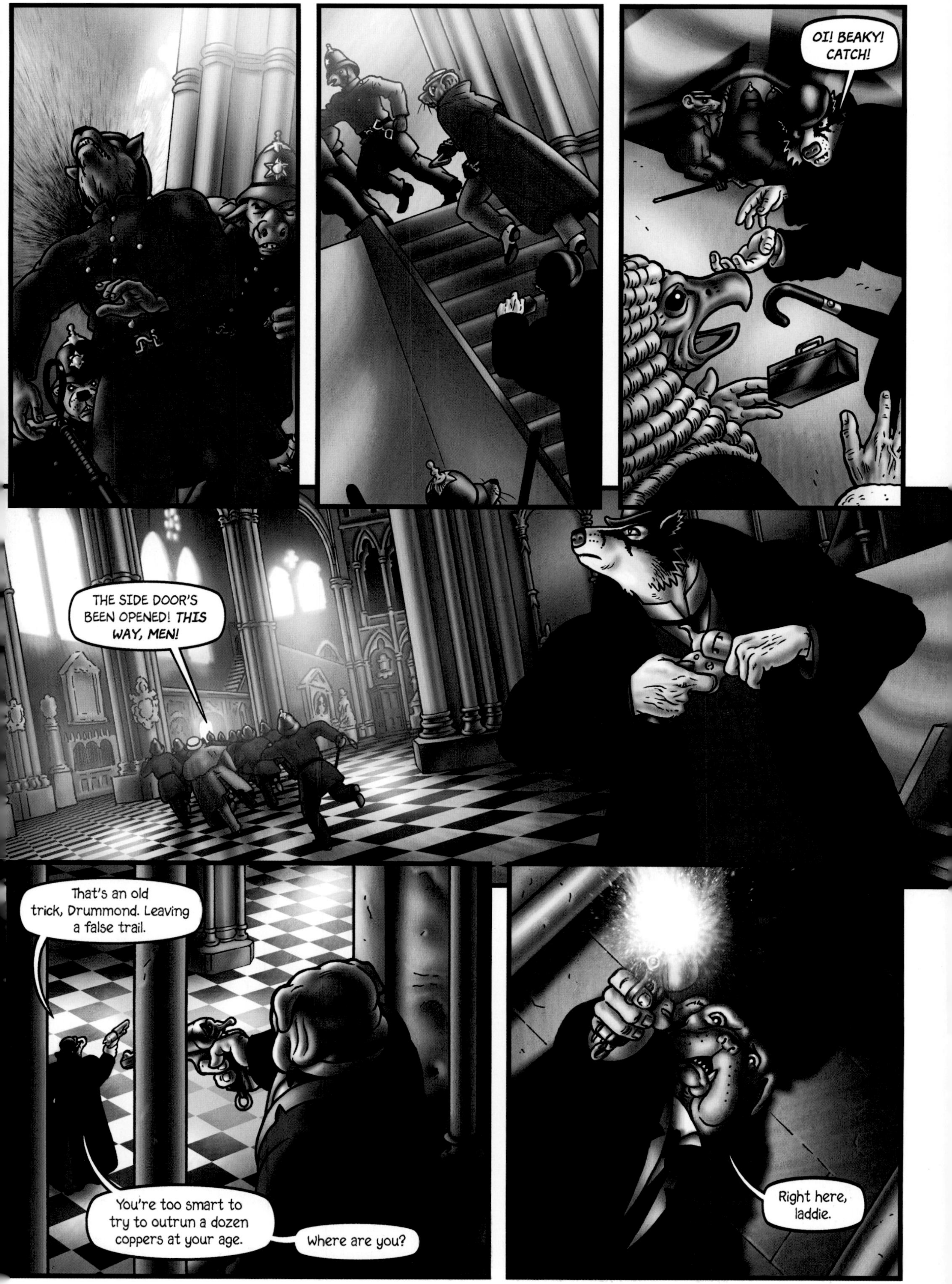
OI! BEAKY! CATCH!
THE SIDE DOOR'S BEEN OPENED! THIS WAY, MEN!
That's an old trick, Drummond. Leaving a false trail.
You're too smart to try to outrun a dozen coppers at your age.
Where are you?
Right here, laddie.

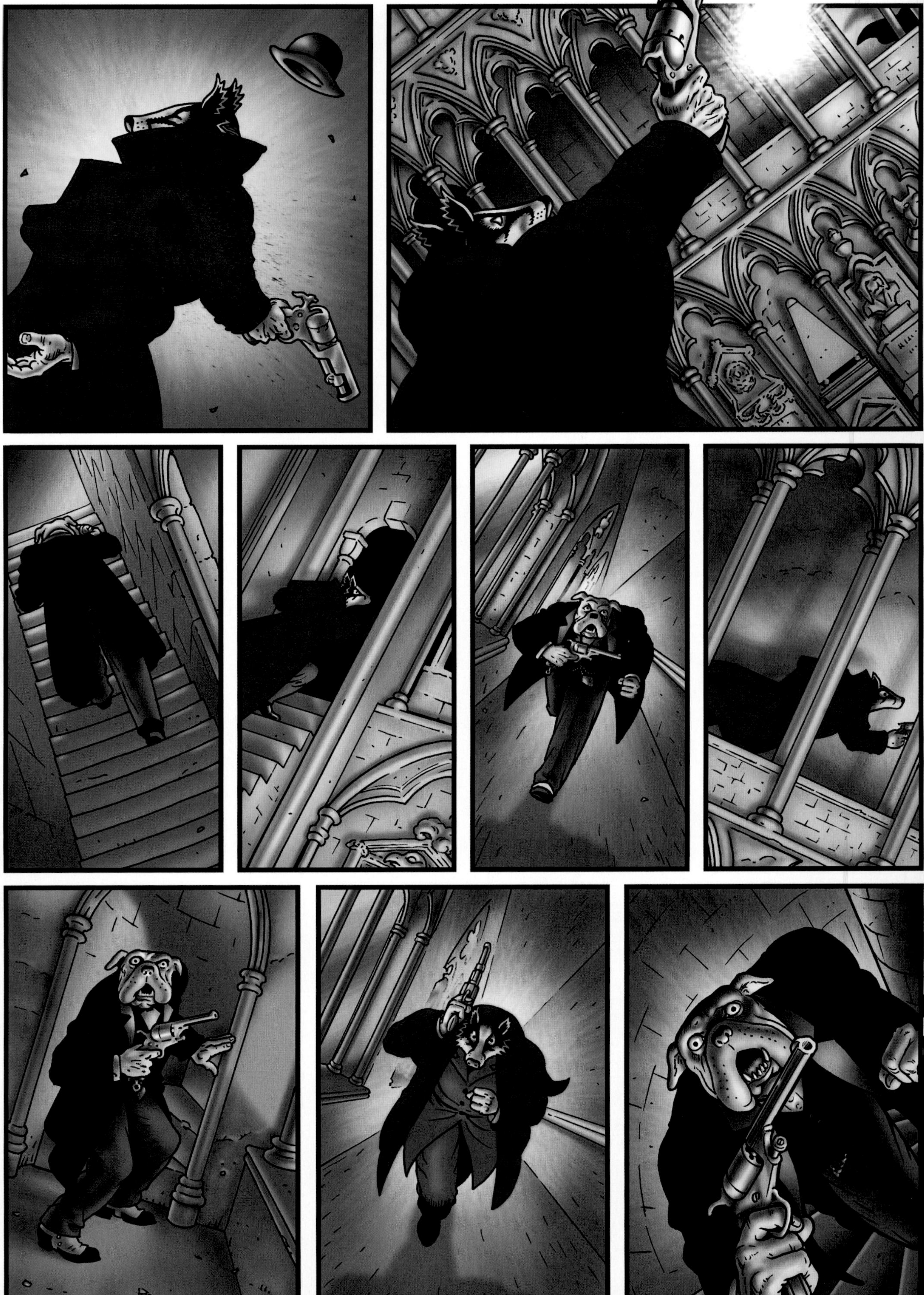

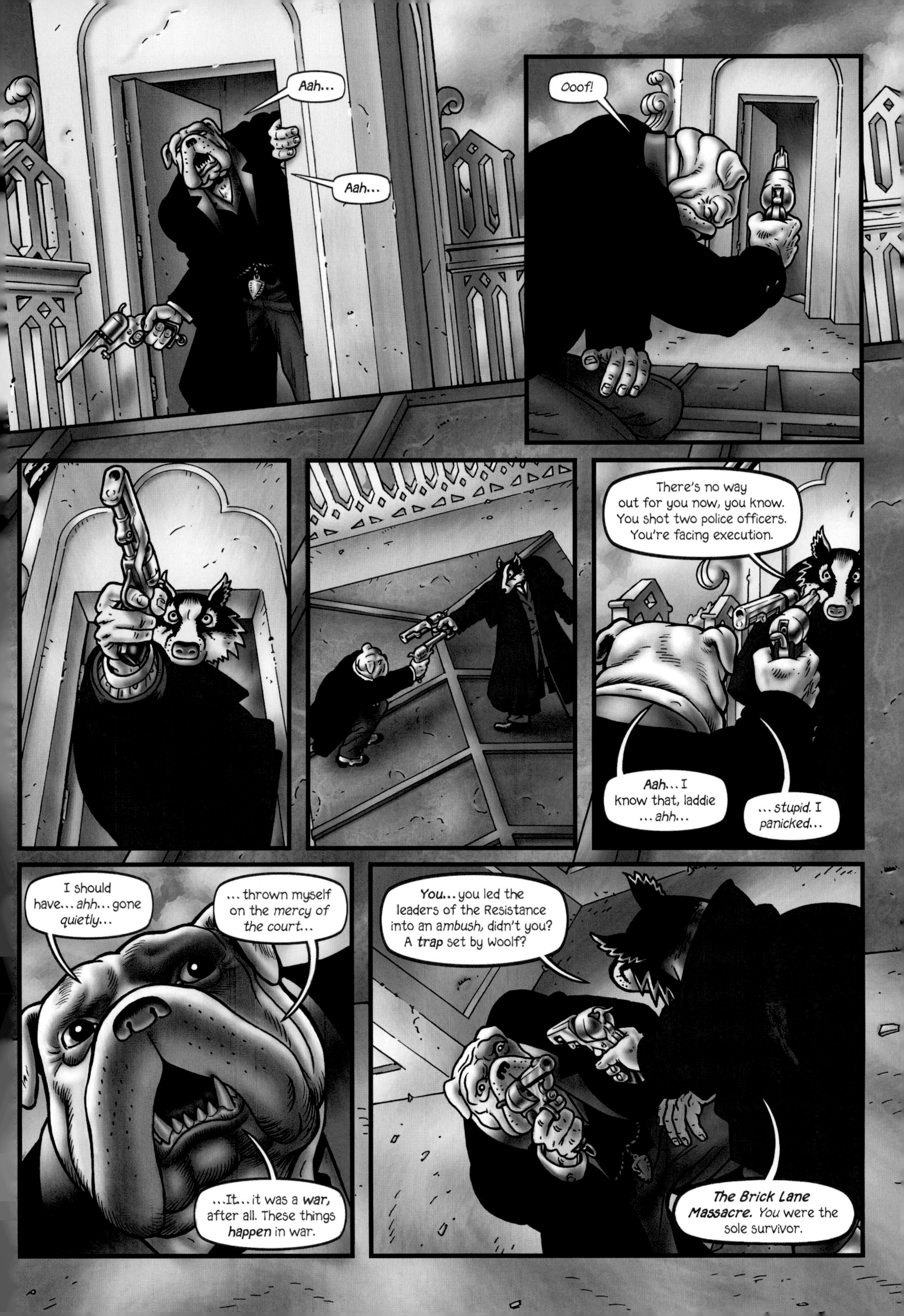
Aah...
Aah...
Ooof!
There's no way out for you now, you know. You shot two police officers. You're facing execution.
Aah... I know that, laddie ...ahh...
...stupid. I panicked...
I should have... ahh... gone quietly...
...thrown myself on the mercy of the court...
...It... it was a war, after all. These things happen in war.
You... you led the leaders of the Resistance into an ambush, didn't you? A trap set by Woolf?
The Brick Lane Massacre. You were the sole survivor.

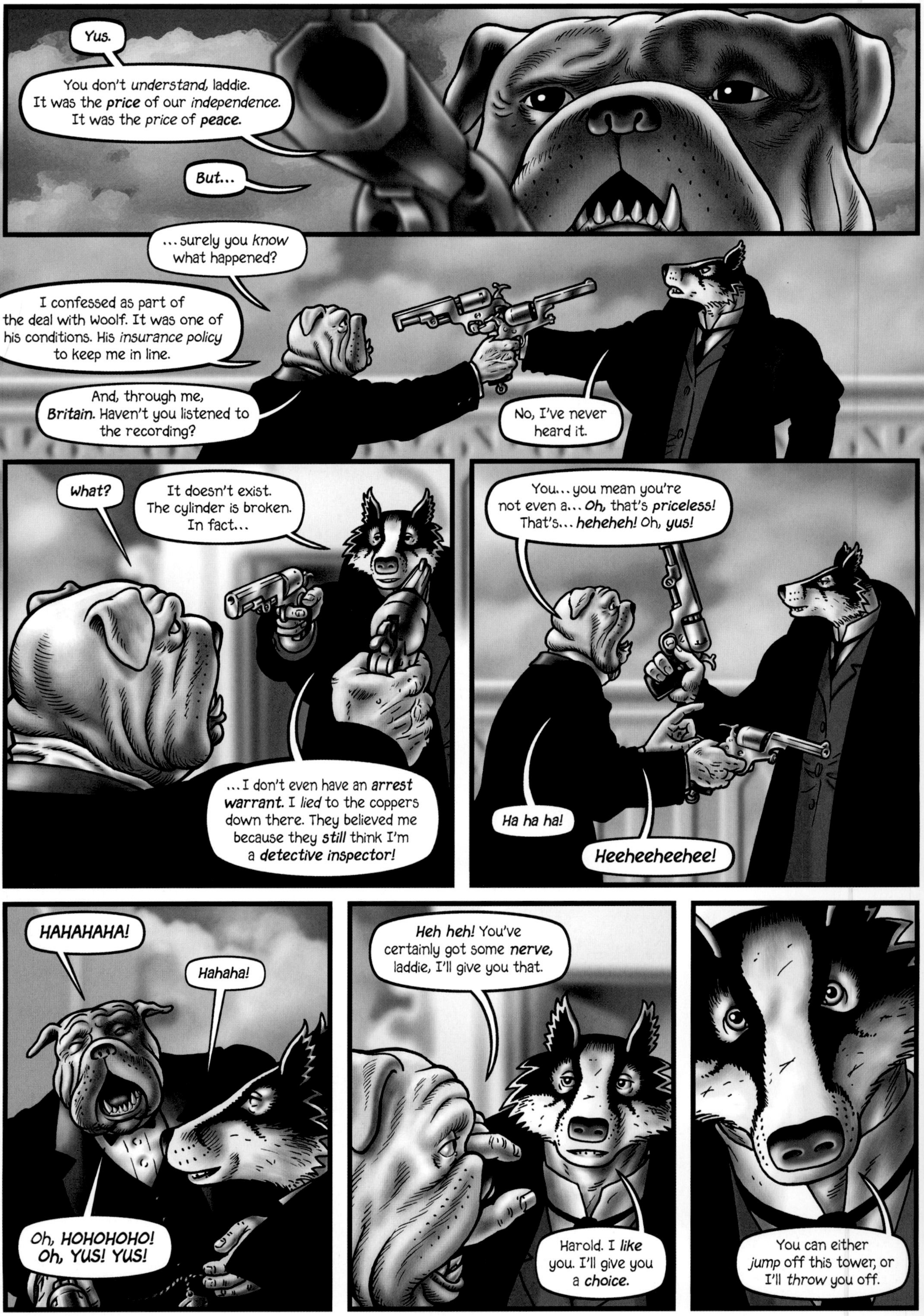
Yus.
You don't understand, laddie. It was the price of our independence. It was the price of peace.
But...
...surely you know what happened?
I confessed as part of the deal with Woolf. It was one of his conditions. His insurance policy to keep me in line.
And, through me, Britain. Haven't you listened to the recording?
No, I've never heard it.
What?
It doesn't exist. The cylinder is broken. In fact...
...I don't even have an arrest warrant. I lied to the coppers down there. They believed me because they still think I'm a detective inspector!
You... you mean you're not even a... Oh, that's priceless! That's... heheheh! Oh, yus!
Ha ha ha!
Heeheeheehee!
HAHAHAHA!
Hahaha!
Oh, HOHOHOHO! Oh, YUS! YUS!
Heh heh! You've certainly got some nerve, laddie, I'll give you that.
Harold. I like you. I'll give you a choice.
You can either jump off this tower, or I'll throw you off.

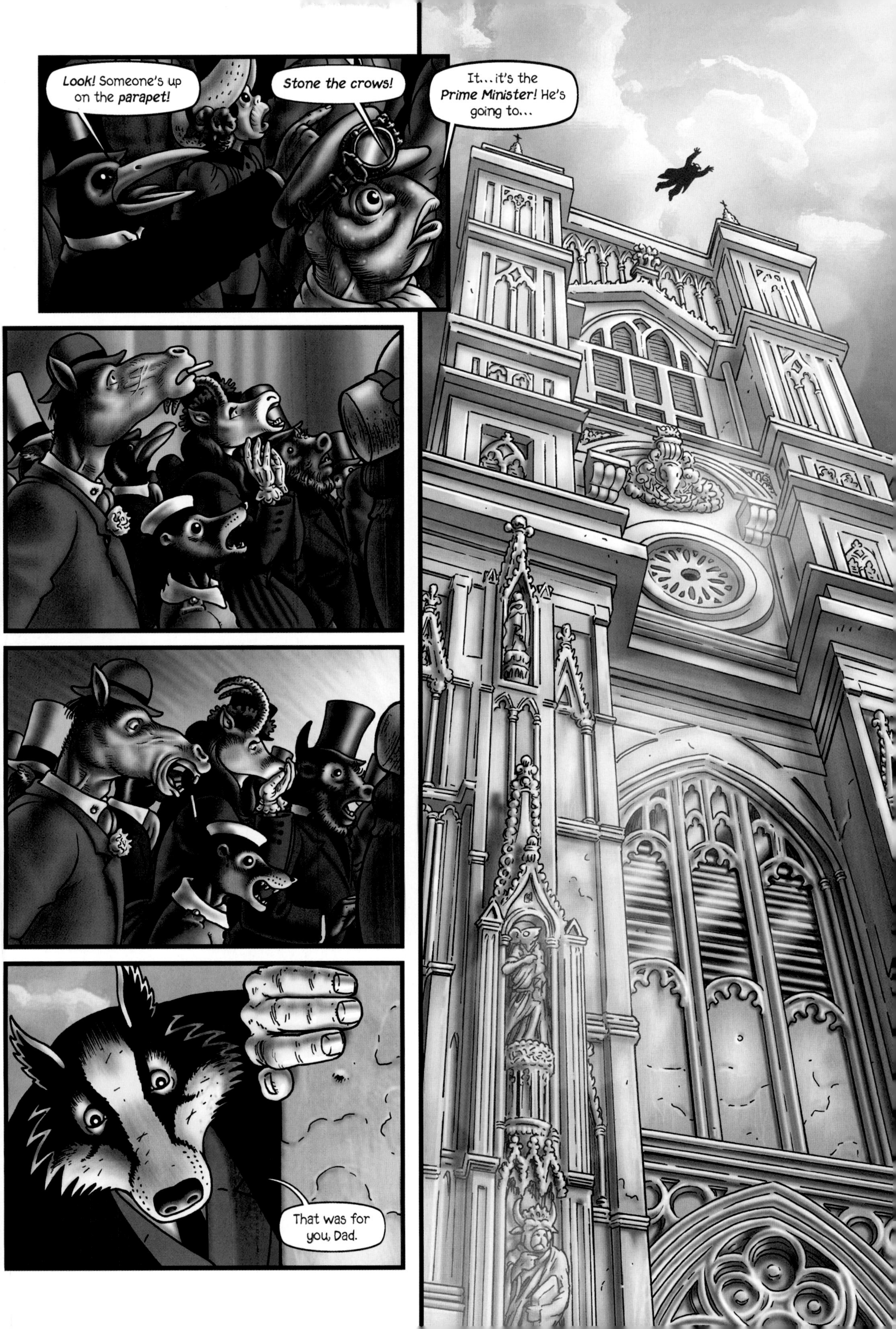
Look! Someone's up on the parapet!
Stone the crows!
It... it's the Prime Minister! He's going to...
That was for you, Dad.

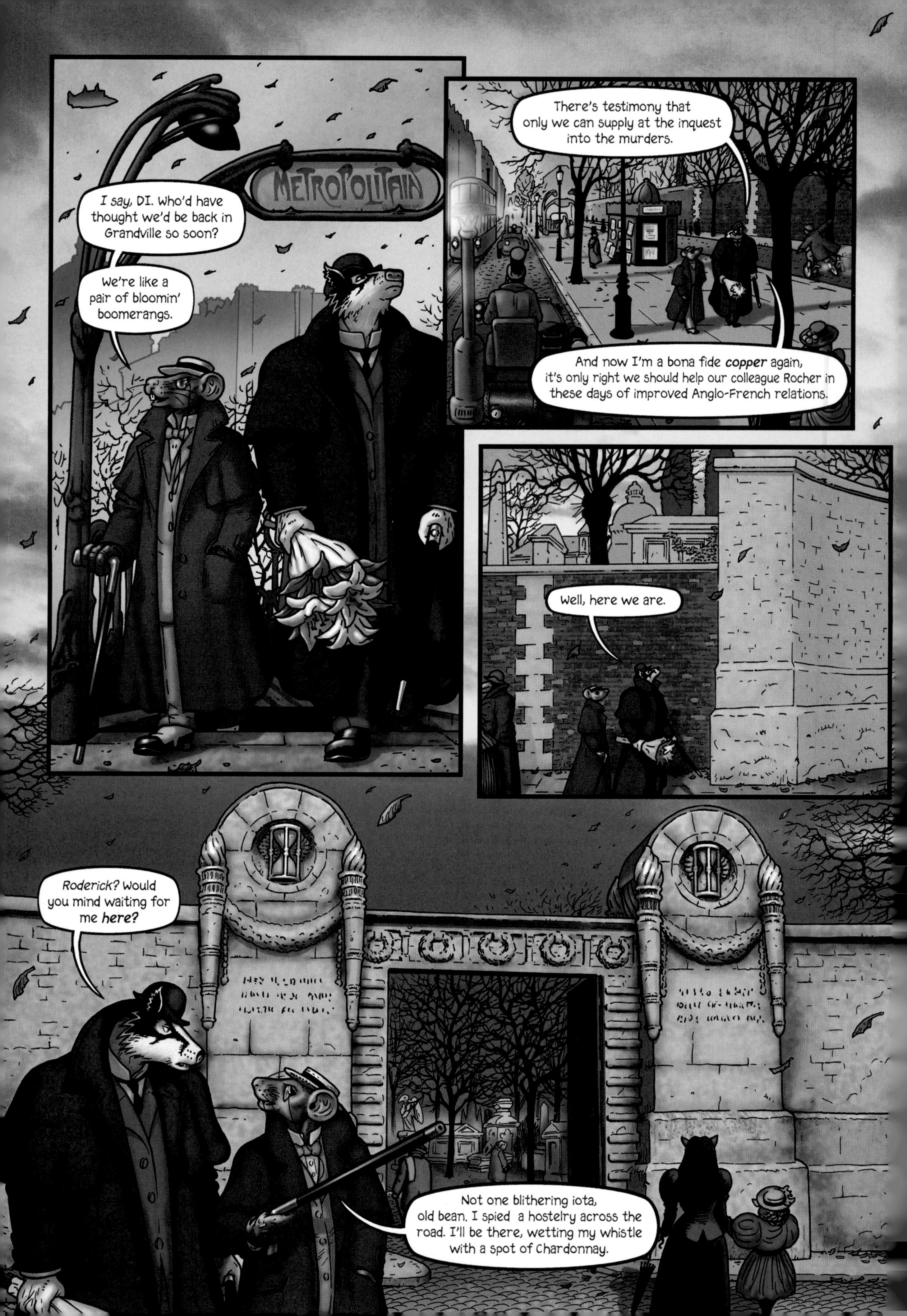
METROPOLITAIN
I say, DI. Who'd have thought we'd be back in Grandville so soon?
We're like a pair of bloomin' boomerangs.
There's testimony that only we can supply at the inquest into the murders.
And now I'm a bona fide ***copper*** again, it's only right we should help our colleague Rocher in these days of improved Anglo-French relations.
Well, here we are.
Roderick? Would you mind waiting for me ***here?***
Not one blithering iota, old bean. I spied a hostelry across the road. I'll be there, wetting my whistle with a spot of Chardonnay.

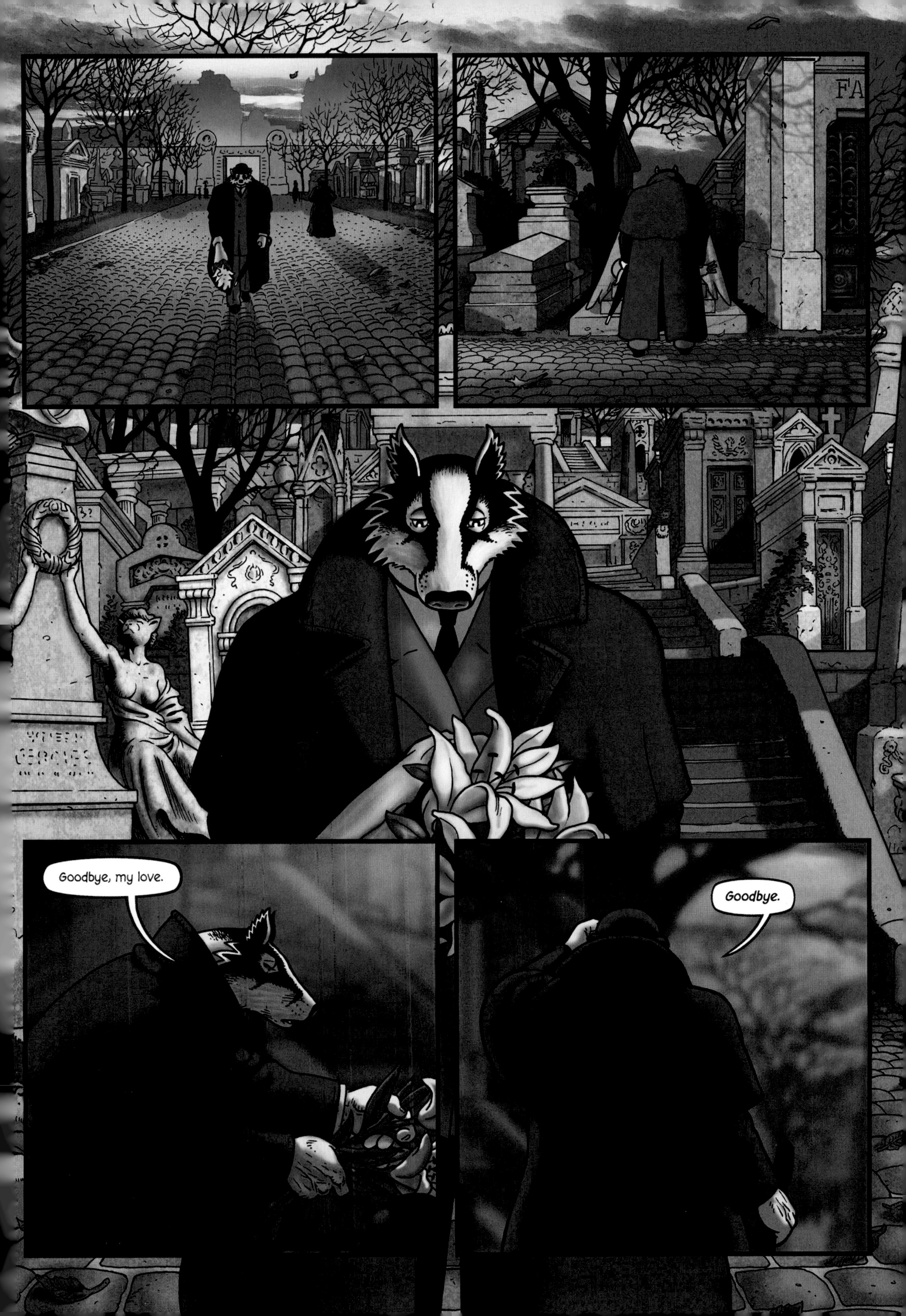
Goodbye, my love.
Goodbye.

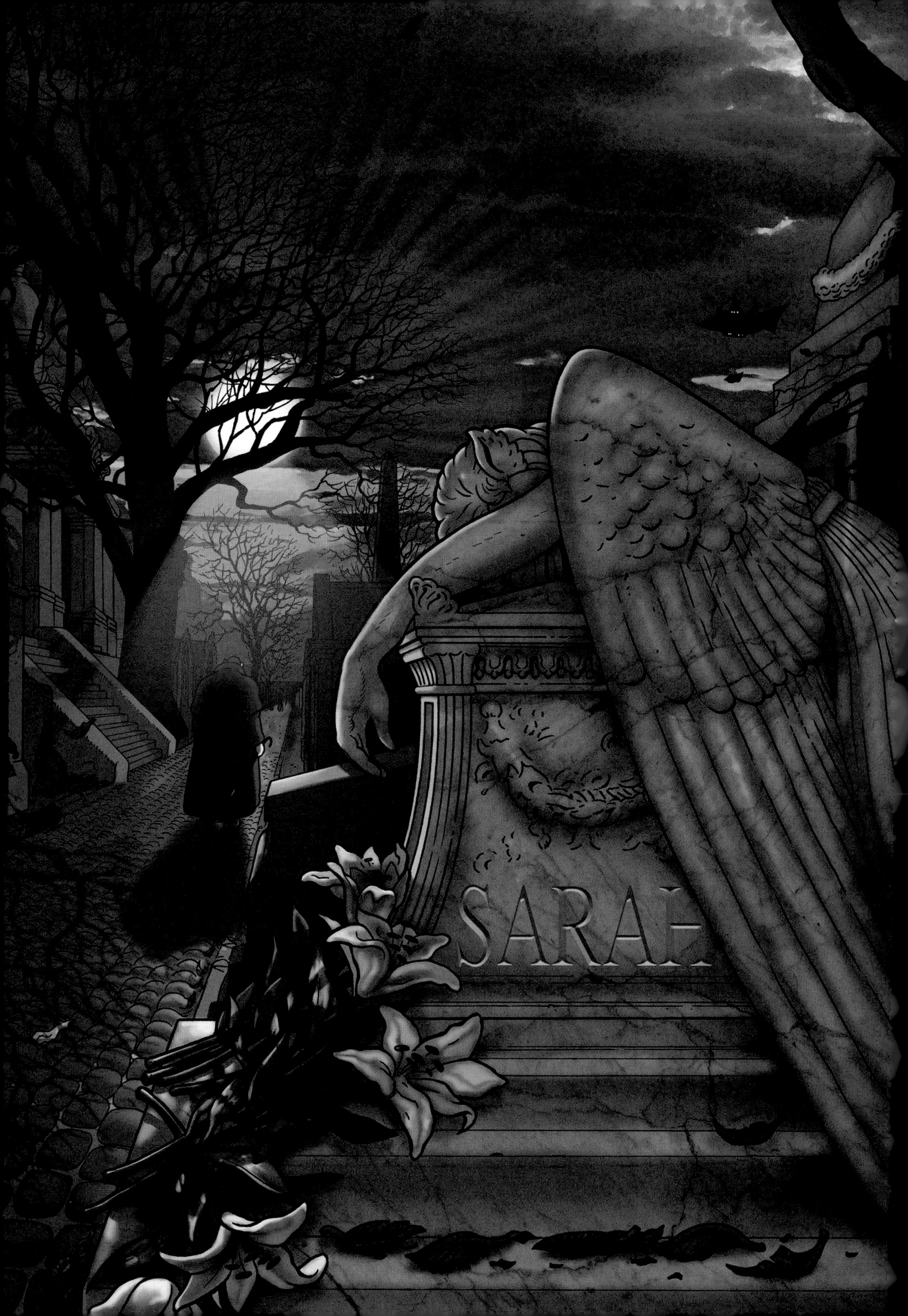
SARAH

Grandville™
Mon Amour

Fin

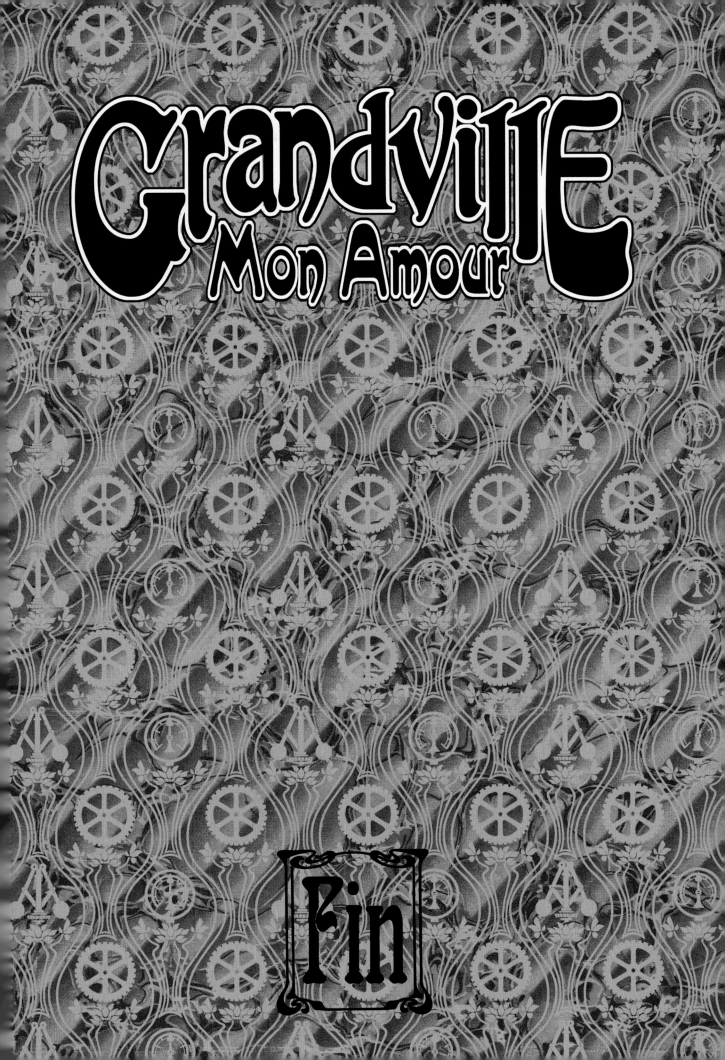

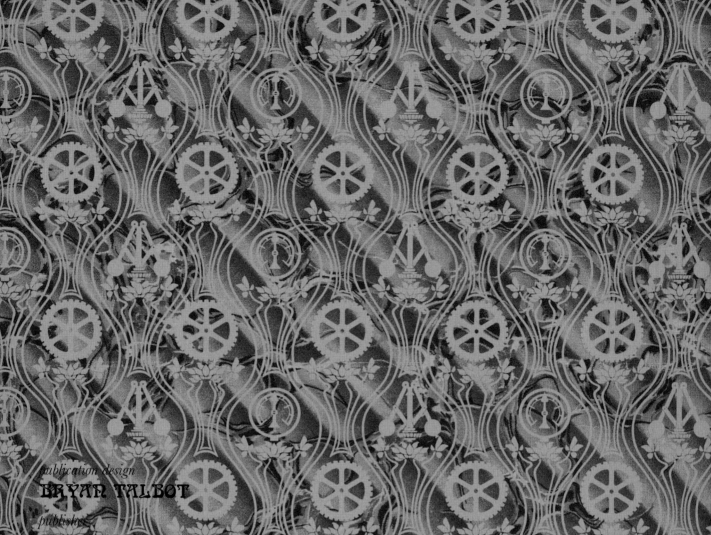

publication design
BRYAN TALBOT

publisher
MIKE RICHARDSON

editor
CHRIS WARNER

GRANDVILLE™ MON AMOUR

Dark Horse Books
A division of Dark Horse Comics, Inc.
10956 SE Main Street
Milwaukie OR 97222

darkhorse.com

To find a comics shop in your area, call the Comic Shop Locator Service toll-free at 1-888-266-4226

First edition: December 2010
ISBN 978-1-59582-574-2

10 9 8 7 6 5 4 3 2 1
Printed at 1010 Printing International, Ltd., Guangdong Province, China

Other books by Bryan Talbot

Brainstorm!

The Adventures of Luther Arkwright

Heart of Empire

The Tale of One Bad Rat

Alice in Sunderland

The Art of Bryan Talbot

The Naked Artist (Prose)

Grandville

Metronome

(Writing as Veronique Tanaka)

Cherubs!

(With Mark Stafford)

Nemesis the Warlock Vols 1 & 2

(With Pat Mills)

Sandman: Fables and Reflections

(With Neil Gaiman, Stan Woch & Mark Buckingham)

The Dead Boy Detectives and
the Secret of Immortality

(With Ed Brubaker & Steve Leialoha)

www.bryan-talbot.com

Eisner and Eagle award winner Bryan Talbot has produced underground and alternative comics, notably *Brainstorm!*, and science-fiction and superhero stories, such as *Judge Dredd*, *Nemesis the Warlock*, *Teknophage*, *The Nazz*, and *Batman: Legends of the Dark Knight*. He's worked on DC-Vertigo titles, including *Hellblazer*, *The Sandman*, *The Dreaming*, and *Fables*, and has written and drawn the graphic novels for which he is best known, including *The Adventures of Luther Arkwright*, *Heart of the Empire*, *The Tale of One Bad Rat*, and *Alice in Sunderland*. He is published in over fifteen countries and is a frequent guest at international comic festivals. In 2009 he was awarded an honorary Doctorate in Arts by Sunderland University.

Illustration by J. J. Grandville

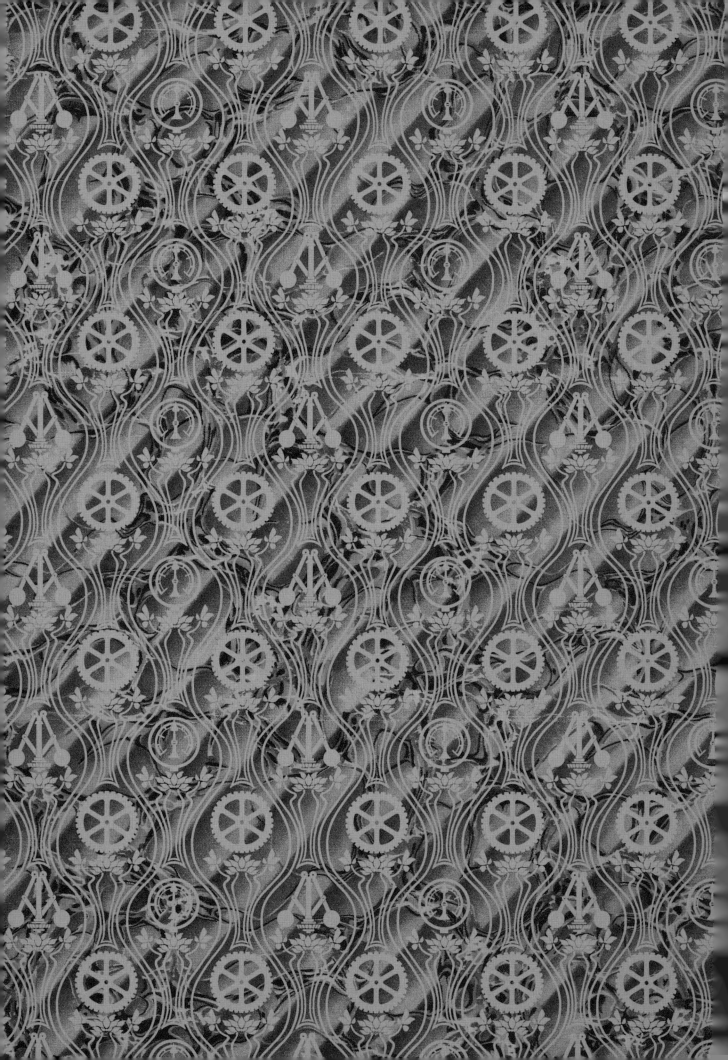